PRAISE FOR AMANDA RUSSELL AND *THE INFLUENCER CODE*

"Amanda is simply a force to reckon with in the influencer marketing industry and without question one of the most valuable marketing experts you will find."

—**Shane Barker**, Forbes Council

"...a game-changing way of viewing the entire category of marketing for the future. I consider Amanda a true pioneer in the field of influencer marketing."

—**Joey Gonzalez,** CEO, Barry's Bootcamp

"*The Influencer Code* isn't just an excellent book, it's a plan for $7+ figure success both at the personal and organizational level. A must-read!"

—**Erik Qualman**, Digital Strategy Expert and best-selling author of *Socialnomics*

"Amanda is one of those rare professionals who has mastered many trades and has provided a positive impact on my course, helping students to 'see the light,' and bridge from books to the real world."

—**Greg O' Brian,** CEO and co-founder, Noodle.Com and Professor, Harvard University

"...an impactful book that will teach you all you need to create and implement an effective influencer marketing strategy."

—**Neal Schaffer,** author of *The Age of Influence*

"Amanda Russell is a force of nature with an indomitable zeal, and it's all powered by a genuine passion and unparalleled insight and experience into a subject very few can articulate better. Amanda BREAKS the Code—couldn't recommend more highly."

—**Simon Kelly,** CEO, Story Worldwide

"The business world has changed. If your company isn't using influencers to grow, you are missing serious opportunities…a must-read for influencer marketing."

—**Mickey Quinones,** Dean of the Robins School of Business, University of Richmond

"Amanda is a dynamo who is redefining how individuals and companies should think about influencer marketing in the modern era."

—**Tom X Lee,** CEO and founder, One Medical

"*The Influencer Code* is what the marketing departments at many schools are missing. With real life stories and pop-culture references, it is engaging, knowledgeable, and essential for understanding what influencer marketing really is."

—**Dr Dana Lascu,** Professor of Marketing, University of Richmond.

"*The Influencer Code* is a must for anyone wanting to stand out in a sea of numbers."

—**Tamilee Webb,** Hall of Fame fitness instructor

"Amanda lifts the curtain and demonstrates how the best influencer marketing is rooted in the basic principles of brand partnerships and how you can apply them to make influencer marketing more trustworthy, more accountable, more measurable and, as a result, more effective."

—**Neil Waller,** Co-founder, Whalar, top Influencer Marketing Creative and Technology Agency

"I stand as one of Amanda's biggest fans and fully recommend her as a valuable, needle-moving asset to your growth."

—**Jim Wolf,** CEO, Ringers Technologies and former president, AIG

"Finally, the essential guide to influencer marketing has been written. Ignore this book at your own risk."

—**Jesse Itzler,** author of *The New York Times* Best-Seller *Living With a SEAL*

"...a master of influencer marketing, and has powerful insights and recommendations to help brand leaders divert their resources away from generating attention and toward increasing influence. I consider Amanda a true pioneer in the field of influencer marketing."

—**Chris Kneeland,** CEO & Co-Founder of Cult Collective and The Gathering of Cult Brands

"...a must-read for anyone that wants to deeply dive into influencer marketing and learn everything you should know about it. A definitive guide for brands, professionals, agencies and students!"

—**Alessandro Bogliari,** Co-founder and CEO, The Influencer Marketing Factory

"Amanda Russell is one of the brightest voices in Influencer Marketing. With *The Influencer Code,* she has created the definitive, how-to guide for practitioners. This book—true to its title—is the code."

—**JoAnn Sciarrino,** Director of Stan Richards School of Advertising University of Texas

"Engaging, thought-provoking and addictive. This book is well worth the read, and a foundational element for your influencer strategy."

—**Kendra Bracken Ferguson,** Founder, BrainTrust and co-founder, Digital Brand Architects

"The first book on the subject I dare to recommend wholeheartedly."

—**Alex Nascimento,** Co-founder at UCLA Blockchain Lab, Faculty Marketing and Blockchain UCLA, CEO 7 Marketing Media

"Amanda thinks about influencer marketing in an entirely different way and can demonstrate what she teaches so effectively (and entertainingly) that people actually get it."

—**Dr. Erin Fall Haskell,** Host/Co-Producer of *Good Morning La La Land*

"In the fast moving world of digital marketing, Amanda stands out as a true expert. With *The Influencer Code,* she DOES spill the code, with actionable strategies to help you break through the noise. If you want to stand out and succeed in today's world, read this book!"

—**James Dalthorpe,** Professor of Marketing, University of Texas and co-founder, BravoZulu

"If you want your business to maintain the status quo, do not read this book. But if you want to step on the throat of your competition and win in the digital marketplace, crack open *The Influencer Code.*"

—**Bill Biggs,** President, Biggs & Associates and COO, Daniel Stark Law

"…unrivaled insight on influencer marketing."

—**Turney Duff,** *New York Times* best-selling author, journalist, TV personality

THE INFLUENCER CODE

HOW TO UNLOCK THE
POWER OF INFLUENCER
MARKETING

AMANDA RUSSELL

THE INFLUENCER CODE

Text copyright © 2020 Amanda Russell

Library of Congress Cataloging-in-Publication
Data is available upon request.
ISBN: 978-1-57826-824-5

Cover and Interior Design by Carolyn Kasper
Cover photography by Kana Livolsi

Printed in the United States
10 9 8 7 6 5 4 3 2 1

CONTENTS

STEP THREE: CONNECT • 203

APPLYING THE PRINCIPLES OF INFLUENCER
MARKETING • 350

Foreword
by Jesse Itzler

A marketing pioneer, a fitness and lifestyle expert, and a model walk into a bar. The bartender says, "Hi, Amanda!"

No, I'm not suggesting Amanda Russell goes to the bar so often she's on a first name basis with the bartender. I'm *telling* you that she's a triple threat—actually, she's so much more than that, and you're about to discover it firsthand.

I first learned about Amanda in 2011 on the way to a fitness boot camp she was hosting. It was right after work; I met my friend Dan Gluck, the founder of Health Warrior, before jogging to West 12th Street together, and as we ran down the West Side Highway, Dan told me about the woman I was to meet. He explained how she'd been a collegiate track star training for the Beijing Olympics when she shattered her femur and had to learn how to walk again. How she'd had to reinvent herself and create an entirely new career, so she moved to New York City with only a used bicycle and one month's rent to her name—that's it. How she'd self-started this entire boot camp we were about to attend on a budget of whatever it cost to copy 100 fliers at Kinkos and the Scotch tape she purchased to put them up on subway platforms, lamp posts, and construction sites. How she was doing it all to pay her own way through business school.

So without ever meeting Amanda, I knew: Grit? Check.

It was a warm spring evening, and we were gathered on a pier hanging over the Hudson River. I looked around at our group of twenty, and it seemed like her clientele ranged from beginner to expert. You know: "*I want to lose twenty pounds*" to "*I want to run through a brick wall without stopping.*" Personally, I was a few months removed from living with a Navy Seal who'd spent 31 days kicking my ass, so I was actually looking forward to being pushed. And Amanda didn't disappoint.

But the most striking thing I remember about that night was the *quality* of people who showed up—a collection of powerhouses across so many fields. Successful by any yardstick, anybody would consider them to be true influencers in their categories. Yet everyone followed *her* lead. I could tell Amanda understood people, what motivated and inspired them, and most importantly, how to get them to act. She was influencing the influencers; clearly, someone I should keep tabs on.

Over the years, our paths would continue to cross; Amanda even became the spokesperson of Zico Coconut Water, a company I'd partnered with and later sold to the Coca-Cola Company. She won the job (with no help from me), but I learned more about her and was able to watch her career take off from the sidelines. As time went on, I began writing my first book, *Living with a Seal,* and launched an online coaching course called Build Your Life Resume. Meanwhile, she was busy building her Fit Strong and Sexy brand into one of the first online female fitness subscriptions platforms, a company she'd eventually sell.

In 2017, I picked up the phone to call her. We needed to talk. I had an idea, in the form of an event called 29029, designed to be the ultimate mental and physical challenge. I'd rented Stratton Mountain for a weekend in October and wanted to see what would happen if you put together some of the "grittiest-push-the-limits" type of people

I knew (and I will say, my rolodex is not for the faint of heart in this category). At the time, this challenge—hike up the mountain 17 times, the equivalent of climbing Mt. Everest, in less than 72 consecutive hours—was something no one knew was even possible. And the kicker? No one would be able to train for it.

So, naturally, Amanda was on my list.

I wanted her involved—wanted the infectious energy, "won't quit" attitude and amazing networking she brings to the table—so I extended an invite. She'd said yes before I'd even finished giving her all the details. It went like: "Hey Amanda, so I'm having this event where you climb up a mountain and—" "*YES*," she said, "*I'm in*." I was happy she was coming. When she arrived, she was prepared and ready to tackle the mountain. And in true Amanda-style, she asked to bring in a whole other group of people from her own network—yet more incredible souls to connect with.

On the mountain, I got to know her on a deeper level. (That tends to happen when you're climbing a steep vertical and pushing limits.) But she wasn't pitching me or selling me or asking for advice; we were just talking—shooting the sh*t. And it only confirmed my first impression of her: she was smart, genuine, a force of nature, with an indomitable zeal…someone I knew I should keep an eye on. I watched her hike up that mountain 17 times straight—finishing well under the allotted time, all while forming bonds and bringing people together.

Amanda killed it on 29029, on many levels. So a few weeks ago, when she reached out and asked if I'd consider writing the foreword for *The Influencer Code*? I said sure, why don't you call me this weekend and give me the elevator pitch.

She did, and I was impressed. She brilliantly articulated how she can help others drive business, break through the noise of fragmented markets and achieve the key to everything—getting action to happen. I already knew Amanda was a top-rated university marketing professor and a serial entrepreneur who's worked with the biggest brands, from Lamborghini to The Plaza Hotel, but what I hadn't realized was that she's also the creator of the world's first accredited university course on influencer marketing. A draft of her book popped up in my inbox right after our call, so I started to read.

Amanda, you weren't asking me a favor to write this foreword, you were providing me with an opportunity—an opportunity to be a very small part of this movement. So thank you.

As for the rest of you, keep reading. Trust me: *The Influencer Code* is much more than a book—it's *the* blueprint for influencer marketing.

—Jesse Itzler, entrepreneur, author,
endurance Athlete and part-owner of the Atlanta Hawks

Why We Need This Book

When you think "influencer marketing", what do you picture? For many of you, the answer might be a pseudo-celebrity with a big social media following—someone who functions as a walking, talking billboard.

You know the drill: high-pressure product placement selfies, breathless testimonials, all-caps coupon codes, three-line affiliate links, and all manner of scammy, spammy, and interruptive calls-to-action.

Some of these posts might seem pretty slick at first glance—it takes effort to look this good—but how do the brands or influencers find out if they've had any real impact on their business goals?

Are all of those followers real, engaged people who actually want what you have? Or just a faceless army of bots? Even if the audience is real humans does the 'influencer' actually exert influence over them? And if so, does that influence translate to the action you are trying to reach with your brand?

Add to this, the increasing number of negative headlines...

"The influencer marketing bubble is set to burst"
"Influencer Fraud Is Costing Brands BIG $$$"
"Influencer Marketing: A Phony Industry Based on False Premises"

No wonder there's so much skepticism! But here's the thing: *all of these thoughts are based on false stereotypes.*

The world is largely confusing attention with influence. Don't get me wrong—as marketers, you absolutely need the attention of your target demographic. But by suggesting that we simply need to get in front of our audience with a great message, a great story, or an incredible product, we're misled.

Simply put, attention is currency; attention is not success.

In believing that attention is all we need, we overlook the most important part—the source of the attention. In marketing, we thrive on attention, but attention without trust is simply noise.

Imagine the following. Notice how both scenarios have achieved your attention, yet with completely different results:

Scenario 1: I recently looked at baby jogging strollers for a friend's baby shower, and now I'm bombarded by all things baby. From my Instagram feed, to my emails—everywhere I look, I see something for an expecting parent or an infant…and every company claims theirs is the very best.

I've seen and even clicked on several of the ads or links, but did not end of buying any of the aforementioned in ads.

Scenario 2: My sister-in-law, who is also an active mom of two, highly recommended a specific baby jogger. I Googled the name, and bought the stroller she recommended.

Result: While many of the ads got my attention, my ultimate behavior (to buy) was a result of the trust I had in my sister-in-law's recommendation.

But why? It's not that complex: people trust people. A brand ALWAYS say their product/service/idea is great.

Advertisements are a notorious turn-off, and if we don't end up just ignoring them, we take them in with skepticism. However, the exact opposite is true when that same list of benefits comes from someone else's lips—especially someone we trust to give us the real scoop.

Influencer marketing is one of the biggest buzzwords in business, and Fortune 500 brands are increasing their investment year over year. The influencer marketing industry is on track to be worth up to $15 billion by 2022, up from as much as $8 billion in 2019, according to Business Insider Intelligence estimates, based on Mediakix data, and that was *before* the exponential growth of TikTok and content creation under quarantine during the 2020 global coronavirus pandemic. So, it's safe to say, it's not going anywhere anytime soon. Seems like a simple solution to success, right? The core concept is simple, but simple does not mean easy.

In the modern market, if attention is currency, influence is wealth. Everyone wants to have the kind of impact it takes to drive action, but a failure to recognize that influence is king when it comes to building a business, leaves you very vulnerable to failure.

In order to leverage the magic of influencer marketing, we must first understand influence.

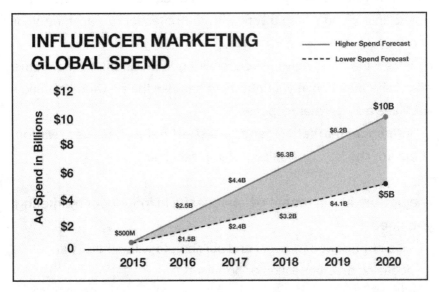

Data credit to MediaKix

It's staggering to watch some of the biggest brands, for all the millions they're investing, fail at one or all of these three key things, which also happen to be the three biggest problems marketers face when it comes to influencer marketing:

- Selecting the right influencer ('right' being the key word)
- Engaging and connecting with the right influencer
- Measuring success of their influencer marketing efforts

Put another way, if you think that garnering a certain number of likes or followers on the platform 'du jour' is going to help you grow your business, you're leaving yourself very vulnerable to the incredible speed at which the market is changing. If Instagram shut down tomorrow, the *true* influencers wouldn't lose their influence.

So why do so many brands get influencer marketing so wrong? And what can be done to turn their efforts around?

This book was born to answer those questions. Influencer marketing is much more than just another a strategy or a tactic. It's a new way to think, and a framework with the potential to transform your efforts. . .*if* you get it right.

Here's the good news: If you're willing to invest a little more time, effort, and intention in your efforts to harness the power of influence, you'll see a far greater response.

Influencer marketing can't be a short game, because *relationships* are the key. Real relationships take time.

The bottom line is that to be successful in influencer marketing, you need:

- The **confidence** to invest and collaborate with others, without focusing on competition or popularity

- The **common sense** to realize that people buy from brands they trust, not just the noisiest brand out there
- The **openness and generosity** to share your own resources and audience with others

In short, influencer marketing is more than just paying someone with an audience to promote your brand. Influencer marketing requires understanding true influence and who has that influence over your target audience. It's not about one-off transactions but rather must be built on genuine relationships. It's not a quick fix, it's a long-term investment.

"[Influencer marketing] isn't a loudspeaker that a brand rents to shout about their message and it's also not a funding source for influencers to take money from brands and not deliver on a marketing brief. This is a marketing partnership between two brands and one where authentic and relevant partnerships drive the most trust and affinity over time."

—Neil Waller, co-founder of Whalar,
Top Influencer Creative and Technology Agency

I've built my career—and helped others build theirs—by understanding the need for this type of relationship and how to create them. And I've put everything together here in *The Influencer Code*, creating a roadmap for healthy, efficient—and above all, effective—relationships between brands and influencers.

The good news is I'm not teaching you anything you don't already know; rather, I'm giving you a structured guide for creating long-term, win-win, always-on strategic influencer alliances, including:

- What influencer marketing is and is not. . .and why the difference matters
- The biggest myths and misconceptions about influencer marketing that get in the way of achieving success
- The four types of influence and how you can put them to work for your brand
- The many roles influencers can play across your business
- Defining the right business goals for your marketing efforts
- Identifying, and assessing the right influencers for your brand and goals
- Selecting the right metrics to track success
- Cultivating a long-term relationship with influencers that moves beyond transaction to shared value
- Facilitating, strategizing and collaborating with influencers to produce high-impact content

You *will* walk away from this book with a 360-degree understanding of influencer marketing, with all the framework and knowledge necessary to help you devise strategies, accomplish real results, and build a reputation as an expert in the process. Throughout my research, I reached out to over 150 colleagues and experts who have run or are currently running successful influencer marketing programs or who are partnered with brands as influencers. I asked them for their insights, case studies, and examples of how companies, brands, leaders, and influencers are successfully using influence—*and* when they're doing just the opposite.

I've filled these pages with stories, examples of influence at work (both good and bad), and key marketing lessons. In school, we're taught to *answer* questions; but as leaders in the marketing space, we need to know how to ask the right questions *and* question the answers—especially when no one else is.

Ready to get started? Let's do this!

DEFINING INFLUENCE, MOVING PAST MISCONCEPTIONS, AND UNDERSTANDING ITS POWER

1

Marketing **is Evolving**
. . .and we can't be left behind

The marketing landscape has changed, and some marketers may feel like they're wandering in the desert. The traditional methods, venues, and strategies marketers have relied on for decades are operating within a very different landscape than they had even just a few years ago:

Traditional media reach is falling off a cliff. As we develop new ways of communicating with one another and consuming information, the channels we've historically used don't have the power they once did. By extension, marketers are losing more of their footing by the day.

Digital advertising is *steamrolling* every other format. This is where those advertising dollars are going! Here, the problem lies in the increasing ad noise on these digital channels. . .i.e., the places everyone went to *avoid* advertising.

Hyper-fragmented markets lead to consumer attention deficit (ADD). Every platform is chock-full of competition for eyes and ears. How do you stand out when everyone is jockeying for attention? How can you hope to grab the attention of someone bouncing between 17 smartphone apps in a grocery line?

There's been humorous, yet entirely reasonable, claims that our current attention span is less than 8 seconds. . .which makes us slightly less focused than a goldfish. (Probably because they don't have those 17 apps.)

Brands can't be in 400 places at once. Even the advertisers with the biggest pockets can't and don't try to be everywhere. So how do you know *where* to go with your limited budget? And how do you make yourself worthy of attention once you get there? If you're trying to be everywhere, you end up resonating nowhere.

Social media's organic reach is all but dead. Social platforms have gone from community meeting places to modern-day advertising channels. Brands aren't getting seen unless they spend—and spend a *lot*. If you don't have an endless budget, your organic impact will be limited.

Content is no longer king. Many marketers still tout content as the solution to all these issues. In 1996, Bill Gates famously said content was king. . .and in 1996, he was right. But in 2020, you can publish the best, most compelling content in the world without any guarantee anyone will see it. Not exactly a royal result, right?

Most important of all: Everyone. Hates. Ads. Dive for the TV remote! Click the little "x" in the browser window! Flip the page! *Anything* to avoid being sold to for a whole minute. No wonder an estimated 30 percent of internet users have downloaded some form of browser ad blocker. What's a marketer to do? Besides watch their budget evaporate before they've made any impact on their prospective customers, that is.

If they're smart, they'll focus on those voices which *already* possess the ability to influence, inspire, and engage the people they want to speak to: **the influencers.**

You *can* break through and succeed in today's—and tomorrow's—marketing environment, no matter where you're starting from. But first, you need to climb into the driver's seat. . .which means it's time to rethink your objectives, reevaluate your metrics and shift from focusing on *transactions* to building *relationships*.

INFLUENTIAL RELATIONSHIPS

Relationships are at the core of influencer marketing, and there are four primary relationship types to consider.

1. **The influencer and you.** This will be critical to your success in influencer marketing: developing a mutually beneficial relationship between you and the influencer you partner with. Starting with a shared set of goals, and a shared understanding of how you'll both contribute to realizing those goals, is crucial to success.

2. **The influencer and their community.** The influencers who have real impact in others' lives know to respect both the communities they've built, and the broader community they're a part of. They take the trust and respect they're given *seriously*, and earn it over time through consistency and value.

3. **You and your potential new customers.** Can you live up to the endorsement you've received? When a customer makes a purchase because of the endorsement of someone they trust, we call it the "Brand Halo effect." You're receiving the "glow" of trust the customer has placed in the influencer. But there's no

guarantee the Brand Halo will last, or that they'll be inclined to make more than a single purchase. It's up to *you* to live up to the promise they see in you.

4. **You and your existing customers.** When you cultivate a relationship with an influencer and their community, your customers may also be exposed to your collaborative content and experiences. If this new relationship doesn't ring true to the customers you have right now, they may feel your brand is headed in a new direction—one which they might not want to follow. That's not to say different customer segments won't respond to different types of relationships and content; they can, and you can also cater to multiple audiences successfully. Your ongoing authenticity will play a huge role in helping them understand that the brand they trust isn't leaving them behind.

I'll give you a personal example—one I'm not exactly proud of—which taught me a critical lesson. When I was starting out in the fitness industry, I was approached by a protein powder company to endorse their product to my community. I tried it. . .and it tasted like a glass of chalk.

I put it in a shaken smoothie, and it was a little less terrible, but then I became curious as to why it tasted so terrible. Upon inspection, the ingredients read like a chemistry experiment. Why would I want to put this into my body?

I waffled about how to respond; I needed the money, but I also worried about what my clients and followers might think.

Was I going to be proud of my brand if I did this? Could I recommend this to a friend—which is how I view the people in my community—if I wouldn't use it myself? Would I be scamming them to make a quick buck?

Well, I'll admit it: I took the money. I knew better, but the double digits in my bank account yelled louder than my common sense.

When I think back to the videos I posted, I do a full-body *cringe*.

I don't sound at all like myself, I don't look comfortable, and the whole thing is so *forced*. Then there was the comment section.

"Um, I thought you were Ms. Healthy Eating?"

"Did you actually taste that crap? Completely gross."

"The ingredient list reads like a chemical lab!"

"I am so gone—unfollowing right now."

I lost the respect of several of my subscribers that day. I followed up with an apology email not long after I posted (and then took down the videos). I knew I had to own my mistake—and owning my mistake actually helped win me back some respect.

Lesson learned: if an influencer cares about the community they've built, they'll be wary about what they're willing to recommend—and that's exactly the kind of invested, passionate influencer you want to work with. You're on the hook to build their trust, just as they've built trust with their own community.

So, what do all four of these relationships have in common?

You can't have a successful relationship without trust

In the end, each one of these relationships depends on one critical and hard-to-foster element: *trust.*

Marketers love to talk about trust, but what does trust actually *mean* in the context of influencer marketing?

We want our customers to believe we have their best interests in mind, and that what we say about our product or service is true—the problem is that people tend not to trust a brand when they promote themselves, any more than we trust when an individual brags about how great they are. We are more inclined to be open and trusting when we hear it from a third party, someone we rely on for the truth. *That* is why the right influencer is so powerful: they can completely transform how a person takes in and processes information about a brand, product or campaign.

The problem is that trust is as hard to *earn* as it is easy to *lose.* That's why influencer marketing isn't like buying an ad or putting up a post on Facebook. In a space full of quick transactions, influencer marketing is about committing the radical act of investing in something long-term.

Think of building a relationship with an influencer like making a new hire for your business. You wouldn't offer just anyone a spot on your team without doing your due diligence first, and you wouldn't be willing to invest in them without considering the long-term impact. Yet the industry has largely been overlooking the same standards and process when it comes to influencers.

Influencer marketing is the modern approach for the modern market

Influencer marketing can be one of the most effective marketing methodologies for both business-to-consumer (C2B) brands and business-to-business (B2B) companies. Not only is this strategy scalable for all budgets, it can reach across multiple aspects of a business, and provides a solution to the "interruption marketing" approach of yesterday.

Influencer marketing allows you to benefit from trust someone else has cultivated. If trust is the key to successful and ongoing relationships, gaining trust through an influencer is a great way to begin building trust with potential customers.

Imagine that you're hoping to launch a new line of dog toys designed to help owners train their puppies. Most dog owners are incredibly protective of their pets, so earning their trust is critical to earning their dollars. Through a detailed search of influencers in the dog training space, you come across a professional who creates puppy-centric videos for new owners.

You don't see them recommending any particular products in their videos, though they use different tools as they move through their training steps. You reach out to ask if you can send them some of your toys to try out with their four-legged clients—no strings attached.

Your toys get a great response from the puppies and an enthusiastic thumbs up from the trainer—giving you the "in" you need to talk about a potential partnership. When the trainer ultimately recommends your toys, you see an immediate response from their followers. Why? The trainer rarely recommends anything except their own methods—so your products *must* be worth the investment.

A trusted endorsement fosters openness to everything from a new relationship to a new product. That's how influencers can help you make the right first (and second or third) impression with the audiences you want to reach.

Influencer marketing enables you to target new niches. If you're having trouble breaking into a new market, or reaching customers with a particular set of interests or needs, building a relationship with an influencer who has the trust of that audience can help you make serious inroads into a new space.

Let's say you have a yarn company: you've done excellent job of reaching out to traditional knitters making blankets, sweaters, and socks for their family and friends. You notice there's a growing group of people knitting as an experimental art form: craftwork that shows up in art galleries and public exhibitions and commands some serious dollars.

If you could get your yarn into the hands of those artists, you'd be adding a new level of credibility to your product—a brand boost that would introduce you to new customers, while adding a new dimension to how your current customers see you, too.

Making a connection with an up-and-coming art knitter would also enable you to become a part of their story as an artist, to learn about their community as they continue grow their audience, and to gain exposure to other art knitters (and their die-hard fans).

Influencer marketing gives you both immediate and long-term value. You gain an immediate boost in your profile when you first create a relationship with an influencer, and you build further trust as that relationship continues to grow and evolve.

Imagine you own a business that sells guitar strings and guitar accessories, like straps and cases. You reach out to a music student who makes thoughtful, step-by-step tutorials on how to change guitar strings, how to tune a guitar, and how to play some basic chords—videos beloved by thousands of followers.

You invite the student to tour your facility, to conduct an interview with your head of innovation about new products about to launch—and to capture it all on video for his audience. You might even invite him to meet and greet fans at your booth at a music trade show. These different points of connection lead the influencer to feature your products in their videos, and to introduce them to his audience.

Over time, he evolves into a music teacher who conducts more formal lessons online, continuing to introduce your products to his new students and followers. You offer to fund some new filming and recording equipment, since he's doing such a fantastic job of getting your products in front of your target market. He's thrilled, and enthusiastic to keep singing your praises: a win-win relationship for everyone.

He even gets studio session work and takes his camera along to talk to other musicians—musicians he shares your products with, and who add another layer of value to the content he creates for you.

Every step of the way, as his community grows, his impact grows—and your impact grows along with his.

Influencer marketing amplifies your multi-channel exposure. Anywhere your influencer is, they create opportunities to share content about you—and their community will do the same. That means you'll be along for the ride on new or niche social platforms, in private groups, at exclusive events. . .everywhere your influencer goes.

The cost and time of adding a new platform to your marketing mix can often be prohibitive, and if you don't know the best practices and community standards, you waste not only time and resources but risk damaging your reputation. Entering a new channel via an influencer enables you to test the waters without jumping in headfirst.

Influencer marketing puts some of the burden of content creation in someone else's court. Influencers are already creating content for their audiences, and every bit of content they create is content you don't have to create yourself. Everyone knows that content creation can eat up a marketer's budget in short order—so let the content pros take that stress off your plate!

Let's say a local foodie takes a snap of themselves enjoying a brew on your patio and tells all their followers that they've found the ultimate place to enjoy a summer sunset. To create this scene for yourself as an advertisement, you'd need to find models, hire a photographer, and figure out which beer would engage your target audience most effectively. Then you'd need to get someone to post the photo with a description that doesn't sound "salesy". . .it just seems a little easier to get to know a real foodie, right?

Influencer marketing gives you content you can re-use. As long as your product still exists and your influencer is still active and well-regarded, you can continue to share the content they create on a recurring basis.

You can also repurpose content across platforms. A speech can become a SlideShare presentation, or be shared as a YouTube video. A YouTube video can become a series of short, punchy clips you include in tweets. A PowerPoint presentation can be divided up to create infographics that can be shared across platforms. The possibilities are *endless.* (Just make sure you have the rights to use it!)

Influencer marketing gives you bragging rights. When an influencer with a strong community uses your product or service, you have an immediate "brag" on your hands. Did supermodel and reality television host Karli Kloss get snapped wearing a pair of your company's yoga pants? You can share that image with, "As seen on supermodel Karli Kloss."

All this took was paying attention to mentions of your product— social listening—to know she wore them. Now you can share that valuable content over and over, through no extra effort of your own.

An implicit endorsement can be huge for a brand trying to generate steam. A future customer might be searching the web for posterior-minimizing yoga pants, drifting from site to site, clicking on several different brands, trying to figure out which looks the most promising. Then they spot a pair of *your* yoga pants they like in their Google results, but they've never heard of you.

When they click through to your site, they're greeted with an image of Karli Kloss enjoying the very pants they've been checking out (and looking great, of course.) They may already have been interested, but now a brand they've known about for mere minutes is instantly validated: *If a supermodel is wearing those pants, they must be good enough for me.*

Why stop there? You can also build that relationship further by reaching out to Karli to share more of your products, because you already know she's a customer.

All this can be yours . . . if you're willing to do it right

Now you know the secret of why the traditional approaches marketers have used for years to win consumers over don't work anymore. People don't want to be interrupted with promotional messaging, so moving forward, smart brands will need to harness the growing power of influencer marketing to break through.

Influencer marketing is not about the one-off ad; it's not a simple quid pro quo transaction. It is a strategy that must be integrated across all areas of a business. It must be an investment, not an "add-on".

In the coming chapters, we'll work our way from the earliest stages of establishing business goals, through to finding an influencer who will collaborate to achieve those goals, to creating content their community will love—all while learning how best to measure your success.

Recap and Review

KEY POINTS

1. **The marketing landscape has changed, and old strategies aren't working.**
   a. Traditional media formats—in terms of both reach and effectiveness—have sharply declined, with digital advertising moving to the forefront of consumer consciousness.
   b. As a result, the market is more fragmented than ever before, making consumers more difficult to reach. Even if you *do* manage to reach them, consumers have developed such a strong aversion to advertising that "tried-and-true" methods are perceived as so much noise.
   c. Organic social reach is all but dead and content is no longer "king."

2. **The solution lies in the power of influencer marketing.**
   a. Influencer marketing is based on influence, which is the power to achieve a desired action
   b. Influencer marketing offers a wide range of important benefits, including:
      i. Opportunities to present traditional marketing messages, using an authentic voice, to an existing audience that is already predisposed to engage and respond positively
      ii. Access to multi-channel exposure, including new audiences and potential niche markets

iii. Both immediate and long-term value through the creation of high-impact, reusable content—developed by the individuals best equipped to do so

3. **To pursue influencer marketing successfully, you'll need to be prepared to manage several key relationships:**
   a. The relationship between you and your influencer(s)
   b. The relationship between your influencer(s) and their communities
   c. The relationship between you and potential/ new customers
   d. The relationship between you and your existing customers

4. **Just as with any relationship, influencer marketing relies on mutual trust.**
   a. The goal of influencer marketing is to utilize the pre-existing trust an influencer has built up in their community to ensure your brand message is seen and engaged with.
   b. Since you're benefiting from (and relying on) trust that someone else has cultivated, your responsibility to maintain a healthy relationship with your influencer(s) is crucial.

MOVING FORWARD

If the benefits of influencer marketing are so obvious and simple, why are we getting it so wrong?

FOOD FOR THOUGHT

What sorts of people come to mind when you hear the term "influencer"? Celebrities? Social media stars? Television personalities? When you consider the definition of influence, do you think a successful influencer requires a social media presence?

2

The Biggest Misconceptions About Influence
And why they're getting in the way of our success

P op quiz! Who has more influence?

Pictured: Barack Obama (left) and a shoe store owner (right).

Ask almost anyone in the world, and the majority will immediately point to Barack Obama. He's a former President of the United States, and he still maintains an incredibly high profile as a speaker and author.

But what if you were looking for the right choice of running shoe to help you train for your first marathon? Whose opinion would you rather hear?

The other guy's not looking so bad now, is he?

(MIS)UNDERSTANDING INFLUENCE

Part of my job as a professor and marketing strategist is to maximize revenue within a budget. We're always looking to get the maximum bang for our buck and make our research go as far as possible, so I'm hyper conscious of paying attention to what works. . .and what doesn't.

Straight away, I found myself running into the popular myths and misconceptions about influencers and influencer marketing. I set out to write the book on using influence for growth, only to discover that *working with influencers is only a small part of a bigger story*. In other words, you can't work with influencers optimally if you're focused on the wrong metrics; i.e., if you don't know what true influence looks like.

Let's begin with the biggest misconception of all: **popularity does NOT equal influence.**

Best-selling author and influence expert Jonah Berger *(Contagious: Why Things Catch On* and *Invisible Influence: The Hidden Forces that Shape Behavior)* explains the difference between the two:

"Imagine a video online that has a million views. What that means is that a million people have seen at least a part of that video. It doesn't mean they've watched the whole thing, or that they've engaged with the video in a meaningful way. What it means is that some set of people have *seen* it.

The more people that view something, or even that like something, the more popular it is said to be. If lots of people buy a certain product, it's popular. If lots of people listen to a song, it's popular.

On the other hand, influence is the power that something has over some sort of recipient. I have a friend who knows a lot about music; he may recommend that I check out a music artist that's popular or unpopular—but if he recommends it, it's going to have some influence on what I buy. It doesn't matter that he doesn't have a million followers online, because I know him and trust him.

Simply put, *popularity* is the number of people that like something or do something, while *influence* is the impact of one thing on another."

Plenty of popular people and organizations have influence over our culture in some way or another. But popularity itself is the *state* of being *liked*, even *loved*—neither of which is the same as being *influential*.

By that same token, **going viral does NOT equal influence.** Let's say you make a video about how your 2-year-old can tap dance on a balance beam and it goes "viral." When it comes to all the typical sought-after metrics on social media—which usually include some mix of followers, comments, and shares—you've hit it out of the park. But what did you actually *achieve* for all that awareness?

Answer: not a lot. And that's why "viral" is a wildly empty metric. A social post can rack up huge numbers and still not drive any sort of meaningful *action*. A bunch of eyeballs does not equate to impact, and being the hot topic of conversation isn't the same as being *trustworthy*.

Organizational psychology expert and best-selling author, Dr. Liane Davey (*You First: Inspire Your Team to Grow Up, Get Along, and Get Stuff Done*) calls out this fallacy:

"People believe they can become influencers overnight by racking up some buzz. To become trusted and influential, it can take *years* of consistently providing value."

Bottom line: just because you have the attention of someone, doesn't mean you have any influence over them. Attention doesn't *necessarily* translate to action. . .and it definitely isn't synonymous with *trust.*

Being famous does NOT equal influence. While popularity is more about being *liked*, being famous is the state of being *known*. And being known is not the same thing as possessing authority or trust. Recall Barack Obama vs. the shoe store owner; the former president's fame doesn't make him one bit more qualified to speak on arch support or durability.

Of course, the former president isn't known for recommending brands of running shoe to his audience. But you *will* frequently see celebrities posting about products on their social channels, which may only be tangentially related to their area of expertise. When this happens, their fans can easily perceive these one-off endorsements as the straight-up advertisements they really are.

Coach, speaker, and author Alan Stein, Jr. *(Raise Your Game)* certainly knows the power of celebrity—given his work alongside NBA superstars like Kevin Durant for over 15 years—and he knows celebrity isn't the key to influence:

"Too many people mistakenly believe you must be famous or a celebrity to be a powerful influencer. In reality, you need to be trustworthy, credible, likeable. . .and you need to *earn* your influence by providing value to those who turn to you. You *attract* your following by *serving* them.

Another big misnomer is that audience size is an indication for influence...interpreting that more followers is better. People assume 10,000 followers are better than 1,000 followers...but it's just not the case. It's the loyalty, support and engagement of that following that matters most."

Neil Waller, co-founder of Whalar Influencer Marketing, puts it brilliantly:

> "Follower numbers don't equal actual reach. They don't give any measure of true influence with an audience and, most importantly, they don't give any insight into the audience composition.
>
> Given marketing is about conveying a message to a specific audience, influencer marketing is worthless if it's not actually speaking to the desired audience, regardless of how niche or broad that audience is.
>
> If you were selling an everyday cooking product would you advertise in Vogue or Good Housekeeping? If you had a fintech product trying to reach a Canadian audience would you work with a very large tech influencer who actually has less than 2% of their audience in Canada?"
>
> By focusing on audience size and reach above all else, the results would be very misleading. To get the most accurate results, concentrate on who you are reaching.

An influencer does NOT need to be an individual. . .or even human! That's right: an influencer is *any* medium that has power or impact on the desired recipient.

Think about this: if the World Health Organization says to stop eating beef because of a disease outbreak, what happens? The world stops eating beef. Stores pull it off their shelves and we are all too afraid to eat a burger. Influencers are most often thought of as individuals, but widen your perspective: they can also be organizations, brands, movements, nonprofits, awards, and schools.

Confusion about influence = confusion about influencer marketing

With our stack of misconceptions that high, it makes complete sense that many modern influencer marketing efforts often don't accomplish their goals.

There are a wide range of strategies that get lumped in with influencer marketing—but they are widely making it worse, adding confusion, and standing in the way to success.

Influencer marketing is not advertising. Advertising is when a brand uses a paid communications channel to convey a sales message. It's fundamentally transactional. Influencer marketing should be much more than a simple transaction, for everyone involved. Plenty of influencer relationships will never see cash changing hands. And even when money *is* involved, that's not where the true value of these relationships lie.

Author, speaker, entrepreneur, and host of *Good Morning La La Land,* Dr. Erin Fall Haskell, points out brands are wasting their time treating influence like advertising:

> "The most misunderstood thing about influencer marketing is brands believing that an influencer can shout out or post about a product and have it will automatically sell, like any old ad.
>
> Having a morning show in Los Angeles, I've had *hundreds* of brands send me free swag. Sock companies, sparkler companies, clothing companies, candle companies, hairdressers, and marketing companies have all reached out. How are any of those relevant to me and my community? They couldn't tell me, either.

The reality is unless the influencer is one hundred percent in alignment with the mission and message of the product it isn't going to sell, period. Influencer marketing is all about bringing value to a community."

Platforms like Instagram are rife with influencers selling products that may or may not have anything to do with their own lives, interests, or expertise—let alone what their community wants, needs, or is interested in. If an influencer holds up a product and a few thousand people hit like, do you think those people are going to buy it immediately?

No way. Yet that's the prevailing mindset, and while a few may, it's just as Dr. Erin says: if the alignment is off, the sales will be, too.

Influencer marketing is NOT social media. This is a *big* one. While social media is a vehicle for *extending* your influence, that's all it is: *a vehicle*. It's a communication channel to distribute and amplify your message. If I call you to have a conversation and I influence you during that conversation, my *phone* doesn't become influential. Yes, social media platforms have the ability to reach a much greater audience than any other communication channel in history—but social media in and of itself is not influence.

Influencer marketing does NOT happen solely online. Influence has been around from the beginning of time—light years before the internet—yet we often position influencer marketing as something that only happens online.

The internet has enabled us to spread messages, connect with more people from further away, and build bigger communities at breakneck speed—but some of the most influential people in each of our lives are not those who boast a large-scale following. They are teachers, coaches, politicians, activists, and artists who see their communities face to face every day.

I recently went to a live class hosted by an Italian chef at my local cooking store. By the time we had finished working through his delicious recipe, every participant was loading up on his cookbook, the $200 knife he'd used (and recommended), and every kitchen on the counter next to him.

Items we thought we needed? Nope. Influenced to buy? 100 percent.

See how that works?

Yet agencies and marketers (and let's be honest, plenty of influencers) are *still* focused on empty metrics like follower counts, views, likes, and comments. These are what I refer to as vanity metrics—they're visible, quantifiable, impressive on the surface. . .and ultimately meaningless. It's easy to understand the appeal: why *not* go with the easiest, quickest way of showing results, especially when clients or bosses are breathing down your neck about showing ROI in a finite time frame?

But by focusing on these 'vanity metrics' we not only fail to get the full story or the most accurate story, we fail to build genuine long-term relationships whose values go far beyond any short term transaction.

Marketing is *not* an exact science—rather, it's a combination of art, social science, and an endless psychology experiment. You're dealing with the forces—conscious, subconscious, and unconscious—that affect decision-making and actions. We can't always explain what contributes to our decision-making, because we're not linear *or* rational in our thinking and behaviors. . .as much as we'd like to think we are.

We act within the complexities of emotion, self-perception, and relationships. . .all of which are constantly in flux. Then, we justify those actions using our own rationale.

That's why measuring influence can't work like any other traditional measurement process you've used.

So what can we do?

Answer: We need to completely shift the way we view influencer marketing.

It's time to transfer the perspective away from that of influencer marketing as a modern-day advertising tactic, to one of building real brand- influencer alliances based on trust.

Pulling from Jonah Berger again, he sums it up well:

"In today's day and age, we've come to see influence almost as a negative word. Marketers are trying to influence us, brands are trying to influence us. . .but influence by itself is neither good nor bad. It's all about the *intent*.

When my best friend gives me a recommendation, it influences my behavior, but it also helps me. It helps me make a better, faster decision than I might be able to make otherwise, to my own benefit."

Real influence is the power of one source on another, resulting in desired action. It is the capacity to have an impact on the character, development, or behavior of someone or something.

If we know what real influence is, our definition of an influencer becomes crystal clear: **an influencer is any medium (individuals, brands, organizations, non-profits) which has the power to affect**

the actions and decisions (real or perceived) of others by virtue of their authority, knowledge, position, or relationship.

If we as marketers aim to begin by understanding where true influence lies and work to develop mutually beneficial long term relationships with those who hold the influence over our market, then we're much more likely to garner the results we desire. . .and achieve the bottom-line business growth we need not only to survive, but to thrive in this increasingly fragmented world.

Recap and Review

KEY POINTS

1. **We have been thinking—and continue to think—about influencer marketing all wrong. Influencer marketing must be based on true influence, which is an outcome, not a job title.**
   a. *Influence* refers to the power one source has on another to affect a desired action. It can also be thought of as the capacity something has to impact the character, development, or behavior of someone or something.
   b. *Influencers* are the force or medium—which can encompass individuals, brands, organizations, non-profits, etc.—which has the power to affect the actions and decisions (real or perceived) of others by virtue of their authority, knowledge, position, or relationship.

2. **Our misconceptions about influence and influencer marketing continue to hold us back.**
   a. Popularity is NOT the same as influence. Popularity is the state of being liked, even loved—neither of which are the same as being influential.
   b. Attention is NOT the same as influence. While "going viral" may result in a lot of eyes on your brand and its message, if it doesn't serve to affect purchasing habits or drive purchasing decisions, then it has not *influenced* anyone.

3. **Influencer marketing is not advertising.**
   a. Advertising is when a brand uses a paid communications channel to convey their sales message.
   b. Advertising is fundamentally transactional, whereas influencer marketing is a relationship—a long-term investment that goes well beyond a one-off paid promotion.

4. **Influencer marketing is not the same as social media marketing.**
   a. Social media is simply a communication channel which allows for the distribution of messages. So, while social media platforms may have the ability to reach a much greater audience than any other communication channel in history—it is not, in and of itself, influential.

5. **Influencers do not need to be an individual...or even human.**
   a. An influencer is *any* medium that has power or impact on the desired recipient.

6. **For marketers to use influencer marketing effectively, what is required is not a change in method—what we need is a change in mindset.**
   a. Current influencer marketing is far too focused on the wrong metrics, which is why so many marketers aren't getting their desired results.
   b. Marketing is not an exact science. By focusing on easily quantifiable metrics like reach, likes, shares and comments, we miss out on the bigger picture—and all the opportunities it offers.

MOVING FORWARD

Popularity doesn't necessarily equal influence, but there are certainly popular, influential people who drive decision making—just look at Oprah. Having a ton of followers on Instagram doesn't equal influence, but there are certainly individuals on social media sites with millions of followers who hang on their every word. So how do we determine when something is influential? More importantly, how do we determine *in what way* something is influential?

FOOD FOR THOUGHT

Would you be inclined to take Tiger Woods' advice on life insurance policies? Do you consider a Wall Street executive's take on active wear when putting together an outfit to wear to the gym? What about your next-door neighbor's recommendations on tropical vacations?

3

The Four Types of Influencers
And why you need to know the difference

L et's talk about how we make our day-to-day choices. Where do we get our recommendations? What shapes our thought processes when we're considering different options? What makes us decide to choose one thing over another, or take a particular action?

One thing is certain—there have never been so many places for us to research the things we're interested in, the things we need or want, or the solutions to our problems. And the way we use all the tools at our disposal can shine a spotlight on our priorities.

One person might want to know what brand of running shoe Usain Bolt, Olympic gold medalist and 100-meter dash world record holder, wears when he trains, but someone who doesn't follow competitive track and field might not even remember his name. Instead, they'll buy the brand of sneaker they see the most fit people sporting at the local gym.

One person might ask their tech-savvy cousin what type of smartphone they should buy, while another might opt for whatever pricey phone Kim Kardashian has in her LuMee case on *Keeping Up With the Kardashians*.

One person might log into Reddit groups to get locals' recommendations about the best rental neighborhood in a city while prepping for an upcoming move, while another won't speak to anyone but their family's longtime real estate agent to get the lay of the land.

A family might see their friends living it up at a Mayan resort on Instagram, and Insta-stalk them for the week to see if the place looks like fun, while another family logs onto Reddit's Disney forums to learn about cruises from die-hard fans.

In each case, the choice made sends a message about what the person or family values, and the way they seek information about the world around them. One person might value a celebrity's pick where another person only wants an expert perspective; one person might want to get the scoop from an experienced community, while another only wants to speak to a trusted family connection.

Whether we realize it or not, there are different types of influence involved in every decision and action, and we can actually segment the different types into four basic categories: celebrity, authority, expert, and affinity.

Without segmentation, we fall into one-size-fits-all approaches that address everyone while influencing no one.

Or worse, it might work for a while—especially if you have a huge marketing budget to throw around—but it won't last, and may even reduce an audience's willingness to engage with future messaging you put out.

This isn't a new concept—influence has always been at the heart of human behavior—yet we still see countless agencies, businesses, and campaigns that differentiate between influencers based solely on the size of their online audience. And they wonder why their results are so poor!

So, let's break down the four types of influence, and why it's important to not only recognize them, but build unique strategies for each category.

CELEBRITY
"Don't you know who I am? You can trust me!"

Michael Jordan (aka "His Airness") is one of the greatest basketball players of all time, and a consummate world-class athlete. He's also arguably the father of modern-day celebrity influencers— long before social media broadened (and democratized) the spotlight.

Nike quickly recognized his potential for impact, and partnered with Jordan to create the iconic "Air Jordan" brand. When his first basketball shoe was launched in 1984, it became an immediate bestseller, and Nike has continued to release new editions of what fans just call "Jordans" every year since—more than 30 iterations to date.

Jordan's face, his flying silhouette logo, and his number 23 jersey are now classic elements of basketball culture, and the Nike-Jordan influencer partnership has become one of the most successful in history.

The collaboration works because Jordan is one of the few athletes who has transcended a team or city to become admired by *all* fans of his sport. He is revered for his athletic prowess, so an athletic apparel line is a perfect extension of his brand. His celebrity also transcends generations, genders, and cultural lines—making him an ideal ambassador for a brand looking for broad impact and relevance.

Celebrities have held influence for as long as there has been a pen, a paintbrush, a microphone, or a camera ready to capture their every move. Whether a celebrity acquires their fame via talent, wealth, association, or notoriety, people are drawn to the power, access, and privilege they possess. And as long as we've had celebrities, we've had celebrity endorsements of products, services, and brands.

These endorsements take a number of forms:

- **Direct advertising.** A celebrity appears in an ad (under their own name or recognizably as themselves) to promote a product or service.
- **Sponsorship.** This is particularly common amongst amateur and professional athletes: a brand provides equipment, products, and compensation to a celebrity to promote their brand.
- **Swag.** "Swag" is the term used when a company's goods or services are provided to celebrities in the hope they'll use or recommend them publicly. This often occurs at awards shows or event "gifting suites".
- **Brand ambassador.** Brand ambassador relationships develop in different ways. A brand might reach out to a celebrity if they use their product, either to provide them with more product, or the means to promote the brand. Conversely, a brand might reach out unprompted to a celebrity who aligns well with their brand and audiences.

Be careful not to assume celebrities have unlimited influence over the hearts and wallets of their fans and audiences. As noted previously, celebrity status does not equate to influence; there needs to be the right alignment of product/brand, with the right celebrity.

As influential as Jordan was when it came to basketball shoes and apparel, when Hanes launched their Michael Jordan underwear collaboration, it completely flopped. Why? Because his celebrity and influence is in the space of athletics, not men's under garments. If we look at who buys majority of men's underwear, it's actually women (girlfriends, wives, mothers), and those buyers aren't looking to Michael Jordan for underwear referrals. The key is to have a natural alignment between the celebrity, the product, and the audience.

So how do you determine whether a celebrity (or any other influencer, for that matter) is properly aligned to represent your product or business?

AUTHORITY
"Do what I tell you because I said so!"

For better or for worse, authority-based influence is one of the most common types of influence in our society. Authority most often comes from a person's position in a company or formal title.

Picture this: You're driving down the road when suddenly you hear a siren behind you, accompanied by flashing lights. You immediately recognize that a police officer is trying to get your attention, so you pull over to the side of the road.

At that point, the officer may leave their vehicle to talk to you, or they may race by to pursue someone else—but their impact on your choices and actions is immediate. You stop your car, roll down your window, and wait for the officer to approach, even though you don't know them or the nature of their business with you—all because they possess the power and legitimacy of a badge.

Authority is influence generated by position or set of powers, often accompanied by a title (like the police officer), that clearly establishes a particular level of control over others. Politicians, business leaders, law enforcement, managers, supervisors, and other similar figures depend on their authority—whether earned or demanded—to get things done.

EXPERT
"You can trust me, because I have training and experience."

Influence via expertise is another common form of influence, often wielded by individuals with a particular type and level of knowledge or skill: i.e. doctors, professors, academics, and so on. An expert possesses a high level of capability, and their status as an expert may be established a variety of ways: a history of successful results, the respect of their peers, a particular certification or title, or a long resume of achievements and commendations.

Imagine that you are part of a crowd listening to a powerful U.S. congressman addressing potential voters. He brings decades of experience working in government compared to his challenger, who is relatively new to the scene. He lists his achievements as a lawmaker, his bipartisan efforts, and all he's done to make his state a better place—while shrugging off his opponent's relatively short list of kudos. He even suggests his opponent's inexperience might make his state a less safe and secure place, fostering the distrust of the crowd.

In a few moments, he's convinced everyone that his experience is his greatest asset—something his opponent can't match.

If a person is interested in a particular industry or space, they'll soon come to know those who can be considered experts in that space. They're the ones who end up on "best of" lists, win awards, and most often receive praise for their work. They are considered credible, both by their peers and by the audiences they attract. When you want an answer to a question or help overcoming a challenge, an expert is a smart first stop.

Let's say you're plotting out how to grow your business, but you're feeling a bit in over your head. Your options may include:

- Plotting your strategy and next steps on your own; hoping you can keep treading water while you figure things out
- Seeking advice from a friend or family member who might know a little bit about what you're looking to accomplish; or
- Picking up a book from an entrepreneur with demonstrated results in helping business owners just like you.

If you're anything like me, you're going to pick the third option—not to mention highlight and dog-ear the heck out of that entrepreneur's book. Their counsel is backed up with real-world results—and results are exactly what we're looking for.

After years of coaching in the fitness space, I know how desperate people can get to move past a plateau in their workouts. Because this is an area of expertise for me, I can make specific equipment or nutritional recommendations—and because they trust my expertise, they are far more likely to make a purchase based on those recommendations.

When I took over the role as Chief Marketing Strategist for Valeo Technologies (a legacy home fitness equipment brand, among other products), my strategy involved researching and targeting the top local fitness professionals across North America. Rather than investing endless ad dollars in social media fitness stars, I chose that our team send our products to the best-in-class local trainers and coaches to share with their clients.

I knew that the local experts wouldn't have the *reach* of a social media star—their communities would more likely be termed "micro" or "niche". But based on my *experience* selling fitness solutions, I believed their recommendations would be exponentially more powerful than a broader, less focused pitch. If a trusted trainer recommends a specific resistance band to a client, along with a specific exercise to do with the band at home, the client will have a good chance of purchasing the recommended band recognizing the product's value in their workout.

Conversely, an Instagram influencer may have 50,000 people hanging on their every word. . .yet they only move 10 units with their resistance band selfie. Why? Because resistance band recommendations either aren't why people follow them or the audience doesn't believe the recommendation is really that valuable for them.

Andrew Davis is one of the leading authorities on content marketing as a speaker and author. If you walked up to a complete stranger in New York's Times Square and asked them who Andrew Davis was, odds are pretty good that they won't know who you're talking about.

But if you went to a marketing, branding, or business conference and asked the same question, you'd get plenty of enthusiastic professionals wondering if Andrew was there, and where to find him. He may not be a global household name, but he's game-changer in his own space and someone I personally look to for info on upcoming trends, and recommendations on what books to read, what websites to visit and what workshops to take in the marketing field.

In other words, we can say that expert influence is unique among the four types of influence in that we can further break things down into "sub-categories." These provide levels of additional distinction that cannot be overlooked when considering influencers for your projects, and which further empower us to craft perfectly aligned messaging for the influencer involved.

In brief, expert influencers can be identified as:
- Insiders
- Connectors
- Activists

Each of these sub-categories develops and uses their influence in different ways—and once you understand which matters to your own audience, you can expertly (pun intended) predict who is going to best influence them.

The Insider: The one with exclusive access

An "insider" is a member of a group that requires a particular type of knowledge, access, or understanding to join it.

Let's say you're a journalist covering the Silicon Valley scene, and you'd like to learn more about Facebook's plans for increased member privacy. You can watch Mark Zuckerberg read a statement about Facebook's vision for privacy at a press conference—or you can find someone in Zuckerberg's circle to give you the candid scoop about Facebook's plans.

By extension, you're suddenly an insider, too. Your colleagues all want the *real* details about Facebook's plans—making your access critical to *everyone's* success.

The concept of the insider is built on the belief that there are two versions of reality: how things seem on the outside, and how they actually are on the inside. We love insider opinions, we love insider jargon, we love insider access. . .and we love the idea that we'll be in on a secret or two, if we play our cards right.

The Connector: **The one who knows everyone**

Connectors have vast networks of colleagues, friends, and acquaintances, and they are passionate about helping others build relationships. They collect connections like someone else might collect baseball cards or stamps: the more hard-to-get and rare a relationship might be, the better a collector they are.

A connector can be a great asset in helping you connect with influencers, or they may be an influencer themselves, with other influential people in their circle. They know the right doors to knock on, the right person to call in the right situation, and the right "in" when someone needs a critical introduction.

Social media has familiarized us with the idea of "friending" or "following" to connect with others. But connectors do more than just run up their numbers; they focus on *quality* over *quantity*. If you want to make inroads in a particular industry, gain access into a certain community, or reach a particular audience, connectors are the ones to know.

Let's say you're looking to launch a brand new product in the interior design space. You rent a booth at a home expo, hoping to meet contractors and designers. As the day wears on, no one stops by, and you're beginning to wonder if you've wasted your entire day—not to mention the exhibitor fee.

That's when you catch the eye of someone who you've watched visit every vendor in the building. They don't know you—in fact, you appear to be the only person they *don't* know. After hearing your quick pitch, they wave over a friend looking for what you have to offer. That introduction turns into great chat, and in the meantime, another couple of people have stopped to talk with the connector. . .and they take a look at your product while they're there.

In the space of a few moments, you've seen more action at your booth than you've seen all day—and your connector might just have changed the whole course of your business.

Connectors exist in every industry, and they have an incredible ability to influence others by virtue of their relationship-building skills. Once you know them, you know everybody.

The Activist: **The one who wants to change the world**

Activists are passionate about a particular cause or issue, and they have a unique ability to draw others in with their passion and commitment to their cause. They are problem solvers, game-changers, and fearless advocates for their beliefs.

If you want a vocal advocate for your product, the activist could be your new best friend. They love sharing their ideas and perspectives because they are confident in what they think, they know how to persuade others, and they believe their efforts have impact.

Online parenting communities are a great spot to find examples of the activist influencer: parents who are passionate about the way they are raising their children. They are eager to build relationships with people and brands who reflect their values, beliefs, and interests, whether they're discussing family leave and flexibility in the workplace, the educational system, or issues around childhood bullying.

If you're willing to align with the work and issues that motivate them, you'll benefit from a strong voice speaking in your favor.

AFFINITY: **PERSONAL CONNECTION**

Influence via affinity is one of the most overlooked forms of influence—
yet it's also one of the most powerful. Affinity is a certain affection
or disposition to trust or favor someone or something, and they are
usually a result of the relationships we maintain with family, friends,
and other trusted individuals we turn to for advice or counsel.

> When I wanted to buy my first car, I looked around at different
> ads and dealerships, but I'd never had a car, and I didn't know
> what I should actually be looking for.
>
> I could have spent hours combing through auto forums on
> the internet and reading the opinions of experts (and self-pro-
> claimed experts), with thousands of comments and rabid
> followers. . .but who could I trust? Were any of these people
> actually worried about my safety and well-being, or the state of
> my bank account.
>
> The real car expert I needed wasn't on the internet. It
> was my dad.
>
> My dad who wanted the best for me; my dad who knew I
> was nervous; my dad who knew I needed something econom-
> ical yet reliable. My dad who knew I wanted to drive a manual
> because it was more fun. . .but who also knew I shouldn't have
> too much horsepower because of my lead foot.
>
> In the end, he helped me make the right decision, and I was
> off to the races (literally!)
>
> (Sorry, Dad!)

Yet the auto industry expects women to turn to celebrities like Danica Patrick: a glamorous race car driver and one of the few women in her sport. Brands bombard her to endorse their products, thinking her image will resonate with younger women.

Is any young girl going to follow Danica Patrick for advice on being a first-time car buyer? Odds are, she's not. They *should* be focusing on the people most likely to influence this decision in a young woman's life: which in many cases, happens to be dad.

The power of affinity is the most often ignored by marketers who see influence as a matter of reach, popularity or notoriety. They mistakenly believe people want to take cues from the loudest voices in the crowd, when what most of us *actually* want is to make a connection with someone we trust deeply, and who cares about our well-being.

Why is it so critical to understand *who* possesses *which* types of influence?

Influence isn't monolithic—there isn't one way to gain it, possess it, or use it. When you understand the different roles influence can play, and the different situations in which influence has impact, you'll be better able to use it in your favor. You can't help people make a certain decision, adopt different behavior, or change their perspective on an issue unless you figure out who has a voice in making those things happen in their lives.

Recap and Review

KEY POINTS

1. **Every decision we make is motivated by a variety of factors—some internal, some external. Those external factors are what we call "influence."**

   a. Further complicating matters, all actions and decisions are unique—and are impacted by different types of influence at different times and in different ways.

   b. Not all influence is alike—or created equal. Different situations and roles create different types of influence for different reasons.

2. **Broadly speaking, there are four basic types of influencers.**

   a. Celebrity: Those who influence through name recognition and/or popularity. This is the most visible type of influence—and the most often misunderstood.

   b. Authority: Those who influence through their role or position. Authority-based influence is one of the most easily observable in our society, and can stem from both respect and/or fear.

   c. Expertise: Those who influence through their prior achievement, specialized knowledge or training, or established reputation of skill. Expertise can be further sub-categorized based on how the expert develops and applies their influence.

d. Affinity: Those who influence through their pre-existing relationship of trust. Typically based on personal relationships, it is easily the most overlooked by marketers and brands.

3. **Understanding the different types of influence—and influencers—is critical for marketers looking to use influencer marketing in their own campaigns.**
   a. Without understanding the different types of influencers—and the areas in which their influence is recognized—it is impossible to effectively utilize influence to drive consumer behavior.
   b. In other words, you can't get consumers to hear your message if you don't know who and what they're already listening to.

MOVING FORWARD

If influencer marketing was based on audience size and attention, it would simply be called advertising. True influencer marketing requires knowing what you ultimately want to achieve, a knowledge of your audience and who actually holds influence over your them on the desired action, and an ability to create long term mutually beneficial alliances with those influencers.

FOOD FOR THOUGHT

Who do you think is more likely to succeed: the person who says "I want to get in shape", or the person who says, "I want to lose 10 pounds over the next eight weeks"?

Which employee would you choose to promote: the candidate who says, "I can increase sales", or the one who says, "I will increase overall revenue by 15% by the end of the third quarter by engaging a new audience"?

INTRODUCING THE CODE

So far, we've talked about:

- The biggest misconceptions about influence today
- The difference between popularity and influence
- The current state of the marketing environment, and why we need influencer marketing more than ever
- The different types and levels of influence, and the roles they play
- How the current dialogue about influencer marketing lacks a consistent framework or structure

Now, let me ask you a question.

When it comes time to approach an influencer—what is the first question you ask yourself?

If you're like most of the entrepreneurs or marketers I know, you ask, *"What should I say?"*

Therein lies the problem: your question has an *I* in it.

That one little word is indicative of precisely the wrong mindset. To get people to align with you, your brand, and your mission, it can't be all about you!

Instead, ask yourself: *"What do I want to happen after they receive my message?"*

If you want to use influence to grow your business, to advance your brand, and accelerate your marketing efforts, it's your job to be an influencer first: in other words, in order to do influencer marketing right, you must be able to influence the influencer.

Influence, at the core, is simply communication with a goal.

I'm about to share with you the fundamental set of ideas that spurred me on to write this book. It's the title of the book, yes, but it's also the foundation—the framework that supports every word. Rather than additional information overload we need organized wisdom.

This is the Influencer Code.

The Code is comprised of three simple fundamental principles (simply but not easy). The vast majority of the marketers, entrepreneurs and brand executives I know either miss or shortcut at least one of these steps. . .and every step you skip undermines your efforts to achieving your goal.

It's no different than a combination for a lock: you can have all the right numbers, but if you miss just one, or enter them in the wrong order, you won't crack it.

From this point on, I'll be walking you through each of the following phases in detail, but let's take a brief look at each one up front, and explore why they are integral to my approach.

STEP ONE: ALWAYS START WITH THE END IN MIND

What is your end game? What is your goal?

As a marketer (or a business owner wearing multiple hats) a strategic approach is critical if you want your efforts to drive action, but you can't build a strong strategy without a clear goal of what you want to achieve. So, before you get caught up in thoughts of, "But wait, what about [*insert crazy success story in which someone says it all happened "by accident" or without any sort of plan in place*], keep in mind that these are the exceptions, not the rule—the equivalent of winning the business lottery.

If you're going to connect with an influencer in an effort to grow your business, you need to know why.

As Simon Sinek put it in his famous TED talk, "How Great Leaders Inspire Action", you should always "start with why".

Influencer marketing is no different.

You have to know the reason you are actually doing all of this: the goal. That means being able to answer questions such as:
- What do you want to have happen?
- By when?
- How will you know when you've gotten there?
- Where do we begin?

In Chapter 4, I'll dig into the differences between objectives and goals, and how to set SMART objectives that will map out where you want to go. Once you are crystal clear on your goals and objectives, it's time to for you to become an observation detective.

STEP TWO: OBSERVE AND IDENTIFY

This is my favorite phase of influencer marketing, because it's where the detective work comes in. Your goal is to first pinpoint what and who influences your audiences—the influencers who have sway over their behaviors, actions, and decisions—and then second, figure out what matters to the influencers you identify. . .and how you in particular can offer them value.

In order to influence your target consumer, you first have to *influence the influencer*, which is why this step is broken into two phases.

Stop brainstorming, stop thinking about what you want to say—and instead, start paying attention. Remember, the best marketer doesn't start with "What should I say?," he/she always begins with, "What do I want to happen as a result of this action?"

Here are the questions ask yourself as you work through this pivotal two-phase process:

Phase 1: Observing and identifying the influencers

- Who is my audience?
- What is important to them?
- What do they value?
- What beliefs do they have around my product or space?
- Who or what is influencing them in ways that are relevant to my space?

Phase 2: Observing and identifying what influences the influencer

- What does the influencer want to achieve?
- What do they value?
- What problems do they want to solve?
- What beliefs do they have around this topic?
- What can we offer them to help them meet their goals or create value for them?

At our most fundamental level, humans are always moving toward pleasure or away from pain—and it's your job as a marketer to discover and act what triggers each.

During this process, make an effort to see the relationship from their perspective. What would motivate them to work with you? If you focus on what you want to happen, you will miss out on learning what *they* want to happen.

"Amanda, who has this kind of time?! I don't have days to research someone, not to mention the hours to conduct an interview!"

We often get caught up in a perceived scarcity of time, thinking we don't have the resources to do our homework and get things right.

But this isn't about pitching a tent, *it's about building a home.*

If you take shortcuts, you'll get what you put in—but if you invest time from the outset, you'll be on solid footing.

Beyond that, practice makes perfect. I'd say that I can gather enough information about a potential influencer partner after an hour or so of targeted searching, and within 5–10 minutes talking to them on the phone, they're telling me the valuable, actionable information I need to help me begin our relationship on the right foot.

If you can make this whole process second nature, you'll not only get faster, you'll uncover better insights and answers along the way.

On the flip side, if you leave *out* this critical process of observation, you end up wasting time trying to dream up the perfect opportunity—one your influence partner is actually going to care about—and miss out on the bigger picture of how you can work together in the longer term.

If you don't know what resonates with the person you're reaching out to, you won't open the door for the kind of long-term connection you want to make—which brings us to our third step.

STEP THREE: BUILDING—AND MAINTAINING—CONNECTIONS

Connection is what builds the magic bridge between your observations and your goals.

The final pillar of the Influencer Code is building authentic relationships with your influencers. This is what saves your efforts from being empty and transactional, and what inspires your influence partner to do great work within your relationship.

When you take the time to set a great foundation and invest in building something of value, it endures. When you throw together something cheap, it blows away with the slightest gust of wind—and after a while, the opportunity cost adds up!

Once you are clear on your own goals, and you know what matters to your potential influence partner, you can create opportunities to collaborate and build your relationship. These collaborations can take different shapes, depending on the strengths and resources you both bring to the table.

If you don't create a genuine connection, it's going to be really hard to create a successful partnership—and if they're just doing it for the money, that's advertising.

As you start to read, you'll see that each chapter of this book has been written to map the tactical steps within each phase of the Influencer Code.

I guarantee you will come out the other end with a profoundly stronger understanding of the value of influence and how to put it into serious action.

As you proceed in your career, keep this book handy— to inspire ideas when you are stuck or facing a challenge. Dog-ear it, mark it up, and come back to it time and again. Not only will it surprise you, you may just surprise yourself!

ALWAYS
START
WITH
THE
END
IN
MIND

4

Setting SMART Goals
It's tough to get a bullseye when you can't see the target

There's a reason running is such a good metaphor for so many things in life. I might be a bit biased, having devoted the majority of my life to it, but I believe this grueling sport is the purest example of how setting the right goals and smart objectives is the critical key to executing on any successful strategy.

Let's take a look at the different ways runners train:

- **Elite runners** make training their priority, and they have a defined strategy to achieve their goals. Since their success is measured by the times they hit for their distance, they don't log junk miles just to run. They constantly set new, key performance indicators (KPIs), then push their limits to get faster. If they want to win an Olympic team spot, they know their objective is to run the marathon at a 5-minute-mile pace. Thus their strategy includes training 6 days per week, at the pace they need to run.
- **Club runners** run to complete a given distance, or log an amount of time spent pounding the pavement. They run to complete the run, to finish the race, and to check that box.
- **Amateurs** spend half their time not really running at all. They're planning their route, walking to catch their breath, stopping to enjoy the scenery, or pausing to let the dog do its business.

See the difference? To get to the highest level of achievement, athletes set concrete goals and articulate their exact training objectives. They have a plan and clear direction—all captured in writing, and then tracked and measured in a training log.

It's amazing how even the highest-paid, most well-regarded executives, marketers, and even influencers will come up with a host of great ideas. . .yet fail to actually *articulate* and *define* their strategic goals before they inject a huge budget into a campaign or plan. Instead, they confuse objectives with goals, and the two are very different. Essentially, an objective is something that guides you on your path to achieving a bigger goal.

Case in point: getting 8,000 comments on one YouTube video or gaining 80,000 new subscribers is *not* a goal in itself, for the simple reason that until you know *why* you want those 8,000 views or those 80k subscribers, it's an achievement without a purpose. Everyone craves the big numbers, but what's the bigger why? What's the result? What have you gained?

Dan Feliciano of Six Sigma Rock Star does a succinct, clear job of explaining the difference:

> "A goal is a brief, clear statement of an outcome to be reached within a timeframe such as 3–5 years. A goal is a broad, general, tangible, and descriptive statement. It does not say how to do something, but rather what the results will look like. It is measurable both in terms of quality and quantity. It is time-based. It is achievable. It is a stretch from where we are now. Above all, it is singular."

In other words, we define a goal as "an outcome statement that defines what an organization is trying to accomplish, both programmatically and organizationally."

Some common business goals are:

- Become profitable by the 2-year anniversary of our launch
- Raise our market share to become the market leader in our category within 5 years
- Be the #1 most recommended brand of XX in the XX category
- Become a solidly booked keynote speaker (defined by 12 keynote talks per year), commanding $30,000/talk
- Publish a New York Times best-selling book and sell over a million copies in one year

Note the *brevity* of these statements. In comparison, an objective, or key performance indicator (KPI), which I'll use interchangeably with "objective", is a milestone that must be attained in order to accomplish a particular goal. In a nutshell, a goal is where you want to be and objectives are the milestones along the way to reach that goal.

To give you an idea of the most common types of objectives that get confused with goals, here's a few I see all the time:

- Sign up for X number of tradeshows
- Buy print ad space in X publications
- Buy X worth of web and social media ads
- Create weekly/daily/monthly content across X platforms
- Increase website traffic
- Win the X award
- Collaborate with X influencer to host an event and corresponding online giveaway
- Produce X videos for a holiday campaign

Again, there's nothing wrong with any of these things—in fact, they're all worth doing—so long as they're *in service* of the goal you want to achieve. But they are not, *in and of themselves*, the goal.

Starting with your goal allows you to work backwards, deciding which objectives are worth pursuing and seeing how each action item can work to get you closer to that goal without getting distracted by every potential opportunity or new idea you come across.

Let's say the owner of a sports franchise is worried his ticket-buying fan base is shrinking. He tells his marketing and sales teams about his concern, and they set a "goal" of fostering greater fan buzz in the stands by increasing the number of t-shirts they shoot out of a cannon at halftime by 50 percent.

They report back to the owner that the fans *love* the t-shirts, and are proudly announcing how they're knocking their goal out of the park.

While fans might love receiving a free t-shirt in the stands, and generate some excitement, getting a free t-shirt shot at you doesn't necessarily lead to any sort of action. Unless you set a real business goal to respond to a real business challenge, your efforts will be more like playing the lottery, than mapping you to a desired destination.

But a goal is only a starting point. You can't draw yourself a map without a destination, and you can't reach your destination without a map. In fact, setting the right kind of goals will make an impact on *every* area of the work you do (and honestly, the rest of your life, too.) In short, a **goal** is what you want to achieve and your **objective** is what will define your success (or failure) in achieving it. We'll begin by walking through my top tips on setting actionable objectives for influencer efforts.

Beware of shiny objects

Hungarian psychologist Mihaly Csikszentmihalyi once said, "Goals transform a random walk into a chase." In other words, goals help you to laser-focus on what's important and keep you from being distracted by whatever attractive opportunities comes your way: the shiny objects.

It's only natural that we get charmed by the sheer number of influencer possibilities that exist on every platform. When we see someone building an audience that looks like it might overlap with our own target market, it's tempting to want to get our product in their hands.

The relationship *could* end up being a mutually beneficial one—but if we don't start with a business goal, we risk wasting our time, money, and energy. By staying laser-focused on our goal, we maintain clarity about the influencers and opportunities that will make most sense to achieve that goal.

The owner of a women's activewear brand I worked with happened to be good friends with a popular fashion influencer who offers engaging styling content on the latest trends for different body types, and she has a huge and enthusiastic following—as evidenced by the thousands of views and likes she gets on each of her videos. Perfect, right?

Except when we dug deeper it became apparent the two brands audiences didn't really align, her audience came to her for a certain type of fashion and weren't into activewear or fitness in general, so while the influence she holds over her audience is real, it doesn't translate to influence in the activewear brand category, and therefore a partnership with her won't help achieve the desired objective.

When we work from a place of goals and set a long-term strategy, we don't waste time on shiny objects, and we achieve much greater long term, bigger picture goals.

THE SMART MODEL
Getting "smart" about what you want to achieve

Imagine going to a networking event, and when your colleague asks how it was, you say: "It was great! I had so much engagement!"

No one would say that; it doesn't mean anything. Did you meet new people and exchange contact information? Field a business inquiry and set up a conversation? Receive some LinkedIn requests or a follow on Twitter?

Yet this vague and elusive term "engagement" is frequently being used in reporting results of marketing campaigns. It's giving influencer marketing a bad name, and it's most often the result of not setting smart objectives from the beginning.

And by smart objectives, we really mean SMART objectives. Not all objectives are created equal, nor are they all equally focused in how they get you closer to your end goal. That's why we use the SMART model, a simple acronym that acts as a checklist when you're formulating your objectives.

Objectives should be:
SPECIFIC
MEASURABLE
ATTAINABLE
RELEVANT
TIME-BOUND

Let's take a look at what each word means, and what impact they should have on setting your objectives.

Specific

Specific objectives can be scary, because they set real expectations. It's much easier to choose a vague target you can fulfill with the smallest possible amount of progress.

Vague objectives include:
- Increase leads (but how many?)
- Increase sales (but how much?)
- Increase engagement (but how? And wait, what does engagement actually mean?)

If you truly want to increase leads, put some firm parameters around *how* you quantify a lead, the *level* of increase you want to see, and *when* you want to accomplish it by: "We want to increase our leads by 20 percent by year-end. We define leads as the number of people who fill out our contact form, and agree to our 15-minute consultation."

With that simple sentence, you've set a specific objective. Now you actually know what you want to achieve.

Specific objectives can also include the answers to questions like:
- Who is going to do it?
- Why is it happening?
- Who is going to keep tabs on our progress?

Measurable

Measurement is specificity's best friend—and as legendary business mind Peter Drucker once said, "What gets measured, gets managed."

If you're trying to accomplish an objective that's critical to achieving your goal , but you're not tracking anything how will you know if you're progressing? There is also an intrinsic motivational push experienced when you can feel yourself getting tangibly closer to success.

Measurement supplies us with hard data, and the answers to questions like:

- How much?
- How many?
- How often?

You can measure an objective in a number of different ways, depending on the nature of what you're trying to accomplish—but if there's nothing to measure, there's no tangible progress to point to. An example of a measurable and specific objective could be to increase your brand's blog readership by 5 percent each month.

Attainable

This is a tough one for plenty of marketers. An "attainable" SMART objective focuses on your ability to achieve your stated goal—making sure that whatever X-percentage increase you're shooting for is rooted in reality. While the temptation is there to reach for the stars, lest you be accused of not trying hard enough, a massive, unattainable objective isn't a motivator—it's a *soul crusher*. You want to challenge yourself, but also to keep a grasp on what's realistic for you, your business, and anyone you partner with.

It's crucial to base your objectives on your own analytics and those of the influencer you're working with—*not* industry benchmarks, or else you might find yourself in over your head.

Let's say you run an interior design studio with four team members. Each month, you each do about $30,000 in client work, but everyone likely has a little time to do more—and if you do a little more than that, you could hire another designer.

You decide to partner with a local design influencer to create some video content around your studio, and share the work you're doing with his very engaged audience. You plan to measure the impact of your partnership in terms of client inquiries he sends your way, and you set an objective for 500 inquiries by month's end.

Sounds great. . .except you've never had more than 25 inquiries a month in years of doing business. Also, your influence partner is going to create 1–2 videos a week for their targeted audience of 10,000 viewers.

500 inquiries would mean that 1 out of every 20 people watching their videos would not just watch the video, but would:
- Be in the market for your services
- Click through to learn more about your business
- Reach out to get in touch.

A more reasonable objective would be a 25 percent increase in your current rate of inquiry via the influencer's videos.

Keep in mind that, while setting your sights too high means you're setting yourself up for failure, setting your sights too low won't motivate you to challenge yourself. Attainability lands you squarely in the middle, and on the road to success.

Relevant

This is where you ensure your marketing objectives map directly to your business goals *and* account for current trends in your industry. If a marketing objective doesn't move you toward your business goals, it's not worth focusing on.

Suppose you're about to launch a startup that connects stay-at-home parents who have several external errands each day with senior citizens seeking ride to do their own errands Your big goal may be to have a thriving, profitable business at the two-year mark of your launch. To make this happen, you set a key objective to raise your profile in the local community so more parents and more seniors are aware of, and interested in your service.

You happen to know a very popular local Instagram star (shiny object alert!) personally that you can get on board to work with your company. Once you've got them signed on, you set an objective of acquiring 2,000 followers on Instagram in the next month.

But is your target market spending time on Instagram? And if so, is it actually possible for you to convert Instagram eyeballs to leads for your specific business?

Relevance helps you take a realistic look at your SMART objective, and adjust the metrics you're using to track the progress more accurately.

Time-Bound

A time-bound objective keeps you on schedule, and puts a healthy amount of pressure on your efforts to ensure you're moving forward.

In other words, set a deadline for achieving each of your objectives. If your timeline is too long or too vague, it lacks the urgency you need to act on it.

For example, which would you prefer?

A) A sales employee who says she is going to increase her sales volume by 5 percent every month, leading to a 30-35 percent increase in half a year?

or

B) A sales employee who says she will increase traffic by 15 percent. . .with no deadline?

Employee A wins by a landslide—and the same principle applies for influencer marketing. Adding a time-frame to your objective is essential in making it SMART.

Using the SMART framework takes a little more time and forethought upfront, but you'll more than make up the time spent with your results. Here are some more concrete examples of how to transform an average business objective into an actionable, motivating SMART objective:

Goal: I want to grow my business.

SMART Objective: I will acquire 10 new clients (measurable) for my custom yoga mats (specific) within two months (time-bound) by launching a social media influencer marketing campaign and offering special discounts (achievable) through each influencer involved. This will allow me to grow my business and increase my revenue to 7 figures (relevant).

Goal: I want to increase sales.

SMART Objective: To meet my sales goal of booking $100,000 in annual orders (relevant), we will hire three new salespeople (achievable) to grow sales by 5 percent (specific) in the first quarter, 10 percent in the second, 15 percent in the third and 20 percent in the fourth (measurable and time-bound).

Goal: I want to improve product quality.

SMART: To meet the company's annual goal (time-bound) of reducing returns to less than 2 percent of shipped product (relevant), a new test and inspection procedure (achievable) will reduce the shipping of defected blenders by 10 percent per quarter (specific), with data tracked weekly (measurable).

Goal: I want to reduce my business costs.

SMART Objective: To meet the company's cost reduction (relevant) goal of 20 percent (specific), management will focus on reducing production errors such as wrong designs (achievable) by 10 percent per month for six months, then 5 percent for six months (time-bound), tracked every two weeks (measurable).

Goal: I want to write a business book.

SMART Objective: In order to establish myself as an industry expert (relevant), I will write a 350-page book on fashion marketing (specific) by writing one chapter of 30 pages per month; i.e., a page per day (measurable). The book will be completed in 12 months, (time-bound) and then I will self-publish on Kindle (achievable).

A good exercise to get started with SMARTening up is take some of your current business objectives—which may or may not meet these criteria—and find ways to make them SMART by adding more detail, setting more concrete measures, and getting them to a more attainable place.

Objective setting is where the *fun* begins

If you feel like setting more defined, measurable objectives is taking the wind out of your sails, trust that just the opposite is true: getting specific about your plans is where the real progress (and the fun!) begins. Instead of dreaming about what might be possible from a collaboration, you get to start building the framework to make it real.

Pablo Picasso nailed it when he said "Our goals can only be reached through the vehicle of a plan, in which we must fervently believe, and upon which we must vigorously act. There is no other route to success."

When you work to define the business objectives that stem from your bigger goal, you become better able to see the foundation of your influence partner collaboration come together.

The clearer your goal, the more defined your business objectives/ KPIs can be, and the easier it will be to identify the right partner(s) to help you achieve them—and build a long-term, win-win alliance.

Recap and Review

KEY POINTS

1. **You need to clearly establish your business goals before plunging into any marketing campaign.**

   a. This means being able to distinguish between your *goals* and your *objectives*. Whether it's to become the most recognizable brand in your field or double your profits within three years, your goal should represent your destination—while your objectives/KPI's represent how you define and measure your goal.

   b. Only once you have a goal in place can you then define things like campaign objectives. These include budget, timeline, metrics, etc. The important thing is to work *backwards* from your goal to ensure you remain on point and on track.

2. **Don't let shiny objects distract you from your goals—or become your goals.**

   a. Keeping your goal and objectives at the forefront will help keep you from being distracted by every opportunity that comes your way. Deviations and shortcuts often end up being more costly than maintaining momentum along your pre-planned route.

3. **The SMART model provides a helpful checklist for setting (and double-checking) objectives.**

   a. Specific: While vague objectives may be more attractive (it's easier to say you've achieved something when it's not clear what that something is), only specific objectives let you set real expectations, establish useable benchmarks and track progress.

   b. Measurable: Every race needs a finish line. In other words, if you can't measure it, you can't achieve it.

   c. Attainable: Shooting for the stars is laudable, but rarely practical. Determine what you can realistically achieve and set your sights accordingly. You'll reach those stars eventually—using a ladder of repeated successes.

   d. Relevant: If an objective doesn't directly contribute to achieving your goal, it has no place in your action plan. There will be plenty of distractions along the way regardless; don't include "shiny objects" in your plan from the start!

   e. Time-bound: Given enough time and resources, you can achieve anything. Unfortunately, we rarely have enough of either and time is the rarest of all. Knowing *when* you're going to do something is just as important as knowing *how* you're going to do something.

4. **Objectives are not speed bumps on your road to success—they are your mile markers.**

   a. Setting these types of big picture goals and SMART objectives *does* take more time and effort upfront. But it *will* make you that much more likely to cross the finish line, saving you time and resources in the long run.

MOVING FORWARD

Consider: you've identified not only those aspects of your current market that have made them your loyal customers over the years, but *also* found a number of comparable markets that you feel could easily be approached, provided you do so with an appropriate campaign that has been tailored to their particular needs and desires. You approach an influencer in that community, put together an attractive campaign, and within a month you've achieved twice your usual exposure on social media sites, three times the average number of hits on your website, and after all that. . .barely a blip in your sales for that quarter.

You don't understand; you did the research, put it into practice, and the resultant campaign had the desired effect of reaching a new market. Yet somehow, you don't have anything tangible to show for your efforts.

Without those tangible results, what have you actually accomplished?

FOOD FOR THOUGHT

You've probably impulse-purchased a candy bar while in the checkout line or made a spur-of-the-moment reservation at an upscale restaurant. But that's probably not how you'd buy your car, or finance your house, or book your vacation. The type and scale of purchase will not only affect your decision making process, but it will also affect who or what will influence your decisions.

5

Beyond the Buzz
Influence and the Consumer Journey

W e've established that to be successful in marketing, you need to know your audience *and* know what matters to them in order to reach them effectively. However, garnering their attention does not mean anything if you can't turn that attention into positive action.

Over the past few years, I've heard too many people claiming that "attention is currency", leading to the misguided perception that getting buzz equals success.

And yes, as marketers we certainly trade and thrive on attention. . . but oversimplifying it this way suggests that getting in front of your audience with a great message means people will go to you, buy from you, and convert to loyal consumers—all of their own accord.

Attention is only part of the equation.

Cultivating immense attention in your niche may increase your subscriber count, create new leads, or bring in increased social media engagement—but that doesn't mean those people will buy from you. And that's the bottom line for any brand: making sales and growing a viable business.

Yes, attention matters, it will always matter, but in order to convert *awareness* into action, we need more than attention; we need them to trust you. We want them to choose us above everyone else, and commit to choosing us in the future.

Attention – Trust = Noise

Attention + Trust = Influence

In fact, having influence is the only way to rise above commodity status and not have to compete solely on price.

Does increasing your audience increase your influence?

So if influence isn't just about numbers—about how many people are aware of you—then what *is* it about?

Influence, most simply, is the ability of a force (person, brand, organization) to cause a desired action. This is what makes building your influence so tricky: you can increase your audience size and level of attention all you want, but if you don't affect the desired action, it won't help you.

Let's say, for example, that you put up a new photo of yourself with a well-known model tagged, and suddenly you have a thousand new followers on Instagram overnight. In that case, you've achieved more attention—you have a larger audience that wants to hear from you.

But if you're a tax attorney, and your professional goal is to bring in more clients, this attention isn't likely to translate to your desired goal of generating more business.

Attention without action isn't influence, it's buzz. And buzz without behavior wastes time and resources. And the scariest part is that confusing attention for influence isn't just an amateur mistake; some of the most high profile brands in the world fall victim to this classic misunderstanding.

PEPSI: A CASE STUDY IN ACHIEVING BUZZ OVER IMPACT

During the 2010 Super Bowl, Pepsi launched the boldest social marketing play of its time. Forgoing their traditional ads entirely, Pepsi elected instead for something entirely unexpected: they became the first brand in the world to divert their *entire allocated budget* to a social media campaign, one which would spread the word about their Internet-based charity contest, the Pepsi Refresh Project.

The results seemed to knock it out of the park. . .at least, in terms of attention in the form of website traffic, social media buzz and popularity. —not to mention the participation of people across the world interacting with the campaign.

It achieved all the things so many influencers and brands *think* they want: the likes, the shares, the comments, the participation—on the surface, seems the advertising agency should win an award. . .right?

But before we give them a round of applause and a trophy, there's one more detail: this is also the first time in history Pepsi *lost* market share, sliding to number 3 in the cola rankings behind Diet Coke.

What went wrong?

First, a bit of background. Pepsi, like many other major consumer brands, typically delivers a glitzy, celebrity-filled advertisement during the Super Bowl telecast. After all, the Super Bowl isn't just the pinnacle of football—it's also provides a world-sized stage for major advertising moments.

No one seemed to know this better than Pepsi, who had produced some of the most memorable Super Bowl spots to date: a sweltering Cindy Crawford sipping on a crisp, cool cola while a couple of adolescent boys look on (admiring the Pepsi can, not Cindy); Britney Spears gyrating for the camera; and so on.

At this point, Pepsi had been advertising during the Super Bowl for 23 consecutive years. So why would they decide to take all the money they *would* have spent on traditional advertising—$20 million or so—and pump it into a social media campaign? Why did the company decide to pull their long-held traditional TV real estate in favor of social media, of all things, ceding the airwaves to their rival Coca-Cola?

In an interview with the *New York Times*, Shiv Singh, head of digital for PepsiCo Beverages America, described the campaign thusly: "This was not a corporate philanthropy effort. This was using brand dollars with the belief that when you use these brand dollars to have consumers share ideas to change the world, the consumers will win, the brand will win, and the community will win. That was a big bet. No one has done it on this scale before."

Let's start with Pepsi's campaign hypothesis:

- Traditional forms of advertising fail to foster engagement and have substantially outlived their usefulness
- The internet has created an environment in which consumer exercises unprecedented control of his/her purchasing behavior
- People are no longer willing to accept the "interruption" model of advertising—they want brands to interact with them
- Marketing should be seen as a "conversation", not a one-way communication
- The objective of marketing communications is for a brand to create "engagement" with consumers versus just making a sale
- Consumers are quickly moving away from brands just out to sell them something, in favor of brands who want to start conversations
- Social media represents the most effective medium for these forms of engagement

- consumers would be validating their engagement-focused choice by helping Pepsi drive meaningful social change.
- By getting consumers to interact with the brand online, the company could gather valuable consumer insights and data.

The campaign goal was to raise brand awareness. And when viewed from a 50,000-foot perch, it was mission accomplished—and more:

- Over 80 million votes were registered on behalf of charities and initiatives
- Almost 3.5 million "Likes" on the Pepsi Facebook page
- Almost 60,000 Twitter followers
- At one point, 37 percent of Americans were said to be aware the campaign existed

So what's the problem? If you dig beyond the buzz and look at what happened to Pepsi's bottom line during this time, Pepsi-Cola and Diet Pepsi each lost about 5 percent of their market share in 2009 (*The Wall Street Journal*), which for the Pepsi-Cola brand alone represented a loss of over $350 million. For both brands, the loss is probably in the neighborhood of $400 million to near half a billion dollars.

While Pepsi may have made some inroads into changing the world, ultimately, they failed to do the one thing they needed to stay alive: *sell Pepsi*. They assumed the big buzz, high levels of engagement and interaction would benefit the brand.

They failed to consider the entire consumer journey—the path of progression which moves from consumer awareness all the way to purchase and loyalty, commonly referred to as **the sales funnel**.

The Pepsi case provides a classic example of how even the top brands in the world, with the biggest influencer endorsements and the deepest pockets, can make the mistake of getting caught up in the awareness (aka attention) stage of the funnel.

Keep your eyes on the prize

While attention gets you seen and can garner buzz, it won't magically inspire people to perform the action you want. Worse, chasing attention forces the wrong metrics. Say you want to run for office. Simply standing in front of a huge audience and waving your arms isn't going to make them vote for you, now is it? Yet so many influencer marketing efforts are based on social media reach, with success determined by a series of metrics to quantify how much awareness they've built. Then, when it comes time to sell a product, they fall flat.

Of course, Pepsi's efforts weren't fundamentally flawed. Charities *can* be influencers in and of themselves, generating plenty of positive sentiment for the brands that support them—but unless that social good effort is well-aligned with the brand, it will fail to do much in the way of connecting with new customers or driving sales.

Let's get into exactly what Pepsi did—and didn't do right:

Pepsi didn't integrate their message into the places their audience attention already was. The Super Bowl commands a massive market share, and even people who don't like the game tune in for the ads. It's like Shark Tank for marketing content.

Rather than spending some of their time and effort where people were hanging out, Pepsi abandoned the trusted medium altogether. In other words, they weren't even in the game.

Pepsi neglected to focus on the ways in which they were influential. Pepsi is, at best, an empty-calorie beverage that people enjoy for fun—it's not a health brand, and it's not a social good brand. The brand was too far off in its messaging; they are not known for being a leader in the world of social good, so trying to force that connection not only felt off-brand to the audience, it garnered negative backlash.

Many people felt if they were really trying to "do good", they wouldn't be selling a sugary, chemical-filled bottle of "poison" to put in people's bodies. The reality is that influence in one place (on consumer tastes and cravings) isn't the same as influence in another (how people do good in the world.)

Pepsi wasn't really part of the story. The video call to action Pepsi created had nothing to do with actually drinking Pepsi, or even triggering the desire to have one. Instead, people were thinking and acting on something completely different than enjoying an icy cold soda.

Pepsi lost sight of the bottom line. Ultimately, marketing must translate to revenue to keep a company afloat. Pepsi Refresh created a flatline where a heartbeat was supposed to be by only considering the very first level of the sales funnel, awareness.

I've said it a million times: it doesn't matter how much *attention* you get if you can't convert it to *action*—or in Pepsi's case, the *right kind of action*.

That's why, in this chapter, we'll look at how to create, plan, and strategically evaluate a campaign by thinking through the *entire* journey—from awareness, through to purchase, and finally post-purchase satisfaction.

ALIGNING YOUR INFLUENCER MARKETING EFFORTS WITH THE CONSUMER JOURNEY

Consumers generally go through stages when they make a purchase, widely known in marketing as the consumer journey, or the sales funnel (often termed AIDA+S). The stages describe how we move a potential customer from their first knowledge of our product to making a purchasing decision about that product.

For the sake of simplicity, I prefer to use "consumer journey rather than sales funnel; the term "sales funnel" is a very old concept which erroneously indicates that people always go through their consumer journey in the same order, taking the same series of steps. With modern 24/7 information access, that's not always the case.

If you're thinking about buying a car, you don't just go out and immediately buy one. You do research to learn what the different options might be within your price range. You consider the look of the car, the reputation and reliability of the make or model, the gas mileage, and how much maintenance it will require.

While a big celebrity like Matthew McConaughey might make you *aware* of the new Lincoln, is he going to propel you to *buy* it? Unlikely.

As you move through your search process, other industry experts— like auto magazines and auto bloggers—may become more influential in determining your choice. The final decision to purchase also usually involves the opinion of someone even closer to you, such as your spouse, parent, or close friend who knows cars.

Most marketers identify some type of journey they use to shape their strategies, even if the names of the stages change. The journey has been updated or revised many times for many different industries and purposes, so it's less about the names than the concepts.

While not every decision or action follows a linear approach that can be directly mapped to the traditional sales funnel, it's the overarching framework that opens up your lens to see your consumers journey and all the influential touchpoints along the way.

There are five classic levels:
- Awareness
- Interest
- Desire
- Action
- Satisfaction (Loyalty)

That fifth level, satisfaction (sometimes referred to as "loyalty") is often overlooked, yet is arguably the most important to your long-term success:

Let's take the fundamentals of the classic sales funnel formula and apply it to influencer marketing using a dating analogy that will ensure you never forget it:

Awareness

You're at a friend's house for a party when you hear a wine glass crash to the floor. You glance over, but you've never met the person who dropped it before. Awareness is neither positive nor negative at this stage; you are simply aware of his existence because of the interruption of the crashing wine glass.

A product mention can come to your attention in many different ways. Whether or not you find it to be of interest or value, you still notice it.

Interest

The glass crashed and now you are aware of him. . .but when you try to identify who this klutz is, you notice that he's tall, well-dressed and attractive. Now you're interested in learning more.

At this point, your opinion could still go either way: he might be obnoxious, or he might just be cute and funny. You decide to have a friend introduce you and to get to know him a little. This stage of the process is information gathering (or as a marketer, the click-through).

Now, as anyone who has dated knows, there's a massive leap between interest and desire. This will be a make-or-break moment for a potential relationship. . .but if the right connection happens, it's *on*.

In terms of the sales funnel, this is the point at which you're looking into a brand with a bit more intention; you may visit their website, do a search on them or ask around. You are ready to learn more, and curious—but not decisive.

Desire

You've actually spoken to him and deemed him worthy of your time. He asks you out, and you're being courted; after a while, you're quite sure you like him and want to see more of him. Ostensibly, he becomes part of a subset of finalists for the long haul—kind of like the final few roses in *The Bachelor* (with fewer sequins and tears.)

In the sales funnel, this is the moment you're actively narrowing down the brands and products you might choose—you've got a set of finalists, and you're almost ready to make a choice.

Action

He's the one! It's a go! You're going to commit. But the timing here is critical: if he pushes for a commitment at the wrong time, you won't be ready, and it won't happen. If he waits too long, your attention will go elsewhere.

In the sales funnel, this is the moment you decide to buy—or take whatever action the brand or product wants you to take.

Satisfaction/Loyalty

Now you're together for the long haul, but the work isn't done. You've got to stay committed to your partner's happiness so they don't feel compelled to find a better partner anywhere else.

This is the critical reason most marriages fail: they take work, and often one party or the other becomes either too comfortable and stops working at it, or they find out one no longer serves the other's needs.

The result? Divorce, or a breakup.

It's exactly the same with brands: we spend so much time trying to get the win and to score that initial purchase, but we fail to nurture and strengthen the actual relationship.

It's much more cost effective and valuable over time to keep the customers you currently have, rather than constantly trying to garner new ones. (Not to mention that happy customers help you attract new customers.)

Obviously, the parallels here aren't one-to-one: your customer's level of commitment probably won't require you to put a ring on it.

However, the phases remain true for every marketer:
- You get on the customer's radar (**awareness**)
- You court them and make them want to know more about you (**interest**)
- You win their consideration (**desire**)
- You receive a buy-in: the customer makes an active choice in your favor (**action**)

But how do you *actually* move someone further down the funnel?

When it comes to the role of influencers in guiding prospects through the sales funnel, it's realistic to note that not every influencer works at every stage of the funnel. Some are good at fostering interest, some know how to build desire, and so on; in broad terms, the use of different influencers at different stages can support your overall mission and help drive your audience down the sales funnel.

It's all about aligning with the right person with the right message at the right phase of the funnel—all at the right time. If you can do that, you'll keep your prospect moving.

Let's take a look at what moving someone through the funnel looks like on a practical level—including where your challenges might occur, and how you can overcome them.

INFLUENCERS AT VARIOUS STAGES IN THE JOURNEY

Let's say you own a café. Your sandwiches are amazing, your customers love you. . .but you need some more traffic through the door to stay afloat. You know that, once you get people through the door, they can't resist what they're smelling, and end up ordering more than they even came for.

You decide to explore the idea of working with an influencer to help build awareness beyond your current customer base, so you can increase your daily customers and generate more revenue.

After doing serious observation and research of your market, you find an influencer (in this case a popular real estate agent) and invite her to your café for a complimentary lunch. To your delight, she thanks you by posting about the sandwich she ate on Instagram and includes a mouth-watering photo. Bonus: she even puts a click-through link directly to your café's site in her bio!

While her audience isn't following her for recommendations on local lunch spots, per se, many people trust realtors to make great local recommendations. From an awareness perspective, the post did well and received a decent number of likes and even a few comments.

The problem is that the agent's territory--and therefore, audience— is a 30-minute drive from your cafe (without traffic)! You achieved awareness. . .and yet your sales didn't move at all. Is it because influencer marketing doesn't work? Nope!

The definition of influence is the ability to affect action—and the two key words are *ability* and *action*. This is where thinking through the whole journey, all the way to action makes the critical difference.

Let's try again.

You discover one of your café's devoted local customers has a small social media following—but what their community might lack in size, they more than make up for in devotion. You see her come in for a bite one day, and you offer to buy her (and her party) lunch if they'd be willing to share an honest review of their meal, and post a photo of themselves (hopefully) enjoying a sandwich and tag your café in the post.

They agree, and tell their segment of the world—including all their local colleagues and friends—how delicious your avocado toast is, all while tagging you from your sunny patio. You "re-gram" the image on your own social media, and thank them for mentioning you.

The value is two-fold: not only is your customer feeling rewarded and appreciated for her devotion to you, she's fostering awareness of you in her own community—awareness that spurs interest because they *trust* their friend's recommendations—and she's provided you with great content to share on social media. Since her friends live in your café's neighborhood, the post is highly relevant, and now they'll have you mind as a choice for their next lunch outing.

But as any savvy marketer knows, you can't rely on being top of mind to drive action, people need a prompt. This is where the call-to-action (CTA) becomes your critical ingredient (it's the avocado in avocado toast, truly.)

Adding a CTA may seem obvious, trivial, or redundant, but making the ask in this instance is the key element that will drive human behavior. Think about the last time you made a purchase at the local grocery store, and at the end of your purchase, the clerk asks if you'd like to donate $1 to local children in need. The little sign to donate has always been there, right above the register, but now that she's actually *asked* you, you say yes. Simple and effective. . .but a fundamental thing too many marketers forget.

When I partnered with Maker Studios (a multi-channel network for creators that eventually was sold to Disney), to grow my YouTube Fitness Channel, one thing the producer told me every single time I filmed a video was to make sure to say, "Subscribe to my channel!" at the end of every video.

"Ugh. . ." I thought, "why do I have to say it *every time*?'" I was annoying myself with the redundancy. It felt needy!

It didn't take long, however, before I learned that the results of "the ask" speak for themselves. When I failed to remind my visitors to subscribe, I'd be lucky to get *any* new subscribers on that video. When I did remember, the subscribe rate would see a notable rise.

The most interesting thing? The ask could extend to other actions, too. If I decided to make the CTA about leaving a comment, people would. If I made the CTA about liking the video, viewers would do exactly that.

In the case of your café, you could get your avocado toast champion to add a message at their end of their post or video saying: "Go in today and get 20 percent off your order with this coupon!"

In a few words, you drive the viewer past salivation to actual action: now they're thinking about coming into your café and purchasing one for themselves, incentivized by your discount offer (because who doesn't love a deal)?

Your results will speak for themselves.

The right influencer at the right time equals the right action

Not every purchase is as simple as grabbing a $6 sandwich in our neighborhood. Factors like a higher price point (say, choosing a college) and higher life impact (such as choosing a surgeon) will require more than simply adding a CTA to a post.

This is where an understanding of how different types of influencers and the types of content and messaging they create is crucial—you need to understand who will have the maximum impact at different points in the funnel, and what other factors can influence decisions.

I'll talk more about macro-versus-micro-versus-personal influencers later in the book (along with the pros and cons of using each) but in general, **macro-influencers** are either mainstream celebrity/household names, or those who have extremely large audiences who follow them, are best at encouraging prospects at the **awareness** level.

Jennifer Aniston is a massive star across both the small and large screens, and a fashion and style icon, to boot—not to mention a longtime tabloid staple. Her advertising campaign with Smartwater featured her sipping on billboards, in magazines, on television, and across her social media channels (and those of Smartwater, of course).

So now you know about Smartwater. But are you going to go *buy* it?

You're likely going to assume, based on Jennifer Aniston's life as a well-paid movie star, that her actions are a paid endorsement and not a statement on what water Jennifer likes most. If you're a massive Jennifer Aniston fan, you might choose it when you pass by it at the supermarket; or, if there are two options and you don't recognize one, you might go for the Smartwater.

But if that's the limit of the influence someone famous like Jennifer Aniston can have on you, who *is* going to have a real impact on your decision to actually seek out or choose Smartwater?

Maybe a healthy living blogger you've followed for ages, who talks about how she believes Smartwater actually tastes better and is more pure than other bottled waters. Or maybe a fitness coach you follow on Instagram who is hyper-conscious about what she puts in her body and recommends Smartwater for the natural minerals to her clients.

You trust these people when it comes to your health, wellbeing and hydration—and if they endorse Smartwater, by extension, you'll soon start to see it as part of that lifestyle.

Macro-influencers tend to be most powerful at the top of the funnel, starting with awareness, through to desire, but they won't necessarily be able to drive action beyond small ticket items (unless we're dealing with the ultimate superfan.)

When it comes to the satisfaction level of the funnel, a macro-influencer will have next to nothing in the way of influence over buying decisions—it's up to the company to see that you stay happy.

Interestingly enough, however, influencers hired by the *competition* can affect your customers' levels of satisfaction, especially if they're not completely delighted with their choice. Macro-influencers are great at creating a distraction—which is why it's very important for any brand to offset that distraction by nurturing their established, loyal relationships, and continuing to provide value.

GET OUT YOUR COMPASS: MAPPING THE CONSUMER JOURNEY

When you're ready to dig into the specifics of the consumer journey for your business, here's a template to help you explore what your customer is thinking about and what motivates them at different phases of the sales funnel—and the different experiences and motivations that guide decisions throughout the customer journey.

	Awareness	Consideration	Preference	Decision/Purchase
What motivates our consumer at each stage?	**"Which brands solve my problem?"** Consumer considers an initial set of brands based on perceptions and exposure to recent touchpoints. *Example: A consumer wants to know which breads are gluten-free. She might read blogs specializing in gluten-free cooking, ask friends, or browse the grocery aisle to find options.*	**"Which brand best satisfies my purchase criteria?"** Consumer weighs benefits, compares brands, and asks others for opinions. *Example: Consumer evaluates gluten-free breads against specific criteria, including: Do others say it tastes good? Does it have ingredients I can't eat? Will my kids like it?*	**"I think this one is the best choice."** Consumer narrows in on the best option. "My local grocery store carries a brand of bread; that sounds good."	**"I'll try it/buy it."** Consumer selects a brand at the moment of purchase. *Example: Consumer purchases bread. If purchase is successful, they may buy again and/or recommend to others.*
What key messages do we want to communicate at each stage?	**Make consumers aware that your product does X.** *Example: Influencers with gluten-free blogs write posts about your bread.*	**Explain how your product does X.** *Example: Influencers write a review of your bread explaining why it's a safe chose for gluten-free clients.*	**Reinforce why your product is a good choice. Show how others use it and like it.** *Example: Influencer posts a sandwich recipe that her kids love, which uses your bread.*	**Make it easy for consumers to buy/try your product.** *Example: Influencers give away coupons for your bread via special offers.*

	Awareness	Consideration	Preference	Decision/Purchase
What content will our consumer respond to at each stage?	**Content should be focused on buyers' pain points (not your brand or product). Consumers become aware of your product via:** • In-store product experience • Expert recommendations via blogs, podcasts, videos • Infographics • Recipes • Articles • Product reviews	**Explain to consumers how your product satisfies their purchase criteria through:** • Blog posts • Demonstration videos • Articles • Product reviews • Word-of-mouth recommendations	**Justify why your product is a good choice using:** • Blog posts • Recipes • Videos • Contests • Shared content • Expert and user reviews	**Make it easy for consumers to buy your product with:** • Coupons • Ecommerce

Now let's take the template for a spin ourselves: you have a subscription clothing business. Your customers receive shipments every month of curated clothing choices based on their style preferences, unique needs, and size profile.

Your target customer comes in a lot of different varieties: different types of women will need or want this kind of service, based on the time they have to shop, how much they enjoy shopping, what kind of retail variety exists where they live, and so on. What they have in common is the need for an easier way to shop—and get the items they genuinely want.

At each phase in their journey—from the moment they learn you exist, to becoming a subscriber, to potentially increasing their monthly expenditure—they're going to want different things at different times and it's your job to provide them all the different options (they likely don't even know) you have. Influence partners—macro, micro, and personal—can play a role at many of these stages, *if* you align their messaging with the journey these women are on.

The type of messaging you would use at the awareness stage is going to be different from the messaging you use at the action stage, which will be different from the messaging at the loyalty stage, and so on.

For example, if you're trying to build **awareness** in the eyes of harried shoppers, a series of Instagram stories in which a fashion/lifestyle macro-influencer is trying on different items from a subscription box will subtly introduce to your target consumer that subscription clothing options exist.

Next, **desire**. If one of your target customers is a harried new mom, a YouTube review from a mom blogger where she has fun trying on clothes with her little ones in her home—without having to deal with crying kids in a store, or fighting traffic, or commuting to the mall, period—immediately comes across as an attractive alternative.

Now, **action.** A friend is given a "try free for a month" code to share on Twitter and Instagram, letting your prospect know that real people—people she knows and trusts—are using your service. And now that she has someone she knows to ask. . .she may be ready to take the plunge.

What next? If your current customers are feeling in a bit of a fashion rut because of their own choices, a fashionista doing a blog post about ways to "blow up your style with what you already own!" would provide you with great content to put on your own social channels and provide value for your consumers. Or you could do a challenge to your existing customers to try a new style in their subscription, share a photo, tag you. . .and voila, 25 percent off their next month.

Not only have you increased their **satisfaction** with their choices, you've turned them into **loyal** advocates on your behalf. . .perhaps even building awareness in your next customer as a result.

You've got the ability now to reach and affect people with much greater precision—something every marketer wants.

THE 3B'S FRAMEWORK

Another Tool for Your Influencer Marketing Toolkit

Freddy J. Nager, founder of Atomic Tango and professor of marketing at USC, has a model he calls "the 3B's" for evaluating the effectiveness of marketing campaigns, and I find it especially helpful for strategizing and evaluating influencer campaigns, Essentially it forces you to think beyond 'reach and awareness', and rather forecast all the way through the purchasing journey to the desired action.

- **BUZZ:** How does a campaign get people to talk about it in a positive way?

- **BRAND:** How does a campaign shape a company's overall reputation and value?

- **BEHAVIOR:** How does a campaign motivate desired bottom-line actions?

Take any campaign, or marketing strategy or idea, and then apply this framework. Not only will it help you evaluate true effectiveness, but it can help you avoid a failing campaign, or further optimize a strategy in the works.

For example, look at how Pepsi did with the 3B's:

- **BUZZ:** Pepsi *killed* it on all of the buzz metrics. . .but the positive buzz was going to the charities, not Pepsi itself. Not a brand win.
- **BRAND:** Pepsi's brand is not about social good. In fact, many parents and medical professionals are anti-soda because soda = empty calories. What does that have to do with social good? Nothing. . .and a single campaign, even if some social good happens along the way, won't change that.
- **BEHAVIOR:** Pepsi generated a lot of attention and funding for charities. . .but failed to sell any of their own product. It's good to do good—but it's bad if your shareholders take a hit to make it happen.

Fortunately for the rest of us, the failure of the Pepsi Refresh Project is something we can learn from to avoid making the same mistakes.

Rather than getting caught up in the buzz, the excitement, and all of the reach metrics that are the focus of "marketing success", I'm here to tell you that true success in marketing isn't about reach, it's about IMPACT. Reach may be a great indicator you are moving towards your goal and/or in the right direction. . .but in and of itself, it's not the goal.

Now *that's* refreshing.

Recap and Review

KEY POINTS

1. **Attention is part of the influencer equation, but it is only a part: attention without a related action is just a momentary distraction.**
   a) Attention + Trust = Influence
   b) Consider the example of Pepsi's Refresh project. A well-intentioned and well-produced campaign, aimed at a receptive (and well-researched) target demographic, but which ultimately failed to drive sales—meaning it ultimately failed.
   c) In terms of the consumer journey, Pepsi scored a perfect 10 on awareness and interest, but the campaign wasn't designed to move consumers that one step further towards desire.
   d) Achieving buzz isn't the same as achieving influence, and engagement doesn't necessarily correlate with—or lead to—action.

2. **Observing, researching and evaluating the entire consumer journey is necessary to identify all the factors that influence your desired consumer—both positively and negatively.**
   a) Consumers move through various stages in every purchasing decision they make, in a process referred to as the consumer journey (or sales funnel).

b) The consumer journey explicitly describes a five stage process, one which is not necessarily linear (or a one-way street) that consumers go through when making decisions:

- Awareness: The consumer has knowledge of the product
- Interest: The consumer is paying attention to the product, believing it has the potential to meet their needs
- Desire: The consumer would like to purchase the product if doing so is possible and practical
- Action: The consumer has completed their purchase of the product
- Satisfaction/Loyalty: Often overlooked but crucially important, the consumer is retains awareness of both you and your product, looking to you to fulfill any further needs they may have

3. **In order to influence your consumer, you have to know what they need, what they want, and why.**

a) You need to become a detective and think about what matters to your audience, where do they go to seek information at every stage of their journey. Who do they trust for information and guidance? What factors will impact their behavior?

4. **Different types of influencers tend to work better at different stages.**

a) To generate *awareness*, macro-influencers are ideal due to their broader reach and appeal.

b) To generate *interest*, it's best to narrow in with a trusted source or a subject matter expert to capitalize on any and all attention you receive.

c) To generate *desire*, unleash your best storytelling influencer to engage your audience, and build on their desire.

d) Generating *action* is something you should be doing at each stage and with every influencer you work. Consumers should never be left wondering where they can go or what they can do to complete their journey. In other words, don't forget the CTA!

e) Creating *satisfaction and loyalty* is part of our new paradigm shift. Remember, we're viewing the relationship with our consumers as long term, and not transactional. That means ensuring we continue to provide content that *builds value*.

5. **The 3B's is a brilliant tool to help analyze, evaluate and strategize the potential (and post-mortem) success of a campaign.**

   a) BRAND: How does a campaign shape a company's overall reputation and value?

   b) BUZZ: How does a campaign get people to talk about it in a positive way?

   c) BEHAVIOR: How does a campaign motivate desired bottom-line actions?

MOVING FORWARD

The right influencers are the ones who have inside knowledge of our audience and impact over them, how could we further leverage them to be valuable across our business? What, specifically, is the value of maintaining a long term relationship with influencers?

FOOD FOR THOUGHT

If there's one thing nobody likes, it's wasted time and resources. There's nothing worse than putting time and energy into a project at work, only to come in on Monday to learn your co-worker was not only working on the same assignment, but they completed it before you did—and did a better job that you could have with twice the time. Not only did you waste time working on the project, you've lost out on time you *could* have spent working on something else. Now, let's talk about incorporating influencers across your business for a mutual benefit and saving you time and money!

6

The Roles Influencers Can Play Across Your Business
Leveraging Influencers Beyond "Reach"

B rand spending on influencer marketing is predicted to reach $101 billion in 2020, per the Association of National Advertisers. While brands are increasingly seeing the value of influencers as a marketing tool, what that number *doesn't* tell us is whether brands who invest in influencer marketing are actually realizing the full potential of influence to transform, advance, and extend their marketing efforts.

In this chapter, we break down various ways you can use influencer alliances to not only scale your marketing efforts and better connect with your target market, but also to grow your business and bottom line.

Remember: influencers come in many different and even unconventional forms. Think beyond the top-of-mind celebrities or macro-social-media influencers who will be harder to connect with and require deep pockets. Micro-influencers, such as subject matter experts, loyal and vocal customers, and employees and leaders who have a strong relationship with their customers, can be some of the most powerful influencer partners. And let's not forget that an influencer doesn't have to be a human, it is any force (i.e. company, brand, organization, team, etc.) that has influence over your desired audience. The proliferation of technology and the dissipation of gatekeepers has given everyone the ability to reach an audience.

It's the bond of trust between the influencer and who they influence that is arguably the most important factor. In the end, you want more than a sale; you want the kind of relationship that fosters brand advocacy and growth.

EDUCATION, RESEARCH & DEVELOPMENT

One of the biggest challenges brands and businesses face is obtaining solid data and information about what their market wants, identifying the best possible way to deliver it to them, and evaluating how it's currently being received.

If you're an executive in charge of product or service development for a brand, you probably spend a great deal of time researching and brainstorming on the needs of your specific audience. That kind of research and creative development can be time-consuming and costly, not to mention riddled with bias, so you need to be as efficient as possible with the process, while still ensuring as much accuracy as possible.

What if you could find someone who. . .
- has already captured your market's attention and trust?
- knows exactly what your market needs, wants and desires?
- is trusted and respected for their taste, opinions, and insights among that audience?
- Knows how to communicate with this audience in a way that garners impact over your market's choices and preferences?
- cares about the kind of product or service you offer?
- wants to offer value to their community?

The right influencer offers a level of insider perspective and insight that can be tough to tap into from the outside, or with third-party research.

Influencers bring a different level of understanding of the audience. They know their frustrations, their challenges, their wants and needs. They're able to tap into a well of opinions and insights quickly and efficiently—in fact, they're capable of assembling ad hoc focus groups to test and evaluate new ideas because their audiences want to interact with them and the products and services they care about.

Influencers can also help your target market envision use cases for your product that they might not come up with on their own—and often even use cases you wouldn't have come up with yourself!

If you're smart, you'll connect with influencers to get their perspective and access at the earliest stages of developing a product or launching a business. You could end up saving a lot of money and effort spent heading in the wrong direction.

Furthermore, when influencers feel their opinion and input is valued in the creation of your brand's evolution and messaging, they tend to feel a personally vested interest and positive sentiment towards your brand.

PRODUCT DESIGN & REDESIGN

Suppose you own a company that makes equipment and accessories geared toward the needs of hikers: backpacks, boots, safety gear, and outdoor clothing. Your backpack sales have dropped in the past few years with a bunch of companies entering the market. In fact, your brand is seen as an "old school" option, according to the sentiment you've gathered via social listening, and you want to shake off that reputation.

You could attempt to redesign your backpack to reflect what your competitors are doing, and hope that you make the right changes to improve how your target market perceives your product—or you could engage with an influencer in the hiking space who is known as a trusted source for equipment recommendations.

You could start by inviting them to test your product on a hike, with no "ask" other than providing you with feedback. Yes, it's risky if they don't like it and decide to share that with their followers—but better to know now and have chance to make improvements.

The key is what you *do* with the feedback you get: you might invite them to make recommendations on what features or functions they'd add (or subtract!) to improve the pack. If they've decided to share the feedback and ask their followers to chime in, you have the opportunity to directly jump into the conversation and work with them to address their thoughts and choose the feedback you should act on.

One thing I always recommend is to create a prototype based on their feedback, and invite them to "road test" it again. In two steps, you've not only gained invaluable feedback from an expert and possibly their followers, but you've also shown that you're committed to evolving and innovating your product—not so "old school".

When the pack is refined and launched, you could name it after the hiking influencer as their signature model, since it's been heavily refined according to their needs and expectations, and even offer to donate a percentage of the pack's sales to park conservation in the influencer's name.

You've now given great nod of respect to the influencer, while further incentivizing them to *want* to share. (How cool is it to have a product they use and love named after them?) What's more, you've also improved, optimized and differentiated your product's value in a highly competitive space. This is the definition of a win-win relationship.

When it comes to fueling product development and design, influencers provide valuable insights, but we must acknowledge that influencers are brands in their own right. Many are increasingly seeking more of a **co-creator partnership** in which you would jointly launch a co-branded product or collection in which they are invested in and have ownership over. This is something to consider, especially if you've spent the time to identify the right influencer and want to continue working with him/her.

This type of relationship is highly beneficial to both sides: the brand benefits from the insider insights into the target audience and built in community, and the influencer benefits by monetizing their community and expertise without having to take on all the backend and responsibility of running the business.

MESSAGING

How many times have you seen a new product come out and thought, "Who are they trying to win over with this?" Even if your product is of the highest quality or considered best in class—it will only sell if it resonates with its intended audience, which happens through effective messaging.

Now, if *only* you had a target market expert to help you come up with the right themes and ideas! They could help you establish how valuable your product is, all while developing a strong connection with your desired audience, right off the bat.

Not only can influencers be critical sounding boards and consultants for new launches or campaigns, they can help you craft or refine your messaging to better target your intended audience. The right influencers know what their community cares about, the way they talk about the things they care about, and what resonates with them. The more insight they can give you on the people you want to reach, the more likely you'll be to hit the right notes with your messaging.

This is an especially valuable strategy when you're working on messaging to target a particular age demographic, culture, or foreign location. If you're a fortysomething business owner, you might not be able to keep up with the latest college-age lingo—but a college-age influencer can help you figure out what resonates without sounding inauthentic.

CONTENT CREATION

Every brand, agency, and entrepreneur has come to recognize (often begrudgingly) that it's not enough to simply be a product or service company these days. If you want to grow and succeed on a more significant level, there's some serious pressure to become a media and publishing company, too—or at a minimum, to start creating valuable content that does more than just sell your product.

Unfortunately, this puts a huge strain on marketing teams to churn out more words, images, and media, resulting in a domino effect of overextension—from the need to allocate bigger budgets for content, to actually having to create and manage all that content you're paying for.

For many companies, it has led to the creation of new positions on their teams, extended (and pricey) agency scopes and engagements, and a stressful, always-on editorial cycle. The shift is tough and jarring, and it's only just begun, because the creation of new platforms and channels every year also means more content.

On the flip side, there's the issue of content overload. Is what the world needs really *more* content?

This is where a collaboration with an influencer who is already creating valuable content is a beautiful match. Influencers can help ease the content load because, at their core, they *are* content creators. It's not a *subset* of what they do—it's what they do and what they are passionate about. They have mastered the skill of doing the thing you're just learning how to do, and they've already won the attention and trust of your audience.

When you bring them on board to connect with your target market, you'll get more authentic and relevant content than any expensive agency or in-house marketing team could achieve—and it's scalable to most budgets, too.

Rather than competing with all the content already out there—while trying to predict what you think will resonate with your audience—look to collaborate with those already doing it. You both have something to offer, and you can go further together.

Growing a *new* audience

A big challenge we face as marketers is finding a way to be heard over a veritable sea of competitors. You can have the best product and message for your market. . .but it doesn't mean anything unless you can actually *get their attention and desire*. It's not enough to have your message roll by, either—you need to find a way to get your audience to *absorb* it and care about it.

Advertising has a come a long way in helping brands target and access their audiences, but recall from Chapter 1 that consumers have kept up with all those developments, too! They're just as savvy about who is talking to them and what they're saying, and will go out of their way to ignore an ad even if the product might normally be of interest to them.

Influencers, on the other hand, have grown an audience that actively tunes into their messages—they're not the ad at the beginning of the video, they *are* the video. The best ones take their credibility in the eyes of their community seriously, and they're not going to share something or promote something they don't believe in.

This means that if an influencer endorses and shares your product, you get direct access to their audience. You're no longer an interruption, you're a recommendation—and that makes all the difference in convincing potential customers that you're worth their time. Another way to think about it is to view influencers as distribution partners.

When you decide to expand to, or launch your business in international or foreign markets, influencers can become especially critical. An influencer who has the attention and trust of a local audience can help you break in much faster—and most importantly, understand the local culture, language, jargon, values and beliefs on a much more intimate level.

Keep in mind, that because of the borderless nature of online reach, influencers communities can often be in places they are not based out of. For example, an American influencer may have a majority audience in China. Do your due diligence to find out where the audience of your selected influencer lays.

Social proof

The happiest place on earth for many women—including me—is a circus. Well, a *kind* of circus: a shoe store with a mega-sale. Think Jimmy Choo at 80 percent off typical retail prices! I call it a circus because if a store actually did that, you'd need a line of security to monitor the lines around the block, not to mention more to tamp down the insanity around the shelves.

You might think that kind of chaos would keep women away, but it's just the opposite: we want *in* on all the crazy (and the shoes!) When we see other women rushing in and reaching for all those gorgeous heels, we want to see what all the commotion is about and join the line–we'd hate to miss out on the sale of the century.

Or let's say you arrive in a new city on a Saturday night. You can't decide where you want to eat, so you head out for a walk to check out the options.

One restaurant has lines around the block and the hostess tells you the wait looks to be an hour; not to mention it looks packed to the gills inside, so finding a bar seat to wait is not an option. Then you see another one, just a few feet away, with no lines at all. You could get a table right away!

Odds are, you're going to get in line for the crowded spot, even if it's not convenient. Why? Because we're programmed to think that if a place is busy and others are lined up, it must be better. At the same time, if no one is at the other restaurant, we figure it's probably not worth our time. . .there must be *some* reason no one else is going there.

This is all assuming we have no insight into how good the food or service is at either place— we don't even use a review app—but that we're making our judgments based on the fact that more people are at one than the other.

Psychologists, sociologists, and new media marketers call this powerful dynamic "social proof." Social proof is a psychological phenomenon where people assume the actions of others in an attempt to reflect correct behavior for a given situation. In situations that are new to us, we tend assume that other people around us—*experts, celebrities, friends, etc.*—have more knowledge about what's going on than we do.

Social proof is at the core of influencer marketing because we often make judgments based on our overall impression of someone—the Brand Halo Effect at work again.

When you're introducing new products to market or reaching for a new audience, social proof is your best friend. When we're exposed to things we've never seen, tried, or experienced, our first response is usually going to be skepticism or hesitation. However, if we're introduced to that new thing by a third party, notably someone we trust, our entire perspective changes—voila, social proof saves the day.

That's where influencers come in. Whether the influencer in this case is a celebrity, a public figure, a friend, a family member, Oprah's book club, or Google, we're going to take their review more seriously than any advertising or marketing campaign the most genius communicator could come up with.

SEO and marketing author Neil Patel maps out five kinds of social proof. You'll notice that all of these are types of influencers in their own right:

- **Expert social proof:** This form of social proof is all about credibility—a recommendation from someone who is expert in a category, industry, or subject matter. This could be a chef recommending an ingredient, a makeup artist recommending a particular kind of brush, or a landscaping pro recommending the best trowel *ever*.
- **Celebrity social proof:** This is the classic advertising strategy we all know and recognize, when a celebrity endorses a particular product, and we jump on board after them.
- **User social proof:** Success stories! Testimonials! Positive reviews! Savvy business owners solicit, elevate, and spread the word when their customers are happy with their products. The smartest ones actually reach out to create content with their satisfied users.

- **Wisdom of the crowd:** Ever seen a "most popular" or "most read" category in a website's content, or a "sort by popularity" option? People want to see what other people are looking at.
- **Wisdom of friends:** This is the strongest endorsement of all—when someone you trust and have a relationship with points you in a particular direction.

When you're about to launch a product, a true influencer advocate to vouch for you can make a world of difference in building credibility, fostering loyalty, and building a community around your brand.

There's a win-win angle here, too: influencers enjoy being seen as insiders and experts on the cutting edge of new products. If you bring them in on the ground floor, you'll be doing their credibility a favor, too.

BUILDING COMMUNITY

While building a relationship with an influencer, your focus should also be on building a community *together* with their content. If you choose your partner wisely, they'll have a natural appeal to your customers, and you'll have a natural appeal to their community: what they care about is what you actually offer, what they talk about is relevant to your product, and so on. Their community can become your community, too.

That's why, when you engage with an influencer to create content for your brand, you'll want to ensure the content they're creating for you is of the same depth, tone, and value as the content they create for themselves—otherwise, members of their community who hop over to check out your content won't recognize what they're looking at.

You want any follower of the chosen influencer to feel a similar connection if they click over to your platform. The objective is that they get interested in learning more, and do things like signing up for your newsletter, following your social media. . .in other words, become a part of your community for the long term.

I have a passion for edgy, fashionista-approved activewear. If you make *and* watch as many fitness videos as I have, it's easy to get bored of the same old colors and styles, so I'm always on the lookout for something fresh to try or wear.

One activewear brand I follow religiously is Sweaty Betty, and it's all because I watched a video in which a fitness trainer was sporting their interesting looking apparel. She did a shout out to the brand of leg warmers she was wearing, and I thought they were cool, so I clicked over to their Instagram to learn where to get a pair.

Now, had I clicked over and *bought* the Sweaty Betty legwarmers, that's already a win by most influencer marketing campaign standards. But it still would have likely been a one-off. Sweaty Betty took things a step further, in a way that had me locked in within moments.

Why? How? Not only did I fall in love with their edgy fitness apparel, but I was immediately drawn to a full platform of consistently great content in partnership with some of the best fitness trainers out there. There was a fantastic mix of inspiring posts and valuable free workout routines. I still subscribe to them today, and because I'm regularly tuned in, they are always at the front of my mind: it's the first place I go for my activewear purchases.

Add to that, I have become a loyal member of the Sweaty Betty community, and when anyone asks what activewear collection I love, not only do I recommend them, I even tell them to follow their awesome Instagram page.

I'm pretty much a walking, talking, exercising billboard for Sweaty Betty. Heck, I've even included them in this book, and all because they built their own community through the communities of the influencers they aligned with.

SEO AUTHORITY

As any marketer knows, search engine optimization (SEO) can be very expensive, time consuming, and highly complex. Even the experts disagree on some of the finer points, and the landscape is constantly changing. You can spend a lot of time and money to chase an algorithm, only to end up back where you started if Google decides to shake things up.

While I won't get into the nitty gritty of it here, it's important to note that influencers can provide scalable value in generating quality natural backlinks for your website—something that unequivocally continues to have a positive impact on your site ranking.

There are a number of ways this can happen, but it's most applicable when you work with influential bloggers or influencers who have their own websites or content access to various high-authority sites, like online magazines or targeted publishing platforms. When these influencers create content and link to you and your products, this generates a high-quality backlink for your site.

Not only that, but these quality links are the gift that keeps on giving: an influencer sharing your link increases your chances of having *other* people share the link. This, in turn, means you have a much greater chance of being found in an organic search, which means higher-authority domains are more likely to pick up on your link and add it to *their* site.

Any way you look at it, influencer marketing boosts your efforts at building a quality link profile—and that gets you seen.

REPUTATION MANAGEMENT/DAMAGE CONTROL

Every brand hits a snag or experiences a hiccup now and then. Even the most popular, customer service-focused companies will occasionally have an interaction go awry, or have a product fail to meet a customer's expectations.

When you're trying to manage the damage from a negative brand experience, influencers can be your 'A team' of defense in helping you regain trust and positive sentiment. Their advocacy, recommendation, and loyalty serves as a counterpoint to complaints, concerns, and frustrations, and enables your brand to better weather the storm.

In this case, these influencers could be well-known figures who advocate for your brand, or they can simply be your loyal (and vocal!) customer base, defending you when the social media mob comes with torches and pitchforks.

Whether the influencers are large-scale and capable of driving mass authority, or they are simply loyal customers who stand behind you and defend your brand when things go badly, the personal voice and support of real people speaks louder than any single voice looking to take you down.

Influencers: the Swiss Army Knife of marketing

Alas, the power of influencer marketing extends far beyond aware-ness; brands who involve influencers as team members, partners, or consultants in various aspects of the business can reap tremendous benefits—everything from incredible content to improved or new products.

At the same time influencers benefit from collaborating with estab-lished brands through the resources, exposure or compensation (or combination) they otherwise don't have on their own.

Now that you're thinking bigger and better, let's get started on our search for the right influencer for your brand!

Recap and Review

KEY POINTS

1. **Fully leveraging your influencers' skills is key to realizing the full benefits your long term relationship.**
   a. Influencers are not advertisements—they are living, breathing advocates for you and your brand. To assist them in authentically presenting your brand in the best light, it helps to include them in multiple aspects of your company—wherever their influence could be beneficial.

2. **Influencers can provide valuable input when researching target markets and developing marketing strategies.**
   a. This can include:
      i. Suggesting improvements to existing products, systems, and services
      ii. Assisting in product re-design or extension
      iii. Co-creating new co-branded product lines to better align with current market trends

3. **Since influencers are expected to help deliver your brand message, it helps to include them in developing your messaging.**
   a. Influencers know the topics, language, and brand positioning that most appeals to their community and can help brands better craft messaging that truly resonates.

4. **One of the primary benefits of working with influencers is the opportunity to share the task of content creation.**

   a. Instead of burning up internal resources, shift the "burden" of content creation to your influencers. In most cases, it's what they're already doing!

5. **Influencers are tremendously helpful at growing new audiences.**

   a. Influencers are distribution partners—a communication channel unto themselves—in that they engage active target audiences, exposing you to them.

   b. Through the use of quality inbound links, influencers help to maximize your SEO and increase your search engine ranking, making you more visible to new consumers looking for more information on you.

   c. Influencers are especially critical in international or foreign market launches or expansions to ensure brand messaging is authentic and natural.

6. **Influencers provide a visible source of social proof for new and existing audiences.**

   a. Social proof refers to the psychological and social phenomenon wherein people copy the actions of others in an attempt to showcase the "correct" behavior for a given situation.

   b. Our first response when we're exposed to things we've never seen, tried, or experienced is often skepticism or hesitation. But if we're introduced by someone we trust, our perspective changes. There is an exchange of trust, as we become more open to this new experience. This is social proof in action, and influencers serve as beacons of trustworthy recommendation.

7. **Influencers are naturally skilled at building communities.**
   a. So long as the content you create with your influencer maintains the same quality and interest as what they've been creating for their community, their community will be inclined to consume your content, too.

8. **Influencers can also assist with reputation management, damage control and rehabilitation, if necessary.**
   b. When things go awry, a high-profile or trusted advocate speaking in your defense can make a big difference in fixing a public relations fiasco or social media flub.

MOVING FORWARD

From what we've discussed so far, influencer marketing seems fairly straightforward: set actionable objectives for your business goals, partner with an influencer who can help you achieve those goals, and create a campaign that will attract your target audience.

Yet identifying the "right" influencer for a brand or campaign is one of the biggest challenges marketers say they face in starting an influencer marketing campaign. There are so many variables to consider in terms of approach, platform, reputation. . .where do we even begin?

The answer? We begin by not getting ahead of ourselves. We begin not with the influencer, but with our desired audience.

FOOD FOR THOUGHT

Can you think of a brand of sportswear that every woman in the world feels she *has* to own to feel stylish but comfortable in her down time? Or a smartphone that everyone software engineer in America wants to buy? Or a car that every person in their mid-20s wants to drive? Probably not.

But what about an unmarried female software engineer in her mid-20s, living on the West Coast, who has a desire to be both comfortable but sporty chic in her recreational time? Have more of a clear picture of who she is and what her purchasing habits may look like?

STEP TWO

OBSERVE
AND
IDENTIFY

7

Influencing **Your Customer**
. . .is only possible if you
actually know them

You can build the best influencer marketing campaign with the hottest names in a particular vertical, but both the influencer and the message must connect with the audience, or you won't see results. You need to develop a deep understanding of your market and what and who will influence them.

In other words, this is where you define your target market.

THE ANATOMY OF A TARGET MARKET

Simply stated, your target market is the group of consumers at which your product or service is aimed, and all too often this is where I see the fatal flaws.

Why? We have a tendency to go too broad in looking at our potential audience for fear that if we get too specific, we will eliminate a or exclude potential consumers . . .but here's the thing: if you try to appeal to everyone, you end up appealing to *no one*.

Seth Godin eloquently rebuts the "spray and pray" mentality: "What actually works in marketing is setting up shop and staying there. Not finding new people for your product, but finding new products for your people."

Targeting isn't meant to exclude—**it's meant to focus**.

The times of generic TV ads trying to speak to everyone are long gone, and casting a wide net generally results in a smaller catch, not a better one. The more focused your audience is, the more tailored you can make your marketing approach, resulting in reaching customers at the exact moment they are most receptive to what you have to say and with the exact messaging the speaks to them.

Use social listening for your target market research

So how do we get to know our target audience? This is where I like to say you put on your detective hat by conducting what many marketers call "social listening".

This is the research process where we gather as much information as we can by observing the landscape and the market to determine who is talking about a brand or industry on social channels, and what they are saying. We also use social listening to surface our ideal market and the influences that shape their behavior.

Now let's take a look at the specific information you'll gather to develop a clear picture of your target market.

Demographics: The basics of your target market

Let's first take a look at the basic demographics that start to make a target market take shape:

- Age
- Gender
- Location
- Income
- Family status
- Education
- Occupation
- Ethnicity
- Marital status

While it's best to start any discussion of target markets by going through the basic demographic factors—they're an easy jumping off point and are familiar to anyone with experience or interest in marketing—I'd suggest you take them with a grain of salt.

My approach to demographics is different from most any other marketing, advertising or sales strategies. In fact, I believe the world has changed so much that placing too much weight on demographic factors will only hurt you in reaching your most optimal audience.

Demographics allow you to see who buys your product, enabling you to gain a clear perspective on the situation they are in, and therefore be empathetic and insightful into to what will resonate with them. For example, a woman making less than $25,000 a year may love fashion, and as much as she may admire or aspire to the fashion Instagram model decked in diamonds and Chanel, she can't resonate, because it's not even an option for her to afford that lifestyle.

Let's take a look at how you might construct a profile, working from your target market's details.

If we are developing a campaign for a college, and our primary goal is to get older Gen Y students to sign up, our base targeting profile might look something like this:

- **Age:** 22–29 years old *(core marker)*
- **Salary:** $10,000–30,000/year *(core marker)*
- **Gender:** Women *(secondary marker)*

While at first glance this data set might seem too overly general to be helpful, it gets you off to a great start with your market.

With just this information in hand, you can dig into your research and:

- Discover what interests and desires people in this basic demographic set might have
- What is actually feasible; for example, a 27-year-old graduate student may *want* a Range Rover, but at a salary of less than $30k, buying one is not reasonable
- Narrow down the research and trends on what top-selling products and services are for 22–29-year-old women making $30k or less
- Scan the local job market for places paying $10–30k/year and ask around (in person) to discover what they're watching or reading online

When you learn about the *top-selling products* for your demographic, you gain a better sense of their priorities, and what they're adding to (in other words, missing from) their lives.

When you learn about what they're *reading and watching*, you're better able to target where you put your marketing dollars, as well as the tone and subject matter of your marketing content. You can also target certain digital ads based on occupation and workplace, giving you a little help with allocating your marketing budget and content.

When you define your target market, simply choose:

- **1–2 core demographic markers:** Data that defines your most likely customer
- **1–3 secondary demographic markers:** Data that fleshes out your core demographic markers

Focusing on a small core allows you to see what's important to your customers, where they spend their time (both online and offline), and what they're exposed to in terms of both media and marketing messages. With this understanding, you can build a basic picture of what ponds you'll be swimming in, and flesh out the types of segmentation (and targeted content) you'll need from there.

Now, here's the key: While demographics can help you narrow things down, relying solely on them isn't enough. You need to know what your audience *cares* about, their needs, their desires, their pain points.

Taking the above example a step further, many different women make under $25,000, but will choose to spend their money in different ways depending on what they personally value. One woman might be driven by status, and believes a designer label will make her more fashionable and beautiful; another may appreciate fashion, but feels that it's all in how it's worn and styled, so she invests in a gym membership, believing that being in great shape is what will enable her to wear anything she wants and feel confident and beautiful.

These factors aren't covered by demographic data, but it's clearly the aspect that most determines how people choose to spend their money. And every individual is driven by a different set of factors.

Think of the last purchase you made. How many of the following factors had to do with different aspects of your purchase:
- **How you shopped** (online, offline, mobile, etc.)
- **What your price point was** (bargain or prestige pricing)
- **Who you were shopping for** (you? your spouse? your kids?)
- **What need or desire you are trying to satisfy** (ex. status, ego, fulfillment, basic need, etc.)

- **The type of research you made for your purchase** (review sites, social media, word of mouth recommendations)
- **Where you shopped** (Wal-Mart or a local neighborhood shop?)

Under which demographic heading would you place these very real (and high-impact) questions? Audiences are getting more segmented and nuanced, well beyond the traditional marketer's understanding of demographics. That means we need to be both proactive and responsive to these changes in the market—and that means going more in-depth in researching target markets.

Psychographics: Getting into your target market's heads

If demographics give you the "who" behind your target market, psychographics help you learn more about the "why"—and how to speak effectively to that "why".

Psychographics refer to determining a classification of people according to their attitudes, aspirations, values, interests and other psychological criteria—essentially gaining what is arguably a deeper, more important level of understanding to help us directly speak to their needs and desires.

Another way to put it is that demographics are things that can be observed or quantified from the outside, such as gender and income, while psychographics are internal attributes or attitudes.

When researching the interests of our target market of young, career women in the last example, we can also be gaining valuable clues into their:

- Character
- Attitudes
- Values
- Interests/hobbies
- Lifestyle
- Behaviors

Let's say that in the course of our research, we notice a significant portion of our target market is sharing posts from the website Refinery29.com.

We can use Refinery29—the tone, the topics, the prevailing attitudes, the conversations—to shape how we market our products and services, because the site acts as an influencer to our ideal customer.

When we know where our market is looking for information, we can do a better job of providing them with what they're looking *for*. The more we get to know our consumer, the more we will be able to recognize trends in the interests and values they share and the influencers shaping their actions.

Let's go back to that young career woman you highlighted and list a few trends or lifestyle markers you might uncover:

- She's making her first big purchases in life (furniture, cars, maybe a first apartment), and stressing out a little along the way
- She's eager to eat organic and "natural" foods (shopping, cooking, and so on)
- She's trying to build a wardrobe on a budget, but she wants a "grown-up" and "classy" style.
- She's in peak 'ambition stage' with her career, and thus has less time to take care of herself through exercise and self-care but

knows the importance of it and is trying to find economical and efficient solutions

- She loves to read *Who What Wear,* follow *The Zoe Report* and watch *The Bachelor* on Monday nights.

These details give you a lot of fodder not only for understanding your consumer, but for everything from product development to content marketing—and a big insight into how you might use influencers to connect with your audience. Good psychographic profiling can be difficult to do, because it requires you to immerse yourself in your market's inner psychology and develop an empathy and familiarity with the target customer.

Some of this approach to psychographics comes from studying how actors immerse themselves in their script studies. When an actor is trying to "become" his character, he digs deeply into every aspect of how that character thinks, feels, lives, and reacts to the world around them.

If you Google "How do actors understand the characters they're going to play?", you'll undoubtedly find some tips to help you gain that same kind of understanding of your market.

GETTING UP CLOSE AND PERSONAL

Once you have a laser focus on who you want to target and what matters to them, it's time to get even more personal, and a great way to do this is by creating **buyer personas**.

A buyer persona is a semi-fictional representation of your ideal customer based on market research and real data you gather about your target market. With your buyer persona in hand, you'll better be able to map out their journey through the decision-making process, and make a targeted plan to speak directly to them.

A detailed buyer persona can be used to inform everything from product development to the nuts and bolts of your marketing strategies and content. It will also help you choose the right influencer or influencers to partner with, because you'll be better able to identify who or what is influencing them.

If you Google the term, "buyer persona," you'll find many different approaches with different levels of detail. You'll even find different terms for a buyer persona, including "pen portrait"—though that term is often used for a more briefly sketched-out buyer persona.

Regardless of what you call it, your goal should be to develop a clear, actionable representation of your ideal customer that allows you to see them as a person (versus a dollar sign) and better understand all the factors that affect their lives and behavior.

A quick note: You could end up creating many different buyer personas, depending on your products and if you plan to serve different markets. For example, you may have a persona for your current consumer (e.g. empty nesters) and then one for the new consumer you are trying to reach (e.g., young couples who don't have kids).

You might find that your buyer personas evolve over time, or that some you create stop being valid, so be sure to make frequent check-ins of your personas and keep adjusting and refining over time. A marketer's worst enemy is complacency, and in this hyper-changing economy we have to constantly be adapting and evolving—which requires serious agility and an ever-evolving growth mindset.

CREATING A BUYER PERSONA
Details, questions, and topics to help you get started

As you start to put your own buyer personas together, here are some of the details and questions you can ask to inform the process. Not every persona needs all of these moving parts, but with some practice, you'll figure out the ones that resonate most with you.

Demographics
- Age
- Gender
- Family/relationship status
- Location
- Occupation
- Income
- Education

Psychographics
- Lifestyle
  - ▶ What kind of work-life balance do they have?
  - ▶ What do they do with their spare time, or for fun?
  - ▶ Where/how do they shop for their needs and wants? Do they set a budget?
  - ▶ Who sets their financial priorities?
  - ▶ What types of media do they consume, and how and when do they consume them?
  - ▶ How do they communicate with the world around them?
  - ▶ How do they interact using social media, if at all?
- Emotional
  - ▶ What are their priorities in life? Work? Family? Recreation? Relationships?

- ▶ What big plans will they be making or executing on in the next decade?
- ▶ What makes them happy?
- ▶ What stresses them out?
- ▶ What would they change about their lives?
- ▶ What do they want that they don't have? What do they have that they don't want?
- ▶ Who do they go to for advice?
- ▶ Who do they emulate/copycat, or simply want to be like?

Some key methods to further your insight as you develop your persona:

Talk to your customers: Seems obvious, right? It's mind-boggling how overlooked this is. We will conduct focus groups, seek expert recommendations and strategies, synthesize data, yet most companies I've worked with aren't actually asking the real humans already buying (and hopefully loving) your product or service. Reach out to some of your most loyal, supportive customers for a quick interview to gain their insights. Ask them a bit about their background to gain a sense of how they fit into the demographics you've discovered, and then dig in to how they discovered you, what aspects of your messaging or marketing resonated with them, why they opted to buy from you versus a competitor, and what aspects of your product they like most (or *dislike* most).

Talk to your internal teams: Your sales team is a gold mine for buyer persona insights. No one knows better than them who is most receptive to your marketing messages, who is most likely to make a purchase with you, and any concerns or obstacles they are trying to overcome with that purchase.

Your customer service team can tell you who is in contact with them most often, how people are using your product, what their challenges might be with your product, and where you might be falling short.

Tweak the forms on your website: Be sure to include some demographic information fields with your newsletter sign-ups, product inquiry forms, and purchase forms. Not every consumer will be willing to fill out an extensive amount of detail, but many won't mind a bit.

The more detail you add, the more clarity you'll have in your efforts to connect with your target consumer. Including a picture or illustration can help you further resonate because it allows you to visually put a human face on him/her.

Armed with a well-crafted persona(s), you can now better inform every aspect of how you create your influencer marketing plan, from selecting the influencers themselves, to the platforms of choice to the messaging and content.

Recap and Review

KEY POINTS

1. **Getting to know your market intimately is the critical first step in crafting a successful targeted influencer marketing campaign.**

   a. In terms of timeline, this phase of market research serves as the transition point between the first and second steps of the Influencer Code. While keeping your end goal top of mind, you then observe and identify key aspects of who your consumer is and what influences their actions on the particular topic at hand.

   b. This phase involves *social listening*: extensive research meant to inform you on both the market and the current landscape.

2. **While researching your target market, there are two key types of information to obtain: demographics and psychographics.**

   a. Demographics (the "who")

      i. Identify 1–2 core demographic markers: data that defines your most likely customer

      ii. Identify 1–3 secondary demographic markers: data that fleshes out your core demographic markers

   b. Psychographics (the "why")

      i. Encompassing everything from individual aspirations to lifestyle choices and personal values, these are the internal influences at play in a person's decision making.

    ii. Observing and understanding these factors at play in your target demographic allows you identify who and what influences them

3. **The importance of talking to real people cannot be overstated.**
   a. Seek out current consumers, industry enthusiasts, even your internal sales team; find out what matters to them, what they find important, and why. You're not trying to reach "the average consumer," you're trying to reach *your* consumer.

4. **From your target market research, create a buyer persona to help you better understand your consumer.**
   a. Combine your demographic and psychographic findings to create a profile of your target customer.
   b. Give your consumer a detailed face. Make them human—because they are! Remember, the goal is to focus on the people who will be your best potential consumers.

5. **Don't worry about excluding anyone or going after 'everyone'.**
   a. By speaking directly to your specific audience, you build a strong audience of people who intensely identify with your brand and, by their nature, become brand advocates.

MOVING FORWARD

Once business goals and objectives are defined, the importance of doing the proper research into your target markets cannot be overstated. The second phase of the code, Observe and Identify, breaks down into two phases: 1) your "ultimate consumer" and 2) Your ultimate consumers' influencer(s).

Too often, we jump into trying to identify influencers before really getting to know our audience. Rather than starting by choosing the influencer, begin by observing and identifying your optimal target audience. By starting with your audience, you will have a much more direct and clear understanding of who the real influencers are over them on the subject at hand.

FOOD FOR THOUGHT

Imagine that you are responsible for filling a new position at your company. What factors would you most consider when making your hiring decision? Their performance in their current position? Work experience and job history? Your impression of them during the interview? Recommendations from past employers and co-workers? Their presence and conduct on social media?

Odds are, you'd prefer to have access to all of the above information. Yet when it comes to selecting an influencer for a new marketing campaign, too many seem content with the equivalent of a 10-minute phone interview before jumping head-first into a new business relationship. That wouldn't fly in any other hiring scenario; what makes us think influencer marketing is any different?

8

Measuring an Influencer's Influence
Identifying and Selecting the Right Influencer

I t's one thing to work with an influencer. It's another thing entirely to work with the *right* influencer.

According to eMarketer.com, 75% of marketers say that *finding* the right influencers is the hardest part of creating an influencer marketing program. To understand the complexities involved with finding a good fit for your brand or campaign, consider the following example:

In the world of entrepreneurs, Gary Vaynerchuk has become one of *the* most sought after influencers in the spheres of digital marketing and motivational advice. Part of the reason for this is that Vaynerchuk stands at the intersection of two opposing schools of thought. On one side, he's known for his glorification of the grind, the hustle and a never-say-die attitude, commanding a huge audience of entrepreneurs who follow him, listen to him, and—most importantly—trust in him to fuel their hustle.

On the other side, those who value education, formal schooling and training see Vaynerchuk's messaging in a cynical light, and don't appreciate his 'free' language style encouraging "the grind" over more traditional means of improvement.

To these critics, Vaynerchuk says, "I'm not a professor trying to sell books. I'm actually in the arena—I'm not in the stands. I'm unbelievably misunderstood by conservative, traditional business people."

While his no-nonsense stance and raw voice may inspire and move a certain group of people to action, a button-up, white collar business or academic institution likely wouldn't want someone like Gary pushing hustle over education. This doesn't mean Gary isn't a mega influencer; it just means his brand of influence may not be the best fit for everyone. His influence lies in a certain "pond."

Answering this question of, "Who is the *right* influencer for my market?" is one I often liken to fishing. . .yes, fishing. To the average observer, fishing looks simple: you round up a pole, hook on some bait, cast your line in the water, and see what bites. And if you're fishing for fun or relaxation, it might well be just that simple—but if you're fishing for any other purpose, things get more complicated.

Professional fishing, for sport or for commerce, starts with knowing what you want, what it looks like, and what you're going to do with it once you've got it. It involves plenty of planning (time of day, the weather, the particular fishing season, the area you're fishing in), specific equipment (your rod and line, your hook and bait choice, your vessel and navigation, how you'll store your catch), and strategy (where you cast off, how you move your line, even the way you reel your fish in).

While you might catch a decent fish with a casual line-drop, a blind catch is based more on luck than strategy, and luck isn't sustainable as a plan—it won't get you consistent results. That's why the pros invest time, money, and effort into learning what works, mastering their craft through practice, and mapping out a strategy so they can optimize from the very moment they've got a line in the water.

Marketing pros take the same approach: while you might occasionally stumble across an opportunity that meets your needs without much effort or forethought, you can't rely on luck to achieve your goals. If you want to use influencer marketing successfully, you'll need a holistic, strategic approach centered around your business goals.

At this point, you have set your overall business goal(s) and SMART objectives for your influencer marketing campaign. To pursue your campaign effectively, everyone across your organization must be on the same page with the goals.

The good news is that each of the previous chapters have walked you through laying the groundwork of the second phase of the Influencer Code: OBSERVE. You are now in a solid position to evaluate which influencers are right for your brand and needs, as well as assess the level of influence they have over their audience.

Having identified your target audience and analyzed their journey to figure out who influences them in the different phases of that journey, you've become a master social listener, an observant detective, and a researcher who understands (a) your consumer, and (b) knows who has their trust and attention.

Weighing out each of the following five factors will provide you with a solid framework for measuring just how impactful a selected influencer will be for your brand, further empowering you to pick the right person for the right job:

Brand Alignment
- Is there a connection between the influencer's brand and our brand?
- Do we share any audiences with the influencer?
- Is the influencer's audience the audience we are trying to reach?

Authenticity

- Is the influencer perceived as genuine? trustworthy? Is their brand ever perceived to be "for sale"?
- Is their voice, advice and the content they share consistent in terms of tone, subject matter, and personality?
- Do they interact with their fans and followers in a tangible, sincere way?

Content Type & Quality

- Is the medium they use to create content the medium we believe we will have most impact on our own target audience (for example, video versus audio versus short form text)
- Is the type of content they produce something we would be proud to have aligned with our brand?
- Do they inspire conversations that bring value to their space?

Relationship

- Is the influencer easy to connect with? Are they responsive and timely?
- Is your product or brand a natural fit for them, or is it going to be a "stretch" for both of you?

Audience

- Is their audience engaged across the body of their content? Do they respond equally to different posts?
- Are there topics their audience responds to more than others?
- Does their audience respond more often in passive ways (likes) versus active ways (comments and conversation)?

UNDERSTANDING THE "R FACTORS": MEASURING AUDIENCE INFLUENCE

The "Pillars of Influence" were coined in 2012 by digital analyst and futurist, Brian Solis. Solis defines the fundamental principles at work in influencer relationships as **reach**, **relevance** and **resonance**—the Three Rs.

Scott Guthrie, Digital Director of Ketchum London, expanded on Solis' concept by adding four more Rs: **reception**, **relationship**, **reality** and **relinquish control**. If you search on how to measure influence, these ideas will be among the first to pop up—communicators love grouping big ideas around a list of words.

You'll note that some overlap with the 5 factors above, given that they are another way of grouping/looking at influence, but they'll do so through the lens of the influencer's audience, specifically. They also serve as a sort of verification checklist. Any influencer you may have pinpointed in observing your consumer's journey should be analyzed against each of these principles.

Here, we focus on the *five* Rs that are most relevant to influence:

1. Reach
2. Recognition
3. Reference
4. Relevance
5. Resonance

Reach. This is the overall total size of the influencer's following across all platforms, as according to metrics like follower counts, subscribers, email lists, and traffic. Reach isn't the be-all, end-all, but it helps you define the *category* of influencer someone is, be it celebrity macro-influence, or personal micro-influence.

Recognition. How easily recognizable or known is your potential influencer in the category you're focusing on? I don't necessarily mean "known" in the mainstream sense, but known to the exact customer you want to reach. Does your target audience recognize your influencer on sight? If they don't recognize the actual influencer, do they immediately recognize their expertise, credentials, or accolades?

In marketing, David Meerman Scott, Jay Baer, and Seth Godin are considered "rock stars": successful pros who are highly recognized and trusted as key leaders in the field. And while a professor of marketing at any given university might not have the same name recognition as these rock stars, people can recognize their expertise and credibility by virtue of their professorship.

Reference. Who else in their field (or outside of it) is referencing their work? Are they relevant and/or influential? Have they been featured on any lists by publications, websites, or organizations in their field—and are those lists credible?

For example, if a real estate firm promotes a list of the most influential real estate agents in the U.S., and the list is primarily made up of their own real estate agents, you can take that reference with a grain of salt. It might as well be a press release.

However, if the National Association of Realtors—a respected and objective organization with members in every state—makes a similar list, we trust that: a) they're drawing from a larger pool than their own payroll; and b) they've got the national perspective to back up their choices.

To be clear: being *referenced* is not the same as being *talked about*. People *talk about* their favorite new recipe, or the shoes they picked out last weekend. When someone is *referenced*, they're being treated as a go-to source and a voice of authority on a particular topic.

The frequency with which that happens and the arenas in which it occurs becomes a measure of their impact and expertise. . .and is absolutely a factor in measuring influence.

Relevance. Relevance answers the question of how closely associated an influencer is with a particular topic. Which influencers show up in your preliminary keyword searches? Which influencers are associated with the keyword phrases that are critical to your own messaging?

An influencer may be "influential" (referenced) and "known" (recognized) in a particular space or for a specific topic. . .but does that space or topic matter to your brand? Relevance defines how closely an influencer's community aligns with your brands target audience, as well as how closely the content produced by the influencer is aligned with:

- Topics of value to that community; and
- Topics your brand wants to be associated with.

It's all too common to see brands choose an influencer because he or she is well-known and *appears* to embody what the brand wants to portray. This was the case when beauty brand Bobbi Brown Cosmetics partnered with swimsuit model Kate Upton for a series of product collection launches. At first glance, Kate might seem like a good fit to sell beauty products to women, given that she's a well-known figure with a reputation for glamorous photo shoots.

Upon closer examination of the model's audience, however, it's clear that many of her followers are actually men in their 30s who like looking at her. . .and who aren't buying much makeup. That doesn't mean Upton isn't an influencer on some level; it just means Bobbi Brown's target audience isn't an audience she can reach on their behalf—and therefore, their product is not relevant.

The more relevant the influencer is to the brand and its target market, the more engaged their audience will be, and the more likely they are to act on your messaging. It's about *quality*, not quantity. In fact, the best influencers won't work with a brand unless the opportunity is relevant to their followers.

Resonance. It's like the old saying about a tree falling in the forest: "If a Facebook post goes out to 1 million followers and nobody comments or shares it, did the post have any resonance at all?" This is the toughest one for many marketers to grasp: does the influencer get *real* and *reciprocal* engagement from their audience?

Resonance is the result of reach combined with relevant engagement—measured by a combination of quality of conversation, comments, shares, views, retweets, referrals, mentions, and so on. Essentially, it determines how much of a response an influencer generates when they post content, host an event, ask a question, etc.

Also remember: not all comments are created equal. You'll want to be sure the comments on their posts are related to the topic at hand. . .and something more tin-depth than just an emoji, or "Cool!"

A quick tip: Offline measures are important, too: when an influencer is featured at an event, what's the turnout like? If they speak at a conference, how are they received? Who shares their content in real time? What's the turnout when they host a book signing? Do people come to see them again and again? If your influencer regularly appears in public, keep their offline engagement in mind.

Your selection of influencers won't necessarily need to align with all of these factors. The ones you prioritize will be dependent on your brand, your goals, your objectives, and your target audience. There are many strong influencers, especially in the business-to-business (B2B) world who don't have much of an online presence or sizeable following—but who will exert more influence than a social star with a seven-figure following. Again, your research will point you in the right direction.

Beyond the five factors, there some additional specific information gathering points to consider when you're identifying potential influencer partners.

GATHER THE INFLUENCER'S INFORMATION

As influencer marketing has become an industry in and of itself, it has become the norm for influencers to be ready and willing to provide information about their audience and community.

Here are a few things you can ask potential influencers for to paint a picture of their impact:

- **Analytics:** Ask for access to their Google analytics, as well as any audience demographic and psychographic information they can collect and extract from their various platforms. This information will also help you determine if they are reaching and engaging with the audience you are trying to reach.
- **Testimonials and reviews:** Keep your skeptic hat on for testimonials or reviews that aren't accompanied by names, photos, or specific details. Anyone can leave a review on a general

website, and any businessperson can make up a fake set of kudos. Specific reviews with specific details by real people? Those are golden, and genuinely tough to spoof.

- **Networks with lasting connections**: Influential people know a lot of people because they focus on making connections that are valuable to them, even to the point of getting to know their connections' connections. More importantly, they add value to the lives of everyone in their network. Think about who might be in their personal network. If they don't *have* a network (outside of an online following), their influence is questionable and/or limited.

- **Past performance.** If the influencer you're assessing is a seasoned digital or social influencer, they should have campaign results, case studies, examples, and references to cover their past collaborations—and you should be able to see some evidence of their success beyond even what they're willing to show you. Don't be afraid to talk to brands they've worked with before. . .in fact, I highly recommend it!

The exception to be aware of here is that smaller, more personal, or up-and-coming influencers likely *won't* have this information. While that means it will be harder to forecast what level of influence they will have, they also won't command as much from you in exchange to garner value—it's a trade-off you can make if it works for your brand and audience.

Measuring influence within the influencer's industry

Here are some specific examples by industry—and don't worry if I don't cover your particular field or market here. This is less about understanding a specific space, and more about how to think critically about an influencer's specific industry, and what translates to impact within that sphere.

Politicians: How many laws have they written? How many bills have they sponsored or co-sponsored? How many active committees are they on? How often are they the dominant voice for their wing of the government?

Organizations: What kind of global/national/local impact do they have? What specific actions have they taken beyond building aware-ness? How have they encouraged their members to interact with them on different platforms?

Authors: How many copies have their books sold? What kind of best-seller lists do they appear on? Who has endorsed their work?

B2B salesperson: How many software programs have they sold to distributors? How many programs are they representing? How broadly used are these programs?

Fitness/wellness/weight loss coaches: How many pounds have their clients lost? How many clients are continuing to lose weight with them? How many new clients come by way of referral?

Coaches: How many games has their team won? How many personal records have their athletes achieved, or how many minutes have they shaved off their time?

Musicians: How many times have their songs been downloaded? How many albums have they released? How many awards have they won? What other higher profile artists have they collaborated with? How has their music been rated or reviewed?

Interior designers: How many clients do they have (besides themselves)? How many projects do they have on the go, currently? How many repeat clients do they have? How many of their clients come to them via referral? Are their clients sharing their projects online in a positive way?

While not every factor or measure will be necessary or applicable to your particular situation, it's important to understand the breadth and depth of what you can actually analyze to gauge influence—and to figure out if that influence is relevant to your needs.

If you choose an influencer on the basis of their popularity, and then try to reverse engineer them into being a "fit", you'll set yourself up for failure every time.

In a perfect influencer marketing world, you have a dedicated influencer marketing specialist, or team of specialists doing all of this research. The problem, most of us don't! It's complicated, time-consuming work.

Spending hours daily to search for new influencers, review their work, their platforms, their history, dig into their metrics, check for any reputational hiccups or competing projects. . ..and all this before even making a connection. . .is a full-time job in itself! Savvy marketers are starting to understand that the long-term payback far outweighs the time upfront when it comes to ROI and real brand growth.

Upfront research is crucial. The shortsighted, one-off "pay-to-post" view of influencer marketing is a fundamental failure, one which hinders performance and prevents influencer marketing from becoming a strategic investment at the board level. You wouldn't hire a new employee from just a first glance, so why would do that with influencers—especially those we want to have stand as public faces of our brand!

Luckily, marketers have plenty of reasons to be optimistic about influencer marketing. Technology is evolving at a staggering pace and agencies are popping up just as fast, offering marketers and brands different tools, methodologies and resources to help identify influencer opportunities, manage influencer relationships, and develop new influencer strategies.

RESOURCES FOR IDENTIFYING INFLUENCERS

While every budget is different, and every campaign differs in scope, there are four main ways to identify online influencers. The beauty of influencer marketing is that each can be scaled up or down, depending on what you want to spend on your search and whether you choose to use an external database, outsource it to an agency, or bring someone in internally to focus on it.

Keep in mind that the landscape of resources available at this stage in influencer marketing is incredibly scattered, and "best practices" are few and far between.

Also, take care that you're not treating "influencer marketing" as an "add-on'" responsibility to someone's (already packed) role in-house—this is a surefire way to turn your efforts into a flop.

At the same time, if you work with an agency, be cognizant of who you are working with, as many of the "influencer specialists" within these agencies are actually just junior-level-employees who will focus on vanity metrics, whether real or fake!

You'll want to oversee your program and manage it closely to ensure whoever is doing the bulk of the work knows what they're doing (and you may want to hand them this book!)

Databases. These are software programs that scrape website content for you, pulling publicly available data according to the particular parameters, keywords, or topics you dictate. These programs enable companies to find, research, and track influencers across the myriad social media platforms (including, but not limited to, YouTube, Instagram, Facebook, Twitter, and Snapchat).

These can be good places to determine the lay of the land, but be prepared to spend time vetting each influencer, and communicating with them directly.

Different services will also demand different fees to use them, or to subscribe, so be sure to do some comparisons up front to get the best value for your buck. A few of the more popular databases to note at the time of writing this book include: NinjaOutreach, BuzzSumo, GroupHigh and Buzzstream.

Manual Search. For a long time, influencer databases were the primary manner in which agencies sought out influencers for collaborations—but general purpose search engines can still offer you some great insights and options.

It's a less efficient process, but critical if you want to truly understand who and what is out there—especially in terms of locating influencers outside of database constraints. This type of search is particularly useful for niche brands with a very specific audience, given that most databases won't capture anything refined enough to meet their needs.

Additionally, most databases are only going to capture the most frequently found names in each category. If you're looking for a "sports car expert", everyone looking to market anything related to sports cars is finding that same hit list when looking for influencers—making the experts that are frequently found harder to connect to (and more expensive to engage with.)

By the way, I don't mean quick a Google session; this is a time to take a deeper dive. Look past the first eight pages of your search engine results, explore the forums and communities, see who is talking, who is being referenced. Go *down* the rabbit hole of who your target audience is listening to. Manual use of search engines and social networks may not require up-front fees or subscriptions, but it is time-consuming. . .and time is money.

Manual search includes:

- **Social media platforms:** There are many, but the biggest players (at the time of publishing) include Facebook, YouTube, Twitter, LinkedIn, Snapchat, Tik Tok, and Instagram. These are established networks where people can create their own identity, connect with other users in different ways, post their own content, and comment on and interact with content that others post.
- **Associations/Groups/Interest networks:** You don't have to stay online! Churches, neighborhood associations, affinity groups, conferences, clubs. . .all of them offer the opportunity to meet all sorts of influencers in real life.
- **Blogs:** Blogs have been a force for community-building for a couple of decades now, though some of their content has shifted from traditional blogging platforms like WordPress onto Facebook pages, and broader content platforms like Medium.
- **Vlogs:** Video-based blogging is extremely popular across many different interest groups, including beauty, gaming, fitness, cooking, and hobbies and occupations of all kinds. Vimeo and YouTube are the places to start searching on your keywords.

- **Forums and communities:** Forums and communities exist for pretty much any interest you can think of. Sometimes they are created using forum software on a dedicated website, such as Techist, Bodybuilding.com, Slashdot, and so on, and sometimes they create meet-ups in places like Facebook or Reddit.

- **Online and traditional media/News sites:** These could include websites by established news organizations like the New York Times, CNN, or Fox News; online giants like Yahoo!, Apple, Google News, and the Huffington Post; or rising stars like Buzzfeed. Don't forget about the traditional outlets of print magazines and newspapers, TV, and radio, either!

When you dig in, be populating a detailed spreadsheet (or note-keeping tool of your own choice) with where you've been, what search terms you've used, when you were there, and any relevant contact info (if you want to follow up). If you don't make these notes as you go, odds are you may not be able to replicate your searches when making your approach list.

Networks and agencies. If databases are on one end of the influencer marketing services spectrum, agencies are on the other. While databases cast a wide net to provide as many potential influencer matches as possible, influencer marketing agencies take an influencer-by-influencer and brand-by-brand approach to each campaign.

A network or agency will actually have a relationship with the influencers, and will require that you use them as a middleman to reach out. They will also take either an upfront fee or an ongoing payment, depending on your arrangement, so be sure to factor that into your budget.

One caution: I interviewed countless influencer marketing agents and agencies for this book, and those conversations made it clear that most of them are still confusing reach with impact, and many had put someone fresh out of school in place as your 'account specialist'. On a practical level, that means they aren't going to give you much more than someone with a certain profile of social media metrics and a vague calculation of engagements.

If you work with one, ensure you get a chance to personally interview the influencer, and ask for results on previous campaigns, and thoroughly do your homework and manual digging. Ultimately, I would only recommend using most agents or agencies as a means to make initial connection to an influencer you may have trouble accessing.

Influencer marketplaces. A marketplace is a two sided-platform that connects brands looking to work with influencers on their social media channels to influencers who are actively working with brands, or considering an alliance. A brand can post their campaign requirements and the sponsorship fee or compensation that they are offering. Influencers are then able to browse these offers to find the best fit— compensation, duration, commitment) for their needs.

Influencer marketplaces provide influencer discovery tools for brands and agencies, and many also include massive searchable databases of potential influencers using clever algorithms to help identify best fits. In fact, more and databases are now becoming full marketplaces, with some of the top options at time of publication including Upfluence, Famebit, Grapevine, AspireIQ, IZEA, Onalytica, Traackr, and Tapfluence, to name a few.

Depending on your specific industry, there may be other methods and places for seeking out influencers. But regardless of what method—or combination of methods—you choose, don't lose sight of the manual human effort component. Whether it's a referred list from an agency or scraped from a database or marketplace, you need to spend the time to dig deeper.

These tools can help you expedite and narrow down a list, but they should be just that: tools to help. Nothing should replace human insight and effort. Just as you wouldn't hire an employee based only on a referral without actually interviewing the person, getting more information and ensuring it feels like the right fit, you shouldn't make influencer choices sight unseen.

Which brings us to the most critical point: just as with fishing, dropping a line and catching random fish isn't good enough—you want to identify the *right* influencer for you in these big ponds filled with many different influencers. Some can be great, some just okay; some are a waste of time and some can even hurt your brand. And it's up to you to know the difference.

Once you've identified an influencer(s) you're interested in working with—by weighing all the various factors to ensure brand fit and target audience impact—there's one final checklist to run down before you make things official. I like to call this the "Red Flag" check, which involves doing a more fine-grain, manual search on wherever your influencer shows up—across *all* platforms. Even if they're primarily active on YouTube or their own blog, they may have accounts elsewhere, or they might be featured in others' content. Failing to perform this type of check might lead to some unpleasant surprises down the road, particularly once an influencer's brand has been publicly linked with yours.

The Red Flag checklist includes:

- Identifying any radical shifts in content type, subject matter, or tone from year to year or week to week
- Locating any content under a different/old username that negatively impacts the influencer's credibility
- Controversial material that won't be a good fit with your target audience. Some controversy can be a good thing—but not if it alienates your potential or existing customers. This includes strong political or religious views in a particular direction, which can be detrimental even when surrounded by content your audience might otherwise engage with.
- Conflicts with other subject matter experts, as well as any broader credibility issues in the eyes of their subject matter community.

Again, locating these potential issues requires manual searches for specific issues—a casual review of the influencer's public face won't be enough to determine whether a *good* fit is actually the *right* fit.

Spotting fake influence on social media

No discussion of identifying and measuring an influencer's impact on their industry would be complete without mentioning the challenge involved in separating genuine influence from manufactured or "fake" influence.

In this crazy, fast-paced world of constantly evolving technology and diminishing barriers to entry, even the most popular influencers face questions as to whether their followers are fake or real, and if their reach actually holds any impact. In fact, "fake influence" is a fundamental problem, and one that is only becoming more problematic in seeing influencer marketing get greater strategic investment.

In 2017, influencer marketing agency Mediakix created two completely fictional Instagram accounts, one supposedly belonging to a lifestyle and fashion-centric Instagram model, and the other to a travel and adventure photographer.

They posted daily to each account to build up a solid foundation of content, and then began buying fake followers for a few bucks per 1,000 "fans". With a fairly minimal investment, each one was at over 30,000 followers within a couple of months.

They also purchased engagement in the form of likes and comments, and noted that the engagement would occur much more quickly, the more they paid.

Once they'd crossed the necessary threshold of followers and engagement that influencer marketing platforms demanded before sign-up, they submitted each account. Then they applied for opportunities to represent particular products, including offerings from a swimwear brand, and a national food and beverage retailer. . .and they were accepted.

Each opportunity for the fake accounts came with some form of (very real) compensation, whether in the form of money or free products—and the brands didn't seem to suspect (or perhaps even *care*) they were working with fake accounts.

Mediakix's experiment proved not just how easy it was to buy fake influence, but how clueless brands were about authenticity in the process.

And as new social media platforms emerge, wannabe influencers are discovering new ways to exaggerate and fake influence on those ones, too—which means there's no end of the deception in sight.

The antidote for marketers is simple: we need to spend more of our time on qualitative measures to figure out if an influencer can really move the needle on our business goals.

Let's take a look at some of the most common measures of influence on social platforms, and how to spot the fakes gaming those measures. I'm going to use Instagram specifically to illustrate each measure here, but trust me: social influence fakery definitely isn't limited to a single platform

REACH AS AN IDENTIFIER

Online reach is an influencer's total number of followers and subscribers. Most brands view this as a fundamental qualifying metric for determining influence, with the argument that it gives insight into the potential number of people your brand, content, and messaging will be exposed to, should you choose to engage or collaborate with the influencer.

How do they fake it?

Likes, followers, views, even comments—you name it, you can buy it. What most people don't realize is how *easy* it is to do so. How easy, you ask?

Journalist Vasily Sonkin discovered the Instagram Likes Machine in Moscow: 100 likes for .89 cents. Now that's some cheap 'influence'!

If you're not in Moscow, do a web search for the term, "machine liker". You'll find a multitude of different software options to help you fake major numbers—as long as you can pay for them. You can even get apps for your phone that allow you to do it anytime/anywhere.

This is how plenty of "influencers" end up with audiences full of bots: fake accounts that perform different types of automated fake actions, depending on their complexity (and cost). Alternately, they may participate in dubious "follow back" schemes—everyone wants numbers. . .but it's not genuine engagement. How much influence can you have over someone—even a real person—who follows you just so you'll do the same?

How can you spot them?

If you dig a little deeper than the numbers, there are some straight-forward ways to evaluate the quality and relevance of a follower base:

- **Do their followers appear to have any relation to their expertise or subject matter**? If you're evaluating a makeup artist's followers, you should look for other makeup artists, or avatars and names that indicate a keen interest in makeup. Fake followers will possess little to no relationship to the nature of the so-called influencer.
- **Do their followers have names and avatars that look overly related to the influencer's name?** Or are they long lists of numbers, or strange usernames and identities that appear to have no relationship to what the influencer does?
- **Does a random set of check-ups yield actual followers?** Click through several of their followers from different parts of their follower list. Anyone with zero posts? Anyone with posts that all look exactly the same, or close to it? Anyone with no followers or low follower counts—but who follow a ton of other accounts? Keep an eye on the follower to following ratio of an

"influencer", too; someone with genuine influence is likely to have a ratio much heavier on the follower side.

This issue is one that plagues social platforms—most notably Instagram—more each year: a New York Times story covered the depth of the "bot" problem on social networks, including a *single* bot seller that had:

- 3.5 million fake accounts for sale
- 200 million fake followers they'd sold to wannabes *and* reality television stars, professional athletes, comedians, TED speakers, pastors and models
- Avatars and bios stolen from over 55,000 real Twitter users, who had no idea what their identities were selling or supporting elsewhere

As long as it's easy and cheap to do so, reach is going to be one of the first areas that social fakers aim to game.

RELEVANCE AS AN IDENTIFIER

If you recall from earlier in this chapter, relevance is defined by how specifically an influencer is aligned with, or mentioned alongside a particular topic. If you search on keywords for your business, you should see their content come up in your results. Likewise, they should be showing up in when you do social listening on key topics for your industry.

The more they show up, the more relevant they likely are to be within your industry—but as with any of these measures, this is still just one factor to take into account as you assess their influence.

How do they fake it?

Great influencers are influential because of their ability to create their own compelling, relevant content that offers value that shapes the thinking or behavior of the recipient on something that matters, or they add their own insights, opinion, and conversation to relevant content they share.

The biggest warning sign for fake relevance is a lack of consistency in posts and frequent posting without depth. Fake "influencers" will use automation or borrowed content to populate their feed with links to give the appearance of activity, without the relevance.

Some might say they do this because of time constraints or for convenience, but regardless, it's not content they care about. . .nor does anyone else.

How can you spot them?

Unfortunately, there's no shortcut to sorting out these fakers. To detect fake relevance, take a closer look at the quality and value they're offering in their content. "Influencers" who share others' content on a frequent basis but don't share any of their own, or users who are clearly being paid to deliver a long stream of branded messages should be seen as a red flag. The frequency and volume of their posts are also likely to be higher than the average account, as well.

RESONANCE AS AN IDENTIFIER

Resonance measures the level and intensity of engagement (conversations, sharing, action) with the posts and content an influencer produces. This metric provides substance because it proves an influencer's followers and commenters actually find the influencer's content interesting.

Consistently high levels of engagement are another sign of a genuine audience—in an audience that is legitimately interested in what that influencer is saying.

How do they fake it?

As with the "influencers" who game their reach numbers, there are various automation tools that make it possible to fake resonance and engagement. The same principle behind reciprocal following applies to reciprocal engagement: "influencers" use automation tools to engage with others' content in a bid to gain followers and engagement on their content in return.

How can you spot them?

Your first step is to look beyond shares, retweets, and likes, into the conversations sparked by their content. Notice I didn't say *comments*, but *conversations:* exchanges that have something to do with the post, someone with more to say than a word or two, or comments that garner a response from the poster or other commenters. Genuine conversation and interaction are indicative of real influence.

Accounts using automated tools to fake engagement will often slip through the net of their selected topics and find themselves engaging with completely irrelevant content—making them fairly easy to identify.

Here are some other handy specifics:
- **Repetitive emoji use.** While the internet loves an emoji or two (or 400), a long stream of emoji-only commenters is a red flag.

Celebrities—even with the blue "Verified" check—do get many of these types of comments. . .but since we've covered how many celebrities have fake followers, that's no reason to believe they're real.

- **Short comments without meaning or context.** *Nice! Lovely photo! Amazing! Looks good! Wow!* Sure, these are comments real people actually leave on photos, but when those are the *only* comments an Instagram account has? You're likely dealing with fakes.
- **Identical comments by different users.** In these examples, we see how the emoji usage, spacing in letters, and word usage is entirely identical to other comments from different users in the list of comments.
- **Repeated comments by the same user.** You'll also see the same fake accounts comment repeatedly, until the comment counter appears to indicate there's a wealth of engaging comments. Sometimes it happens just twice; sometimes much, much more.

Not exactly the authentic engagement you're looking for to build your brand.

REFERENCE AS AN IDENTIFIER

As I mentioned earlier, reference is an authority metric that assesses how influential an individual is deemed to be within their community or space based on the references of others to that influencer or his/her content.

This requires a deep dive into interactions between influencers—which isn't something you can do without searching all the places their name or social handles show up.

As a result, this is the hardest metric to game with automation tools or shortcuts, because it relies on peer validation; i.e., other influential users referencing their content. If a metric is hard to game, it's also one of the most powerful.

How do they fake it?

Many of the automation tools that help "influencers" increase follower numbers *also* give users an option to add particular accounts to lists if those accounts mention a topic of interest.

For example, someone looking to increase their influence in "female empowerment" may use an automation tool that not only engages with content around the topic of women's empowerment, but *also* adds content mentioning hashtags related to women's empowerment (e.g. #womensrights #empowerher) to a Twitter list—both efforts serve to increase follower count and, in turn, their "influence".

This is why being featured on a number of lists (Twitter, in this case) isn't always an indicator of influence.

Also, be on the lookout for "influencers" who join a pod of users who comment, mention, and re-share one other's content and posts to boost the appearance of real reference. These reciprocal arrangements are the opposite of sincere, spontaneous engagement.

How can you spot them?

Again, this is the hardest metric to fake, because it focuses on valid references and mentions within a community of influential users. But with social listening, good old fashioned Google Search, and the right relationship management tools, brands can delve deeper into the influencer network to identify and analyze genuine relationships between influencers—which is the only real way to gauge authority.

SHALLOW MEASURES = SHALLOW IMPACT

It's easy to fake "influence"—and if you're a marketer who isn't willing to dig past the first impressions, you're going to end up with an "influencer" partner who won't help you achieve the results you're looking for. I've used Instagram as an example of easily faked social content here, but there are many more ways and places that fakers attempt to elevate or inflate their popularity.

The big lesson? You can't base your measure of influence on a single number or metric alone, particularly in terms of easy actions such as followers or likes. Become a detective and dig into a number of factors and indicators, including thoughtful comments, real conversations about the topics that matter to you, and content that says something fresh to an audience that genuinely appreciates it.

That doesn't mean you should throw analytics or data to the wind—but rather, you should use it as a supplement to build off of in your research, rather than the primary foundation for your strategy and tactics.

Take the time to really get to know your influencers: meet them when you can, start building rapport and getting to know them as a person. Get to know their audience, learn who is really listening to them. The more you know them, and what they are actually doing, the more you will innately get a sense of their impact and who is the recipient of that impact.

There are so many intangible traits and factors you can miss if you rely on hard quantifiable data alone, which admittedly makes up a big part of why we marketers love social media—the ability to put metrics around human behavior, and label it as influence.

Admittedly, it takes time, effort, and experience to get to the point where these vetting processes are second nature. I've seen firsthand how the predominant mode of thinking—the one-off, shortsighted approach to influencer marketing—has become *the* central issue hurting the influencer marketing industry's credibility and growth potential. As marketers, we must think differently about the entire concept of influencer marketing—think bigger, and in ways which facilitate moving towards long-term investment mindset. When we approach this process as one of building mutually beneficial relationships that can function across entire organizations, ones which include both the influencer's brand and the entire consumer journey—we will begin to see the full range of opportunities offered by influencer marketing.

Recap and Review

KEY POINTS

1. **Finding the right influencer is like going fishing—the more diligent your approach, the better your results.**

   a. Having already done the groundwork of observing your target audience (which includes who influences them), you are in a solid position to better select the right influencer(s) for your brand *and* assess their level of influence.

2. **There are a number of important factors to consider when selecting a good-fit influencer.**

   a. Brand alignment: Is there a pre-existing connection? Do you share any audiences in common?

   b. Authenticity: Are they trustworthy? Acknowledged by their community? Are there any issues with the way they present themselves or their message?

   c. Content: Is their content of a quality that you would want associated with you and your brand? Is it appropriate for your current and intended audiences?

   d. Relationship: Are they easy to connect with, to get in touch with? Are they professional in their dealings, punctual with deadlines?

   e. Audience: What level of engagement does their audience demonstrate across all platforms involved? Does the influencer elicit active responses (comments, shares) or only passive responses (likes)?

3. **When evaluating an influencer for a role in your company, it's important to evaluate how much influence they hold.**

    a. We evaluate an influencer's level of audience influence using the five R's:

        i. Reach: Determined by evaluating a number of metrics including follower count, subscribers, website traffic, etc.

        ii. Recognition: How well do audiences know the influencer? Do they know their name, their face, their credentials?

        iii. Reference: How often do other influencers (or peers in their field) refer to or promote their work?

        iv. Relevance: Is the influencer a household name in their community, or just one of many? Will their name come up in a search of their field?

        v. Resonance: Does the influencer's content receive consistent, reciprocal engagement from their audience? Is their audience active and visibly interested in what the influencer has to say?

4. **It is equally as important that you learn how to accurately spot "fake" influence, or influence that seeks to artificially inflate these metrics.**

    a. Nothing could be simpler than purchasing fake followers, subscribers and commenters. Scrutinize social media accounts to determine whether their followers appear genuine and engaged.

    b. Do they consistently put out original, interesting content? Or do they generate fake relevance through excessive reposts and link sharing?

   c. Do they actually engage with their followers? Do those followers reciprocate? Or are the majority of their responses simple, off-topic or automated?

5. **Improvements in technology have given rise to new methods of finding influencers, including:**
   a. Databases
   b. Networks and agencies
   c. Influencer marketplaces
   d. Manual searches

6. **Each industry has its own specific actions you can use to identify influence.**
   a. Specific pieces of information to gather to ensure good compatibility include:
      i. Analytics
      ii. Testimonials/reviews
      iii. Networks/connections
      iv. Past performance
   b. Brands may also choose to hire internal experts or outsource to an agency.

MOVING FORWARD

By working alongside influencers to help them create compelling content for their audience, we create a consumer journey that does not end at purchase—but rather continues to build an ongoing relationship that provides them satisfaction and earns us their loyalty. And, much like an influencer, there are a variety of different ways that consumers can actively participate in that relationship—actively showcase their loyalty—in a way that makes them influencers in their own right.

FOOD FOR THOUGHT

You're thinking about applying for a job at a new company. You've heard their commercials on the radio, you've looked at their website, and you've asked your friend who works there what they think of management, the culture and their working conditions. Which source of information are you most likely to trust?

And if your friend tells you it's a fantastic place to work—the best job they've ever had—how soon after do you make your decision whether to apply?

9

Brand **Ambassadors 101**
Putting a spotlight on insiders, customers, and influencers

B rand ambassadors—sometimes called brand advocates—are receiving increasing levels of attention as influencer marketing becomes more popular, but since the two marketing processes largely overlap, it can be confusing.

Let's start by reviewing the concept: a brand ambassador program is when a person or collection of people are selected by a company to advocate for a brand's product or services. They share the brand's messaging with their networks, and lend their reputation and personal endorsement to an organization—to their mutual benefit.

Brand ambassadors can be loyal customers, traditional or digital influencers, or employees. Ideally, they are people who love your brand and can speak about your offerings on social media or in person with genuine enthusiasm.

Compensation for brand ambassadors can be highly variable by brand, but it usually comes in the form of one (or more) of the following:

- Commission on products sold
- Up-front fees paid
- Free products
- Gifts

- Inside access to special events
- Marketing or production support

Brand ambassadorship is often considered a critical tactic for leveraging your "micro" or even "nano" influencers , especially when you don't have a big budget to supplement content with paid promotion, it's scalable.

Brand ambassadors are:

- powerful and meaningful (when engaged well)
- loaded with potential to support the brand's marketing and business goals
- a long-term investment—when used properly

Where the confusion begins is when marketers see ambassador programs as something *separate* from influencer marketing. An ambassador or advocate program is simply one way to formalize an influencer agreement and make a partnership a long-term relationship—which is what influencer marketing should be.

Simply put, transitioning an influencer into a brand ambassador role is a way of making your relationship "official". The influencer and the brand are committing to build their relationship over an extended period of time—an exclusive arrangement that will give them the freedom to explore new angles for content, and to optimize every touchpoint and opportunity they share.

Some of the most powerful instances of brand ambassador-ships happen without being planned. Just the other day, I was approached at a restaurant by a table of ten women holding a baby shower. They gushed over the coat I was wearing, and wanted to know where I'd bought it. The coat was actually from a client's boutique (shout out to Red Bird Boutique in Austin!)

In that moment, I was a walking, talking billboard. I could've easily shared the name of the boutique and left it at that, but as a brand ambassador, I was able to guide the conversation to a more compelling place, and create a high-impact call to action.

I told the ladies about the unique story behind the exquisite shop, and how they provide a complimentary styling service to help customers find just the right pieces for them—a benefit that more than pays for itself. I gave them the name of the owner, and told them to tell her I'd sent them. I knew she would take great care of them!

On the spot, they decided to head there after lunch. One of the women even mentioned she was a fellow Austin business owner; she ran a home decor and gift shop. I suggested the two owners should collaborate, because they were both targeting the same audience. . .and would you believe there's already a collaboration in the making?

None of this interaction was planned. Rather, it was another example of the organic opportunities that arise when you're aligned with a brand in the long term.

In fact, many full-time professional influencers are now focusing on long-term brand ambassador alliances versus one-off posts for random brands.

IDENTIFYING EXTERNAL AMBASSADORS
Connecting with customers, enthusiasts—and even critics

In *The Customer Advocacy Playbook*, Sujan Patel of Web Profits offers some seriously persuasive numbers to argue for the value of ambassadors recruited from a brand's loyal and happy consumers:

- 84 percent of millennials don't trust traditional advertising
- 74 percent of customers identify word-of-mouth as a key influence in their purchasing decision
- 88 percent of people trust online reviews written by other consumers as much as they trust recommendations from personal contacts

While every happy customer *can* potentially be part of your ambassador army, not all of them will want to engage in an active, visible way with your other customers or potential customers. Nor should they have to, and certainly not on demand. Some may also be more low-key or quiet recommenders and connectors—but there's still a place for them.

Just about every customer has what it takes to be a great ambassador for you in the right context with the right infrastructure. One way to identify your best potential customer ambassadors is to segment them into subsets (bearing in mind that some customers may overlap in different categories).

Your happy customers

This one is pretty obvious, but plenty of brands don't take the simple step of engaging with the customers who love them most.

Get started by reaching out to your support and customer success teams to identify customers who are very satisfied with your product and/or services, and make a connection through a special outreach or offering. They've already provided you with their feedback or kudos, without any special benefit extended their way. You could offer a special coupon code, access to a "roped off" product or swag section of your website, or even a unique product or service offering.

Hotel and resort chain J.W. Marriott uses geofencing technology to identify social media posts by customers staying at their properties, and reaches out through "M Live" teams around the globe to offer those customers special privileges or access to special events, like a free spa treatment or a day cruise—all in real time.

Not only does this spontaneous outreach result in more happy posting from delighted and surprised social users, it deepens customer loyalty in existing Marriott customers. It also gives Marriott a chance to do service recovery in real time if a customer vacation is going awry—never a bad thing.

Your NPS Promoters

NPS stands for Net Promoter Score, and refers to an online survey you send to your customers. NPS surveys are usually related to customer success and finding the right product/market fit, but it can also help identify potential brand advocates. NPS surveys query your customers on how likely they are to recommend your product to others, on a scale of 1–10. Customers who respond with a 9 or 10 are described as your "promoters."

Marketing automation platform Hubspot uses an NPS score at the end of their customer support journey to gauge what went well in the interaction. . .and what didn't go well. Their team can then reach out to the customer to find out where things went astray and make the situation right—or discover how they're getting it *right*, and build on their successes.

Customers who receive a follow-up on positive feedback are undoubtedly great ambassador candidates, along with customers who feel their concerns were heard and resolved.

Your "social butterflies"

Look for the customers who are actively singing your praises and sharing your content on social media, especially if they do so on a regular basis. Who is retweeting you? Who is commenting on your posts? Who is interacting with your content?

Make a habit of searching your brand name, your product or service name, and your category on channels like Twitter and Instagram to see who is talking about you already. (To learn more about how to make these discoveries, head back to Chapter 6, where I talk about social listening).

The point is, if people are willing to talk about your product without any extra encouragement from you, an ambassador relationship can only increase the depth, frequency, and quality of their posts.

Your "regulars"

A "regular" is a person who returns to visit your content again and again over a longer period of time. In contrast, when people are searching for a particular item, or deciding on a purchase, they tend to make lots of visits to your website in a short period of time. Potential and existing brand advocates consume content more consistently over a longer period of time.

You can find your regulars by watching and tracking your repeat visitors. See if they regularly open your e-newsletter, attend your webinars, or interact with your content in any way. While you'll need to track and trend these visitors over a longer period of time— minimum 6–12 months—you'll have some exceptionally qualified leads for your ambassador program when you're done. Also be sure to observe the length of time repeat visitors spend viewing your content. A regular visitor to your blog who spends 10 minutes on a single blog post is taking time to read the entire post—indicating a high level of engagement and interest.

Once you've identified these types of users—even if they've never made a purchase from you—reach out with a special ambassador opportunity, product, or service offering to reward them for being an active part of your community. It may be just the thing they need to get them to actually make a purchasing decision in your favor.

Your critics

Yes, you read that right: critics have *incredible* potential to become your brand advocates. Social review sites like Yelp have given business owners the chance to identify who is talking about them, and to directly respond to reviews of their product or service.

Sure, some owners have used this opportunity to argue with the customer publicly—never a good idea—but many also reach out to offer a comped service or some sort of benefit, if the customer is willing to give them another try.

That's the other big benefit of participating in review sites and forums like Yelp—disgruntled customers can revisit and update their reviews if they've had their concerns resolved. When a potential customer sees an owner interacting with a customer in a positive way, perhaps resulting in an updated review, odds are they'll be more likely to give that business a shot.

I become a bit of a princess when it comes to staying at a luxury hotel. If a hotel is deemed as being 5 stars and charges the high prices to go with it, I think it's fair their customers expect 5-star service and quality. When they come up short, I don't hesitate to tactfully make it known. And my favorite hotel in the world is the George V in Paris; I had dreamed that one day, when I 'grew up', I could stay there. . .but when I did, it didn't start off so great.

During my first visit, I landed after a delayed red-eye flight (*literally* red-eyed) with a strained back and a bad mood. I had let them know I would be arriving early, and they assured me they could accommodate me with an early check-in. When I'm landing in a foreign city after an overnight flight, I always ensure that I can get into my room early, even if it means I have to purchase an extra night.

However, upon arrival, my room was not yet ready, and I was told it would not be ready for three hours. This seemed like an *eternity* in my current state—especially since I had made such a specific request in advance. Offering a free drink was not going to give me satisfaction. . .in fact, it made me even *more* annoyed.

I proceeded to make it work by toiling away for several hours on my laptop in the hotel restaurant, but at the end of my visit I wrote to the hotel about my experience. Instead of ignoring me, or giving a generic, "So sorry about your experience but [insert excuse here]" response, the hotel manager wrote me back personally to apologize, and to insist on comping part of my stay—no small sum!

That personal outreach made all the difference in resolving my concern, and suddenly I felt like I *mattered* to the George V. As a result, I have become a walking, talking brand advocate for the George V ever since, and continue to tell this story 10 years later.

The takeaway is that, even if you might initially disagree with a customer's critical feedback, you can use it to your benefit in two ways: 1) embrace it as a learning opportunity to improve your product or the way you deliver it, and prevent negative feedback from future customers in the process; and 2) demonstrate that you value your customer and want to act on their feedback—which is the first big step towards converting them from critic to advocate.

FOSTERING INFLUENCE FROM THE INSIDE OUT
Discovering your internal influencers

Employees, by nature of working for your company, are "insiders'". Remember that special type of expert discussed in Chapter 3 (page 42)? Your leadership and your employees can become instrumental brand ambassadors because people believe they know the real inner workings of the company—and if they love it that much, it has to be worthy of their trust.

However, achieving advocacy from within is not as simple as grabbing employees and forcing them to act on your marketing behalf. Rather, employee advocacy has to be a result of the employee's true belief in and love for an organization, product, or brand. . .not a mandated policy.

A quick Google search will yield many articles and books about how championing your employees is the answer (or part of the answer) to marketing and giving your brand a human voice. On the surface, it makes sense: who knows your company better than the people who work there day in and day out, and who are already being paid to work on your behalf?

Employees possess a unique ability to both earn and reflect trust—something every brand needs to thrive. They also have the exponential power to reach audiences and networks more widely and deeply than a brand can on their own.

The problem lies in the question we ask when we learn of the value of employee ambassadors: "How can I make my employees participate?"

The answer: *You can't.*

Why?

Well, for one thing, you don't "make" them do anything. To be successful, brand ambassadorship can't be a mandate, just as you can't dictate company culture—you have to develop it. It has to be the result of what's actually going on in the organization, including your support infrastructure, your brand integrity, and the way the people on the inside actually feel.

When you force a practice on your employees, it leads to resentment and inauthenticity—and people can see right through it. You may be able to fool a few in the beginning, but over the long-term, this strategy never wins. And once you break that trust, it's all over.

Rather than trying to enforce advocacy as a tactic, we should instead focus on fostering a culture in which employees *actually* love your brand, are proud to work there, feel valued, and want to talk about you.

Take the time to learn about the members of your team on a personal level. What matters to them? What motivates them? What do they value? These questions let them know you care about more than having them punch a clock.

As marketing expert Amber Naslund puts it, "If you're looking for people to regurgitate brand messaging verbatim and never flex their own voice and perspective out in the market, you've lost before you've begun." While actual business operations and types of employees and roles vary from company to company, there are an unlimited number of ways to open the door and create winning brand advocate programs for your employees.

The following are a few proven ways to approach it:

Consider all the ways employee voices can fit into your communications. The opportunities can be as endless as your employees want them to be: profiles and testimonials on your website, social media, print materials; product demonstration videos; social channel takeovers; quick "day in the life" posts on Facebook Live or Instagram Stories; panel discussions at customer events; and so on.

Recognize the social media stars already in your midst. Do you have employees who actively follow your social media channels, and retweet or share your content? Are your employees already sharing their pride in your brand, or telling positive stories about their work-place experiences?

These folks give you the ability to start from "square two". Give them the tools they need to help you do your work: there are many software programs, services and systems designed to make the pro-cess of creating, curating and sharing content easy and seamless for employees. Whatever you do, making it easy for your employees to participate is *crucial*.

Provide social media education and training. Providing them with the tools isn't enough; the best tools in the world won't work if people don't know how to use them easily and optimally. Give them the sup-port they need to be comfortable.

Send out a "get to know you" questionnaire. You'll discover plenty of content for fun, employee-centric posts by asking them about their interests, passions, and pursuits—and then following up on their answers with fun employee profiles for social media. You'll also get a sense of the born storytellers in your midst.

Find the balance between freedom of expression and "mes-saging". This is the hardest part: creating a sense of structure and guidelines around appropriate messaging, while also allowing creative freedom.

The most effective employee ambassadorships occur when you trust your team to communicate in a way that's both authentic to themselves and valuable to your brand—and this can only happen when employees have a deep passion, satisfaction and belief in the brand.

Create employee profiles that bring your key marketing messages to life. The FedEx and Adobe examples on the following pages demonstrate the value of telling a compelling story while *also* affirming the brand messages both companies want to elevate.

In other words, you don't have to always rely on them to create content and share; rather, include and showcase them in your content.

Want to highlight work-life balance at your company? Share what your employees do when they're not in the office. Want to highlight commitment to your community? Spotlight an employee's work for a cause, and show how you've supported that work through volunteer days and donation matching.

As part of a Women's History Month initiative, **FedEx** chose to produce a series of "Profiles in Trucking", highlighting women of different ages, different backgrounds, and in different places by offering them a chance to tell their story of driving for FedEx, including the path that led them to work for FedEx and the benefits they've enjoyed while being part of the FedEx family.

Not only did these blog posts position FedEx as an employer committed to gender equity, they reminded customers there was a real person inside each of their ubiquitous white delivery trucks.

Software giant **Adobe** is exceptional at facilitating employee advocacy. It all started when they noticed an employee's Twitter account sent more traffic to their website than their own official account (kudos for social listening) and decided to start including employees in their social presence after. Instead of censoring or silencing the employee, they created a program to inform and train employees on how to interact appropriately on the company's behalf on social media.

They also launched the Adobe Life blog to tell the stories of different employees in an accessible, warm way—and to strengthen Adobe's employer brand, one benefit-highlighting tale at a time. For example, a recent post told the story of a member of Adobe's corporate team, Michael Harmon, and his successful efforts to adopt a child from Bulgaria with his family.

In addition to having authentic heartwarming content that puts a human face on Adobe's brand, the post also provided an opportunity to highlight Adobe's top-notch adoption benefits—something many potential applicants might be looking for, or would at least view in a positive light.

"Chief Ambassador Officer": The power of the social CEO

Chief executive officers have always played a significant role in steering and shaping a company's brand from the inside out, but the rise of social media has enabled many CEOs to play a strong role in their company's external messaging, too.

Elon Musk of Tesla Motors is a classic example of how a CEO can "become" his brand to the world. . .for better or for worse. Renault-Nissan is the largest maker of electric cars in the world, but many people would assume Tesla takes that title, because they are much more visible in the media.

According to a social engagement study of automotive brands by TalkWalker, Tesla generates over three times the engagement of the next-best performing automotive brand on Twitter, Toyota.

A big part of that engagement has come about as a result of Musk's high-profile involvement in social media. He comes off as brilliant, passionate, driven, and unpredictable in his frequent tweets, giving the brand a human voice—a brand impression that ultimately shapes consumers' impressions of Tesla itself.

Elon Musk is Tesla, and Tesla is Elon Musk.

During the live streaming/tweeting of their Model 3 launch, Musk was front and center as the voice of the company, sharing posts on social media to his 15+ million followers and making a huge difference in facilitating engagement and driving further reach for each of their posts.

The flip side of Elon's activity on social media is that Tesla takes a hit when Elon's own personal brand takes a hit. For example, when a clip of Elon smoking marijuana on Joe Rogan's podcast went viral on social media, Tesla's stock went down.

Big mistake? Tesla shareholders might feel that way. But many brand devotees love how candid and real Musk is, even when his exposure sets him up for controversy. In a crowded market, Tesla stands out with a human face.

Musk claims he's never done any marketing, PR, or advertising, yet I argue he is one of the *best* marketers out there. Whether you love him or hate him, you can't deny that he puts time and effort into interacting with fans and critics alike on social media on a daily basis, and that he humanizes his brand by being present and responsive, and by providing interesting, valuable, and thought-provoking content.

Sara Blakely, founder of shapewear and clothing company Spanx, is a far less controversial social CEO who also maintains a high profile in both social media and the mainstream media, on top of her company's strong social profile. In fact, she's pretty much a household name, not only for her power business acumen, but she's the pinnacle of role models for female entrepreneurs.

Blakely is also a groundbreaking influencer marketer. She built her business by sending samples of her initial products to important people to court them as advocates. This included tastemaker extraordinaire, Oprah Winfrey, who ultimately sent cameras to feature Blakely and her products, giving her the boost of a lifetime for both her brand awareness and sales.

Blakely told her crazy (and inspiring) story to *Inc.* magazine:

> "Just as I was running out of money and just as I was running out of friends to help me promote this business, Oprah Winfrey called.
>
> As an entrepreneur there is no greater call, *especially* when you have no money to advertise. I actually get the call from her show. I had sent Oprah a gift basket in my very first slot of Spanx prototypes, with a handwritten note, 'You've been inspiring to me, and here, check out my invention'.
>
> And apparently, Andre, who dresses her, put them on her, and she's worn them pretty much every day, since. So, I get the call from her show. They say, 'Sara, Oprah has chosen your product as her favorite product of the year.'"

Today, Blakely is one of the youngest self-made female billionaires *ever*, with Spanx doing in excess of $400 million in profit each year. Some CEOs might opt to let someone else take care of the marketing at that point, but Blakely's role as the approachable face of the brand—through both the primary Spanx accounts and her personal accounts—adds depth, color, and personality to Spanx's broader brand personality.

This means Spanx doesn't need to court some sort of social media star to do the talking for them; Sara *is* the personality of the company, and the company is Sara.

Just as she created her first product to meet her own needs—cutting the legs off of her pantyhose to create some underwear that wouldn't be seen under white jeans—she continues to interact with fans as though she's "one of them": a successful, vibrant woman who has bigger things to think and dream about than visible panty lines.

Not every founder or CEO is cut out for the online *or* offline stage, mind you. Some may not have the charisma or energy for it—even if they'd like to.

Bottom line, no one will ever care about a brand as much as its founder—so if you have one with the drive, desire and personality to advocate for you, it's worth it to invest in her/him

Connecting your customers with company leadership

There is a unique power in enabling your customers to go "right to the top". In other words, by allowing people to get an insider view into how the company is run from the top leadership, it acts to humanize the brand and garner trust. Here are some easy ways to get leaders involved with customer engagement: **Give people a peek into company culture.** Capture video or images of company leaders interacting with employees in professional environments, and use that imagery to accompany messages about company vision and values. Don't settle for visuals taken at a company meeting, with your leadership at a podium, however. Get them into the environments where real work is being done, so customers can see that they exist beyond the boardroom.

You could even invite your customers to a company open house where your leader does a meet-and-greet or mingles with attendees. Be sure to take lots of pictures and video, and share them on your website, and via social media.

Give people a chance to interact. A live Twitter chat, Facebook live, or Instagram live moment with leadership offers customers a way to connect more directly with the folks in charge. Be sure to set a time limit and plan some structure for the moment, to ensure you're creating content that's both bite-size and compelling enough for customers to view again.

You could schedule a time each week for a leader to personally respond to comments across platforms, whether it's Yelp reviews or an Instagram comment. Not only will you impress the heck out of whomever gets the response, but everyone who sees the review will be influenced by that personal touch, too. I've actually chosen to book a hotel or salon when I see a negative review—and then see the owner or senior leader personally respond!

Give people a chance to give feedback. Create videos with leadership asking a conversation-starting question about your products or services, and asking for customer feedback. Not only will this give you valuable data to iterate your offerings, but it shows that your company is listening to the folks who have made it a success.

In times of crisis, flip it on its head. Give people an apology. No brand is perfect, and they all experience mistakes and negative feedback, whether it's an upset customer complaining on Twitter about a long line, or a mistake big enough to make national headlines. It can be tempting to sweep it under the rug, or to give a canned public relations-composed response, but a direct note or video from the CEO or senior leader, will put a more personal face on your reconciliation efforts and undoubtedly hold more impact.

CREATING A BRAND AMBASSADOR PROGRAM

Brand ambassadors will usually have another label that aligns them with any other kind of influencer—macro, micro, internal, etc.—but the key to helping them shine in particular is creating a structure that both helps and rewards them for being your advocate, and achieves mutually beneficial results.

When creating an environment for your brand ambassador, you need to use the same methodology as any influencer partnership, because that's exactly what it is:

- **Focus** on your overall goal, because every aspect of your strategy and tactics should map back to that goal
- **Observe** what your ambassadors can do (and would *like* to do) to achieve that goal, and how you can offer them value for their advocacy
- **Connect** with them by putting a program in place to nurture and deepen the relationship over at least a year—or longer

If you're not doing all three of these things when you reach out, chances are you'll end up wasting your ambassador's time *and* yours, and potentially put a dent in your good relationship.

It helps to walk through this one step at a time. First, think about your goals and what you expect or want from your ambassador.

Here are a few examples of actions to consider:

- Refer new leads/customers
- Provide a testimonial
- Attend event(s)
- Create organic content: letting them run with an idea of their own, in a medium they're comfortable with
- Write a product or service review
- Share or comment on your company's blog, or even write a guest post
- Provide targeted feedback on current or new product features
- Help promote a company event
- Respond to a negative social media post
- Answer other users' questions in a support forum
- Identify and recruit other potential ambassadors who love the brand

Be sure to tailor your plans to the ways and places your ambassadors are already interacting, rather than try to drag them to a different platform. For example, if they're active on social media, create opportunities for them to share your messages on social media. If they're not, find a way to include them in an event, or on your website.

Once you know what you want them to accomplish, your next step is to figure out what your ambassador wants. In other words: what's in it for them?

Now looking beyond your own goals, OBSERVE. Ask yourself the following questions:

- What are the personal/professional goals of your ambassador?
- What does he/she value?
- What kinds of resources does he/she need/use in daily life?

- What perks, special benefits, or increased access can we offer our ambassadors to add value to their experience?
- How can we give them a role in refining our product or brand experience?
- How can we publicly include their story in our brand story to affirm what they mean to us?
- How can we make advocating for us easy, seamless and natural?
- Do we have the infrastructure and resources to support our ambassadors? For example, are we offering to edit their content? Produce it? Educate them on new technologies or social media platforms to help them grow?

Ultimately, you want to deepen your relationship with your ambassadors, to get them excited and motivated to share their positive brand experiences with you, and to produce content that reflects that deepened connection and excitement.

Remember, **great brand ambassadors are the result of a great overall brand experience**.

Let's look at a real industry success story from Kentucky-based bourbon brand Maker's Mark. Maker's Mark had grown wildly in popularity beyond Kentucky by the early 2010s and they were struggling to keep up with production. A 2013 decision to start diluting their whisky to meet that demand in 2013—a choice they quickly reversed after consumers cried foul—put a dent in their reputation with old fans and potential new consumers alike.

From the company's first days, founder Bill Samuels had eschewed traditional marketing in favor of deepening existing customer relationships, and letting word-of-mouth do the rest. What advertising they *did* do was in collaboration with Doe-Anderson, a Louisville-based marketing firm, since 1973.

The time had come, however, for them to make a more intentional outreach (and make amends!)

With an eye to building on Samuels' original approach, Maker's Mark asked Doe-Anderson to figure out a way to reconnect with, and reward their long-term fans—and connect afresh with the ever-critical millennial audience.

According to Doe-Anderson CEO, Todd Anderson, the agency went forward with ten guiding principles:

1. Always treat our customers as friends.
2. Consumers own the brands and they want to reinforce their ownership.
3. Tell our friends exactly what we want them to do.
4. Be interesting and people will talk about it.
5. Everyone in the organization must play a role and embrace the mission.
6. Exceeding expectations is a full-time job.
7. Surprise and delight is more powerful than a reward
8. A peek inside the tent creates the conversation.
9. You have to keep it special. It is human nature to want things that seem hard to get.
10. You can't be halfway in the game.

Principles worth memorizing for many brands, frankly!

These principals formed the base of their wildly popular and ongoing Maker's Mark Ambassador program, which reaches out to known bourbon fans and expressed Maker's Mark fans—online and in-person—to offer:

- Elevated product offerings like personalized bourbon barrels: each barrel has 30 ambassador names engraved on it, and ambassadors get regular updates about how their bourbon is aging
- An exclusive website for Ambassadors to log into, with special discounts;
- An Ambassador app for iPhone or Android that provides even more convenient access to their online discounts and benefits
- Ambassador-only events in different communities, and at their distillery, including a tour in which you can get your own bottle dispensed from your barrel
- Ambassador-only merchandise, including glassware and clothing that advertises their love of the brand
- Wildly 'Instagram-friendly' holiday gifts

While all of these perks are great, what makes the program truly special is that Maker has taken the time to truly get to know the influencers chosen for the ambassador program—finding out what matters to them, and how to add value to their lives through each channel This is evidenced in their efforts to make the program consistently active and compelling in their ambassadors' lives.

As a result, Maker's Mark's Ambassador program gets significant coverage on blogs and social media, too, providing the brand with a wealth of fresh content throughout the year.

Even when Maker's Mark attempted to dilute their product *again* in 2019, the outcry—and second reversal of the plan in six years—actually fired up their ambassadors to defend and promote the whisky as the dust settled.

That's loyalty.

While some companies opt for a less formal partnership and allow any enthusiastic customer to sign up, if you are creating a structured program in which you're delivering substantial value to your ambassadors, it's important to have clear expectations around deliverables, performance, and compensation.

Using an affiliate commission structure can be straightforward—ambassadors are only compensated for any sales they make—but other forms of compensation, such as fixed payment, free products, production support, marketing assistance, and other resources should have requirements in place to help keep their budget and investments in check.

Requirement-driven brand ambassadors are tasked with complete certain actions for your brand within a specific time frame. Most often, these types of brand ambassadors are influencers with a highly engaged and desirable target audience.

We don't go too in-depth on compensation structures in this chapter; we'll be covering it in greater detail in Chapter 12). For now, the important part to note is that brand ambassador programs are really just one way of formalizing a long-term influencer relationship. It's these agreements and contracts that spell out the mutual requirements and expectations made of the parties involved.

THE POWER OF USER GENERATED CONTENT
Putting your brand in front of fresh (and receptive) eyes

We're going to be diving much deeper into influencer content creation in Chapter 14, but any discussion of brand ambassadorship wouldn't be complete without a mention of User Generated Content (UGC).

I like to think UGC as the digital, printed or recorded version of word-of-mouth. According to marketing expert and social media agency founder, Tyler Anderson, User Generated Content is any content created about your product or service by other people, including your customers, potential customers, and your employees.

This content can be anything from photos on Instagram, to reviews on sites like Yelp, Google, and Trip Advisor, to demonstration videos uploaded to YouTube, to blog posts, Facebook rants, Snapchat Stories, and Twitter shout-outs. They could be glowingly positive—or they could be an opportunity to respond to a complaint or concern in a transparent way. As channels evolve and new ones crop up, there will no doubt be new types of UGC for you to share with your customers and prospects.

When content or referrals come from real consumers, they are automatically more *impactful*—which means they hold more *influence*. Everyone is a brand, whether they know it or not, and smart organizations are looking to connect and align their brands with the personal brands of their customers and employees—for advocacy, for engagement, and for brand management.

As someone who admittedly has no patience and needs constant stimulation, wasting time at appointments—specifically doctor's appointments—makes me crazy. The problem is right there in the name of the place they stick you: the waiting room!

During one particular appointment, it looked like I was going to be stuck waiting for an hour, so I did what every digital marketer does—I opened up Instagram and began scrolling, swiping, liking and even throwing out the odd comment.

One of the people I follow on Instagram is a woman named Heather Scott. I follow @HeatherScottHome because she and I share a love for beautiful interior design, and because she is an incredible interior designer in Austin, TX, where I live.

On this particular day, Heather happened to post a picture of a living room she was inspired by. It was a simple single-frame picture that featured the most beautiful black and white King Henry VIII chairs. Heather also tagged the maker of the chairs, a small independent furniture maker and re-upholsterer located in a tiny Texas town.

I had never heard of this furniture maker, nor did I know reupholstering chairs like this could even be an option. The small independent furniture maker was certainly not SEO optimized, which means they never would have shown up in a Google search, even if I'd known what to search!

As I saw this post, I thought, "*How unique! Definitely not something you could get out of a Pottery Barn catalog. Heather has such exquisite taste—I need to find out who makes this.*"

I took the natural next step: I clicked on the tag of the maker, which brought me to their Instagram account. I spent some time window shopping their recent posts, filled with beautiful, unique pieces and talented work that breathed life and beauty into vintage objects.

My admiration and curiosity led me further to their website, where the owner had a short video explaining their story, their process, and their passion in detail. He was so sweet and charming and full of passion.

Right then and there, I called him and commissioned him to make me two chairs similar to the ones referred to in Heather's photo. In less than 15 minutes, I went from being totally unaware his company existed to buying two of his pieces (which, by the way, have generated their own referrals from guests at my home).

To me, this is the perfect example of the power of a customer as an influencer. In this case, Heather Scott was the consumer, who did 100 percent free marketing for the furniture maker by producing great authentic content. When consumers or employees are happy with their experience, products or services, they are most often happy to vouch for it—which is an easy and seamless way to create content that users might actually care about!

Cultivating high-value UGC

Start gathering this content by searching your brand name and the products across different social platforms and review sites, and then sharing and elevating positive mentions.

Don't stop there, though: get creative about generating more UGC. You might decide to offer a **referral or affiliate program** that encourages social posting, or offer a **free service upgrade** for a testimonial, or other types of direct **rewards** for publicly sharing their experiences with you.

You might also opt to create a **contest or giveaway** that offers free or special product offers for sharing how your products have improved their lives, or even for the best creative or unexpected use of your product.

Tracking attribution is never easy (see Chapter 13 on measurement and tracking), but whatever you decide to do, ensure you have mechanisms for gathering feedback—that means in-store or in-house, anywhere you appear online, and anywhere you are "out in the wild". Send out surveys after every purchase, or after a customer service interaction, not everyone responds, but those who do can help give you key insight into what's working and what's not. Consistently be sharing your social channels and contact information broadly, and welcome customers and prospects to get in touch.

After all, one of the best ways to learn what people think of you is simply to ask—and then put those influential comments and stories to work for you.

Recap and Review

KEY POINTS

1. **Brand ambassadors are simply one way of formalizing an influencer partnership—it is not a separate field.**
   a. Brand ambassadorship refers to any influencer marketing effort that involves putting a formalized program around those who advocate your brand.
   b. There are many types of ambassadors who can advocate for you, ranging from industry experts and loyal customers to great employees.
   c. Brand ambassador programs typically involve some form of compensation ranging from free products and gifts to commissions on products sold.
   d. Typically, these ambassadors are what's referred to as micro- or nano-influencers, but are nevertheless very powerful when properly utilized.

2. **By elevating your customers, you can create brand ambassadors from the inside.**
   a. When looking for people who are willing to say positive things about your brand, there's no greater place than the people who already know and love your brand: your happy customers!

3. **You can also work to turn your critics and naysayers into your best advocates.**
   a. Individuals critical of your brand provide you with a huge opportunity to turn things around by showing them an enhanced brand experience (and winning them over in the process).

4. **Internal brand ambassadors are employees, CEOs and other elements of your existing company that act independently to promote and support your brand.**
   a. To achieve successful employee ambassadors, you need to foster a culture in which people are truly happy and believe in the company.

5. **Building a great ambassador programs works the same as building any influencer relationship—it only works if it follows the Code.**
   a. Give your program a solid foundation by starting from your business goals and thinking about what you want your ambassadors to achieve.
   b. Observe and identify your potential ambassadors, determine what they value, and how can you offer them that value.
   c. Connect by creating a structured program that consistently offers value and builds a relationship with your ambassador—one that will last long term.

6. **Part of creating a structured program means establishing the requirements that your ambassadors need to fulfill and the benefits your ambassadors receive.**

a. While some companies opt for a less formal approach, optimizing your ambassadors means mapping out both what you *expect* from the ambassadors and what you *provide*. This avoids any miscommunication.

7. **User generated content (UGC) is a valuable—and often ignored—resource for driving engagement and creating brand ambassadors.**

a. User generated content is the equivalent of digital word of mouth—in other words, non-mandated content created on behalf of your brand. As such, it's more trusted than brand generated content.

b. There are many ways to incentivize and cultivate UGC, which include, but are not limited to:

   i.   Affiliate or referral plans
   ii. Free service upgrades
   iii. Rewards
   iv. Contests and giveaways

MOVING FORWARD

Step Two of the Influencer Code, Observe and Identify, is very much about 'getting all your ducks in a row.' Market research, influencer vetting, and a comprehensive inventory of your external and internal influence opportunities is necessary to ensure you're taking full advantage of every available resource at your disposal. This step tells us what people want, what we have to offer, and which influencers can help us get from point A to point B—and back again.

Step Three of the Influencer Code, Connect, involves the building of a relationship or partnership with the influencer. It is an interactive process, not a transaction in which you create mutual value through mutual interdependence and collaboration between brands, influencers and customers.

FOOD FOR THOUGHT

Everybody wants something for nothing, but nobody wants to give anything away for free. Makes sense; nobody enjoys being on the bad end of a good deal.

If only there were a way to exchange two items of equal value, but have both sides end up with more than they started, but sadly, that's just not possible. 1 + 1 can't equal 3. . .can it?

STEP THREE

CONNECT

10

Crafting the Irresistible Influencer Opportunity
The Perfect Partnership Starts With a Genuine Connection

You've found your ideal influencer. They're *perfect* for you. So, how do you show them you're perfect for *them*?

THIS IS WHERE THE MAGIC BEGINS

You've put the right goals in place, identified the target audience you want to reach, spent time hanging out where they hang out, reading what they read, and researching what matters to them—and in the process, you've established the key prospects who are influencing those individuals.

When engaging an influencer, you have to bring your "A game". It's just that simple—yet at this critical juncture, far too many brands and agencies consistently drop the ball. This is where we transition from Step Two of the Code, Observe and Identify, to Step Three: 'Connect'. Taking everything we've learned about our influencer candidates (most notably their goals and motivations) we craft a mutually beneficial collaboration opportunity that not only engages, but provides serious value to both parties.

This all may sound like common sense, but trust me—after years of being on both sides of this relationship, this is often easier said than done, particularly given the prevailing mindset of modern marketing to treat these types of exchanges as transactional.

Remember, influencer marketing must be seen as a marketing approach based on building relationships, as opposed to completing a single transaction. It is about identifying, establishing, maintaining and enhancing relationships—both with customers and with influencers—so that the objectives of all parties involved are met. And this is something that can only be done through the mutual exchange and fulfilment of promises.

In fact, I'll go as far to say that **the greatest influencer relationships you will ever have won't involve the exchange of a single dime.**

This likely goes against *everything* any self-proclaimed influencer, agency, or marketer has told you. In fact, I know of many highly esteemed marketers who are adamant that you *must* pay, and pay *very well* for influencer relationships. . .and that, ultimately, you "get what you pay for."

That's true of many things in life—but in this case, putting the focus on money alone is what will lead you down the path to one of the most common mistakes in influencer marketing. This is what is meant by a paradigm shift: we're changing how we think and approach influencer marketing, not to chase a trend or exploit a new strategy, but simply because relationship building and maintenance are fundamentally the core of influence. By reframing our approach to influencer partnerships as one of value creation, we ensure that we don't confuse our long-term strategic objectives with short-term tactical implications.

To be clear, I'm not talking about a short-term engagement, one in which both brand and influencer go their separate ways after the campaign or collaboration is over. There's nothing wrong with that—sometimes brands *need* a little extra boost for a new collection or launch of some kind. But if the intention isn't to build a longer-term relationship, then it's not influencer marketing. Call it "influencer advertising".

It's like dating: do you want to bribe someone to go out with you because you offered incredible concert tickets, a fancy trip, or a spin in your sports car? Or do you want someone to go out with you for *you*—the *real* you, not just what you own, or the cash you flash?

That said, most influencers aren't going to promote a product or represent a brand solely out of common interest or appreciation. Their time and energy is valuable, and they know it—and offering to "pay them in exposure" is a great way to get ignored.

True influencer marketing is an exchange not of cash but of opportunity—the chance to form a *mutually beneficial partnership*, one where *both sides win*. That is the essence of the third pillar of the Influencer Code: creating a connection.

In short? Never do an "ask"—**craft an opportunity**.

In the early stages of my online fitness brand (Fit, Strong, and Sexy), I didn't have much of an audience, or money to spend driving eyeballs to my workout videos. But I knew what I *did* have: the knowledge, ability, and passion to create valuable exercise programming, and the on-camera presence to engage an audience.

I needed the help of others who already had the audience I needed, or the resources to help me to grow my presence. That's why I did what most of us do: I immediately started reaching out to fitness experts, YouTube stars, wellness brands—and anyone else who I thought might share a like-minded audience—and presented *my* brand, *my* mission, and *my* goal. I was excited, and I wanted to get moving.

I asked them to help me by sharing *my* content, being a guest in one of *my* videos, or reviewing *my* program.

The response I received was like a deflated Bosu ball. I was shut down, at best. . .if I even got a response.

Do you see the problem?

My, my, my, me. . .it was all about *Amanda*, and how they could help *Amanda*.

I came off as *needy*. I made the entire conversation about what I wanted them to do for my career.

That's when it hit me: if I wanted to get someone's attention, I need to give them a reason to actually care about me—or, to be more specific, to show them what I can offer them. . .especially if we don't have a pre-existing relationship.

If you *can't* actually deliver, word always gets around. . .and no one will want to work with you

The "it's not about me, it's about you" mentality is what will enable you to not just start a conversation, but create a foundation for a strong alliance. And yes, that does mean each opportunity has to be developed according to each specific individual's needs, and that you'll have to dig deep and get creative.

"Amanda, that sounds time-consuming!"

I know, but trust me: the relationships you build will be worth it.

I call this process being an "opportunity detective":
- **Identify the problems, needs, and challenges** of the people or brands (or influencers) that have the attention of the audience you want.
- **Explore ways you can help** them solve their problems and grow their business.
- **Think beyond a single transaction** or one-off hit.

- Ultimately, **figure out how you can help them grow *their* influence long-term.**

In many ways, this process serves as a culmination of every element of the Influencer Code up to this point. By observing and identifying your influencer and their needs, you essentially put yourself in their shoes and imagine the end goal they *could* work towards. . .provided they had you to help them along. That element, that missing link that prevents them from developing and expanding further—that's you. And once you've determined that, you've found that key connection, that perfect opportunity.

When you're selecting someone to approach, it might be tempting to look for the biggest or most established fish in the pond. But bigger isn't necessarily better; there are so many incredible content creators, experts, and brands with powerful offerings out there, and they're just as eager to succeed as you are. If you can spot real talent, you can get in on the ground floor of their ambition and aspiration, and work *together* toward your success.

This is *exactly* the model energy drink brand Red Bull has taken with the athletes they sponsor and promote: they view sponsorship as a two-way process—one that's all about collaboration and relationships.

From the outside, you might assume Red Bull only hires or endorses high-profile athletes or fitness influencers; in reality, the opposite is the case. Red Bull believes it's essential that the "opinion leaders"—their term—the company works with are the right fit for the brand, and they put their energy into identifying up-and-coming influencers in sports, music and gaming.

Their goal is to find talented people on the rise *before* they make it to a bigger stage—and in the process, help grow the influencer's influence. Whether they're deepening engagement with their existing audience, growing their profile among new and relevant audiences, helping them improve their performance through better training, coaching, equipment, and the like, or offering unique experiences to raise their game and create higher value content—they're adding value for their influencer.

I N 2014, RED BULL worked with the then largely unknown but up-and-coming Australian surfer Sally Fitzgibbons to film a documentary about her participation in the surfing training camps which they funded. Through this partnership, Sally not only grew her surfing skills but also gained increased visibility and exposure to Red Bull's audience, benefitting from the validation of being backed by a global brand.

The surfing camps also benefited from the valuable promotion and content both Red Bull and Sally provided. They in turn reciprocated by sharing and amplifying Red Bull's content, introducing *their* brand to new audiences in the process.

So, what did Red Bull get out of it? Not only did they gain a host of valuable content to engage and delight their audience, but they gained lifetime loyal advocates out of athletes like Sally, who grew into an iconic female surfer.

In the final analysis, we see Red Bull athletes growing to be bigger brands faster than they ever could have on their own—providing Red Bull with content and marketable success stories without a single dollar changing hands. What's more, it provided Red Bull with tangible evidence that their forward-thinking practices towards potential influencers offered powerful rewards in the face of little to no risk. By taking on the role of influencer scouts, much as one might scout promising athletes for college or professional teams, marketers stand to create powerful and lasting relationships with up-and-coming influencers in developing communities.

It goes back to Red Bull's core promise to "give wings" to an individual's ideas and goals.

If you ask any of the athlete-influencers they've worked with how they feel about Red Bull, you'll get an immediate expression of genuine loyalty and affinity. They are eager to give back to Red Bull—which goes to show that when you aim to provide real value and give more than you look to receive, it most often does come back around, and you can achieve more, no matter how big or small you are when you start.

Case in point: *If you want to go fast, go alone. If you want to go BIG, go together.*

WHAT MAKES AN OPPORTUNITY IRRESISTIBLE?

The answer will differ depending on the influencer and the context, but the list below provides an excellent checklist of elements and ideas to consider when crafting an opportunity.

Affirmation and exposure

Influencers build their audience by being seen and/or heard talking or acting on what they love or what's important to them. Your goal should be to convey how much *you* love what they do, or how much you've learned from their work—and then offer them the opportunity to be featured on your platforms as an expert.

This approach works best if you have an established brand reputation, or you've got a significant enough following to make the effort worth their time. You'll also want to make the opportunity uncomplicated and undemanding, right off the bat:

- A 20-minute interview that you write up into a profile or story on your blog
- A video chat that you edit into a series, or use as a single video that highlights their expertise
- A call that becomes a podcast

Whichever format you choose, the final product needs to be professional enough *and* complimentary enough that they're proud to share it with their own community, too—the key to expanding your audience, and getting your name out in front of new people.

Recognition as an expert advisor

Influencers love sharing their opinions and perspectives on the topics they know best—in fact, that's how many of them become influential. Tap into that tendency by asking them directly for advice. Some simple conversation starters include:

- How did you get started in your field?
- What's the most important trend right now in your field?
- If you could have done something differently coming up, what would it be?
- What do you wish you'd known then that you know now?
- What advice would you give someone just starting out in your field?

Their answers could end up in an article, a video, an in-person panel at an event, or a Facebook Live series. . .you name it. You could even collect questions from your followers—or theirs—to be answered in a post or video akin to an advice column.

You could even go one step further by formalizing an advisory relationship. Ask them if they would be willing to serve as an advisor to your business along with other like-minded influencers. You can host virtual or in-person quarterly meetings to get their perspective on relevant trends or shifts in the marketplace, or to learn how to better meet your community's needs.

This is exactly what the internet community Mogul did—and in the process, grew to be one of the biggest global online hubs connecting women to top-trending content, including articles, videos, jobs, events, and products.

They began their growth efforts by reaching out to experts and influencers with authority in those trending topics, and offered them the Mogul platform as a place to showcase the work they were doing.

Yet they didn't outright ask these experts to contribute—thus adding another obligation to their lives. Rather, they offered a designated account representative to curate the amazing projects, books, content, and other endeavors each one had in the works, and then offered to personalize and feature some of their best pieces—along with links to work they could highlight on their behalf.

They were also made aware they would be among an esteemed panel of experts—allowing them to immediately capture the attention of other expert influencers being featured. Each contribution would also gain an extra layer of authority simply by being aligned with other experts on the site and being recognized as a leader in their field by Mogul.

In response, most of the experts went above and beyond, providing more content, more value, more interaction, and references and recommendations for Mogul.

How did Mogul benefit in return? Not only did they garner a multi-faceted online hub of always fresh, valuable expert content across multiple categories, they won over the cumulative audience of each of the individual experts. And all that without spending a dime.

There are multiple reasons this strategy works well:
- You're positioning their expertise and seal of endorsement alongside your brand—the Brand Halo Effect at its best.
- You're building a relationship that gives the influencers a vested interest in your brand or mission, making them more likely to want to continue collaborating with you.
- Because they've got the attention of the audience(s) you want, when they decide to talk about you, it's both a byproduct and a bonus.

One important thing to remember is that if the relationship becomes too demanding, or feels like they're giving more than they're getting, the influencer is likely to lose their enthusiasm for working together. The goal is to make it easy for them to provide expertise by keeping the commitment as reasonable and beneficial as possible.

Mogul recognized this and set up an option for influencers to send over articles they'd already written, giving their editors the work of re-purposing them. Or, if a contributor had something she wanted to share, but no time to draft it herself, Mogul offered to interview them—saving them the time and effort it takes to write up an article. For many on their roster, Mogul became the first place they'd go when they want to give an opinion, share an article or discuss a new project.

A paid business opportunity that blossoms into multiple opportunities

One excellent way to begin a relationship with an influencer is to get in touch to find out what their fees are for different types of up-front engagements, and then consider how they could fit into a customer event: as a spokesperson, a speaker, or as part of a panel discussion. This approach enables you to leverage equity from an established influencer in the space who isn't motivated to sell to your customers—thus creating a more valuable experience for the audience.

You also get direct access to the influencer and the chance to share your mission, values, and goals with them in advance to get them up to speed. You can use this time to focus on getting to know what drives them, what they need, and how you can support and connect with them further.

"Amanda, didn't you just tell me the best relationships aren't paid. . .and now you're telling me to hire people?"

Yes—but the hiring is *not* the end goal. It's a stepping-stone to open the door to a relationship. At the highest echelons, most macro-level influencers will not be inclined to partner for mutual benefit or exposure; people and brands are already clamoring for their endorsement, advice, and attention all the time, and they've only got so much to give.

However, it's important to note that for some influencers, especially in the B2B space, it is the influencer's *objectivity* that is the basis for their influence—meaning they are perceived as lacking bias towards any brand over another. For example, a concierge immediately loses credibility if the client knows he/she is simply recommending a restaurant because he is getting paid to do so.

Here's a powerful example: **Kathrine Switzer** is the most legendary name in women's running history. If you don't know her story, here's a quick (and inspiring) recap: Kathrine registered for the Boston Marathon in 1967 as K.V. Switzer, hoping to work around restrictions that had kept women out of the event. By using just her initials, the race officials wouldn't realize right away that she was a woman.

She ultimately ran one of the most iconic 26.2 mile races in history, after publicly battling an official who tried to force her from the course. Her bold move to not just enter but fight her way through despite the struggle made her the face and champion of women's running. In fact, Kathrine is often credited with having changed the sport of running forever. Now she's a best-selling author, an Emmy Award-winning commentator, a social activist, and an in-demand speaker on the evolution of women in sport, and health and healthy aging.

The American Heart Association (AHA), recognizing an audience overlap with Kathrine—given that one of their key missions is to raise awareness about women's heart health—reached out to hire her to speak at various events, including their annual *Heart Ball* and the prestigious *Go Red for Women* luncheon. They believed having her name on the invite as the keynote for the event would raise the profiles of the various events, and ultimately increase turnout. . .and it did!

That's great, right? Many would call the arrangement a success strictly by that standard. . .but that's not where the benefits ended!

The American Heart Association began the relationship with Kathrine by hiring her to speak at some of their events, but the longtail benefit came through the continuation and growth of their ongoing relationship, which was only viable because of the paid speaking contract.

Their initial contract opened the door to build a stronger connection, to get to know one another's needs, and to develop a mutual interest in how each could help benefit the other. . .including an introduction to Humana, one of the AHA's key sponsors.

Kathrine, was not only able to make a big comeback in the public eye as a result, but she was also able to sell more of her books, grow her online profile, and to get booked to speak at multiple global events—on top of being involved in a cause she continues to be incredibly passionate about.

Humana has raised their profile in the eyes of their customers and prospects, many of which are aging Baby Boomers who "see themselves" in Kathrine's story.

Through it all, Kathrine continues to build her influence in the healthy living, senior living, and women in sport spaces. Pretty much the definition of a win-win, wouldn't you say?

Exclusive access

People love to feel like they have special privileges or status, and providing exclusivity is one more way to make things more desirable. In this case, exclusivity means giving access to influencers who meet a certain criterion (for example, access by invitation only, or entry to things money can't buy, unless you are a certain influencer).

As with the Red Bull example earlier, a high value offer might be exclusive access to events, complete with the chance to be featured or showcased in front of the attendees. This can take the form of VIP access to events, conferences, trainings, new/exclusive product demonstrations or samples and corporate executives.

This last one in particular, access to corporate executives, can be quite attractive to the right influencer. One of the benefits that stood out for me most when Lamborghini reached out to ask me if I would join their advisory board was that I would have the opportunity to interview the CMO and CEO for my own work (which included content for the very book you now hold). Having that access felt like the ultimate seal of support, and I've become a die-hard Lamborghini advocate as a result.

Recognition as a VIP customer

The benefits of championing your customers were already discussed in Chapter 9, but it's worth mentioning them here, in the context of how they can help you create opportunities. If you sense they have the potential to be an influential voice for you, why not up the ante a little?

As a quick refresher, the first step here is to OBSERVE: look for customers who are talking about you, and then figure out why they value you, and how you could help them fulfill their goals in a broader sense. This bit of listening will give a sense of who to reach out to, and who might be open to partnership.

When you think about creating opportunities, keep in mind that, just as with every influencer, every customer is different; while there are certain guiding principles that are universal when creating win-win value, how you approach each customer needs to be 100 percent tailored to that person or organization. This specificity is the key to turning a *good* customer relationship into a *great* one.

The following ideas might inspire you as you consider influencer opportunities with customers:

- Offer personal rewards in the form of product or gift cards for their brand advocacy, recognizing their value to your brand.
- Garner their feedback in product development—again, people like to have their opinions valued, and when you ask for their feedback, they feel ownership and value. They'll also be excited to tell everyone they were part of the process when you launch a new product, or improve on an older one.

- Give them VIP status as a customer. Status is something we all crave innately, whether it's hopping onto a plane first, having special product access, being labeled as a prized customer, or getting invited to exclusive events.

Beauty retailer Sephora's Beauty Insider Program is one of the most popular customer loyalty programs in the beauty and cosmetics space. Marketers and retail experts often cite them as a case study of how to turn customers into advocates and influencers.

While, plenty of other stores in the space offer loyalty programs, like Ulta and Bath and Body Works, it's the depth and creativity of Sephora's offering that puts them head and shoulders above the rest.

Here's how the Beauty Insider program works:

- **Three levels of Beauty Insider:** Sephora devotees can become a Beauty Insider for free, a Very Important Beauty (VIB) after spending $350 in a calendar year, or a Sephora Rouge at $1,000 and up. The levels are dependent on customer spending, and each one increases access to exclusive rewards and additional points as you rise through the ranks. It's tough to get to the Rouge level unless you really, really love makeup and skincare. . .but that's exactly why customers love it so much. Rouge customers are known for touting their near-status or celebrating when they achieve their status on whether on Twitter, Snapchat, or on YouTube beauty vlogs. The #VIBRouge hashtag is always humming.
- **Multiple rewards for increased status:** The Beauty Insider program also has a points-based reward program that provides discounts trial-size products for members, but that's not where the benefits end. VIB and Rouge customers get early access to

new products, special discount codes at key spending moments in the year (especially the winter holidays), full-size product rewards, and access to exclusive in-store events.

- **Increased status in their online community:** Everyone knows who the "Rouges" are on Sephora's community boards. They get top billing anywhere they share their opinions, and their reviews and comments are also flagged with their status across the site, giving them extra weight.

The results of the program are clear: if you search the term "Sephora Haul" on YouTube, you'll find hundreds of videos from professional makeup artists and amateurs alike sharing their recent purchases, what they've chosen to do with their points, and what products they're most excited about trying or purchasing. When they release new products to their Rewards Bazaar on Tuesdays and Thursdays at 9 a.m. PT, the social media buzz is immediate and the sales follow.

While Sephora still advertises in traditional media, their real power is in their legion of lip gloss-addicted advocates across the nation, sharing their favorites, finds, techniques, and positive brand experiences—online, in-store at special events, and one-on-one with their family, friends, and complete strangers who want to know where they got their lipstick.

While you might not have the resources to set up a tiered reward system or a massive online community, the important takeaway is to create additional value through exclusivity. The scale isn't what's important; you can align the benefits you offer with the resources you have to work with.

The lessons to be learned from Sephora's example are:

- Provide real, tangible benefits for being a brand loyalist;
- Give brand loyalists a way to identify themselves as such to like-minded shoppers and aficionados; and
- Balance exclusivity with strong community building to keep every level of customer coming back for more—and striving to rise up in the ranks

The feeling of being a "true" insider

Here's the hard truth: we're all narcissists on some level. Humans are just wired that way. That's why social media has taken the world by storm: we love thinking about ourselves, talking about ourselves, and seeing how everyone else responds to what we share. As with the classic cocktail party advice, you can make a lot of friends just by *listening*.

Want to get on someone's good side? *Listening* is the premium ticket. Rather than trying to get people interested in you, show an interest in them. Suddenly, you're the most interesting person in the room!

Everywhere you go, take the time to be curious, to ask questions, and to show genuine interest—not the sort of interest that comes before an ask, but interest that comes from genuine curiosity and concern.

My "NYC Bouncer story" has become a favorite of mine. Like most big cities, the inner New York City social scene can be *highly* exclusive—if you want into the top clubs, and you're not a celebrity (or don't have an inside connection to get you on their "list"), you might as well be trying to get into Fort Knox.

The true gateways to NYC's most exclusive clubs? *The bouncers.*

I actually came across what I call "befriend the bouncer approach" accidentally one evening while I was on the way to a bar next door to a new club with a line longer than airport TSA at the airport. Now, I'm extremely impatient, and the thought of waiting in line for longer than 5 minutes gives me anxiety.

While we were checking out the line, I happened to see a girl arguing with the bouncer. She was getting aggressive and belligerent, but he handled it so well. I was genuinely impressed. I commended him on his calm, cool, and collected approach, and asked him how often he deals with social climber freak outs. He was game to tell me a few stories and I continued to pepper him with questions. It was so interesting!

After a few minutes, he offered—I didn't ask, he *offered*—to invite me, along with my party, into the club. We truly didn't go up to him with a motive, but by being curious and thoughtful, we made him feel heard, and made ourselves noticed. The key? It wasn't phony and he knew it—*we genuinely connected and he wanted to help me out.*

Once you create that kind of connection, it creates a domino effect. In this case, the doorman also worked at another club and hung out with other bouncers. With him as our ally on the social scene, we had all the connections we could possibly need for a fantastic NYC nightlife.

So, the next party you go to, the next coffee shop you sit at, the next time you strike up a conversation, be curious, have a few questions ready. Ask someone about what they do, what they're passionate about, or what they think about a particular topic or issue. . .and see where it takes you.

You may end up kissing a lot of proverbial frogs along the way, but you'll find some princes in the mix. . .and you'll also likely also end up with some great friendships.

Or, as my dear friend and 35+ year Hollywood PR veteran, Cynthia Lieberman, always says, "Hang out in a barber shop long enough, you're going to get a haircut."

That's the ultimate win-win!

A connection far bigger than an endorsement

You might want to sit down for this next one, because I'm about to contradict everything you've been told about influencers and the products they endorse.

A great influence partner does not have to be passionate about your product.

Yes, you read that correctly—in a world where everyone and their Instagram feeds are screaming about passion, I'm telling you it's not *that* important.

In fact, this is one of the first things most influencers and marketers will tell you. And sure, it helps to find people who are already locked into what you have to offer, because their messaging comes pretty naturally—and they're easier to find.

But I will forever argue against overstating passion—a stance I back up with a very real argument.

Shown here is the team I worked with at ZICO; that's Bill Lange on the far left.

In 2010, I landed a pivotal opportunity: to take over as the face of ZICO Coconut Water from none other than supermodel and household name, Molly Simms.

The first campaign we launched became one of their most successful, as did our partnership. In fact, it resonated so deeply with their audience that they began to use me as the face of the brand at the international level, and for several years beyond the scope of our original relationship.

Instead of our initial one year/single campaign scope of work, they continued to renew it annually for several years all the way to the point at which they sold to Coca Cola.

Sounds great, right? What a boost for growing my community and my profile as an influencer in the health and fitness space!

But here's the irony: I hate coconut. The meat, the water, the milk. . .any part of it. I don't even like things that have the *flavor* of coconut. I wouldn't drink it (ha!) even if you paid me.

Eyebrows raised yet?

Let me explain. While I didn't love *coconut*, I loved what ZICO *stood for*. I knew the benefits the product provided for so many, the values of the company, and most importantly, the team of real humans who worked there.

Everyone from the founder of the company, Mark Rampolla; to the CMO (shout-out to Bill Lang, who I still adore to this day, and who I credit with so much of the greatness of my experience with them); to the field marketing team who I worked with day to day. ZICO and I became a family of sorts, and I knew and felt how they cared about me personally—beyond just my ability to 'organically include' a product shot in one of my YouTube fitness videos.

They *completely* supported the growth of my own brand and career, and made it clear they would be there for whatever I needed. If there was a way for them to help me, they wouldn't hesitate; in fact, they'd often get on the ground with me to help find ways to do bigger things. We had monthly, and sometimes even weekly calls to update each other on what was going on in each of our worlds—from events and campaigns, to brainstorming ideas and product feedback.

While my contract may have had a specific set of tasks in the beginning, I threw that list out the window as our relationship progressed into a genuine partnership, going above and beyond to sing their praises at every chance I got. In fact, they were so important to me after the first three years that when they changed directions with their marketing and the amount allocated for my role in the budget was reduced, I agreed to maintain the same level of work with them *regardless of pay.*

There go your eyebrows again!

But that's how much value I saw in our relationship.

I can't even list the countless ways I spread the word of ZICO to anyone who would listen. Whenever I taught a workout class, I would bring ZICO for all the participants. I would tout and insert the benefits of ZICO in articles I wrote, from my personal meal plans to articles in major publications like the Huffington Post. I happily attended ZICO sponsored events—such as The Hamptons Super Saturday, the high-profile, exclusive shopping event for true A-listers—where ZICO had a booth, and I offered to personally give out water and lead workout sessions. . .no payment required.

We both understood that every opportunity, whether it came from me or came from them, was mutually beneficial to our growth. And we kept up to date with frequent check-ins, keeping our calls consistent even if there wasn't anything 'hot' on the agenda. Just by checking in, we could always find new potential opportunities to grow.

Remember: relationships are complex and take time and effort to build, but they're absolutely worth it in the long run. You'll never have a more powerful advocate for your brand.

A long-term relationship

If you're going to put all the work into building an alliance with an influencer, don't sell your efforts short by neglecting to turn your partnership into a long-term relationship. The right influencer can be a boon to your business for years to come.

In his book, *Brandscaping,* Andrew Davis talks about a missed opportunity by one of the biggest brands in the world—IKEA.

Mark Malkoff, a New York-based comedian and filmmaker found himself temporarily without a home while his apartment was being fumigated. While brainstorming a solution, he came to the sudden realization that most of his home furnishings had come from IKEA—and that gave him an idea.

He pitched his local IKEA in Paramus, NJ on a win-win trade: they would provide him with a temporary living space on their show floor in exchange for a series of short videos, which would provide IKEA with fresh content for their website and social media channels. Their PR firm, Ketchum, agreed to the arrangement, and Mark moved right in.

Over the course of a week, Mark uploaded 25 videos in the "Mark Lives at IKEA" series, which attracted more than 1.5 million views in the first week alone. The campaign attracted a ton of media attention, with Ketchum estimating that they garnered 382 million positive brand impressions, all on a budget of around $13,500.

Those are stats any marketer would die for. . .but a week later, it was over. Mark moved back into his apartment, and never worked with either IKEA or Ketchum again. It was the most successful marketing campaign in store history, resulting in web traffic and sales increases across the board. . .only to end as a *'one-off'* because there was no plan in place to keep the momentum going. It was a transaction, and once it was completed, both parties left it at that.

There's nothing wrong with a short-term spike in sales and the attention garnered was positive, but consider the possibilities if they had thought longer term. There's no guarantee that future collaborations would have been as successful, but to see all that potential go to waste is truly unfortunate.

A quick note on compensation: By now, you know that effective influencer marketing can't be reduced to a simple transaction, and I stand by that when it comes to building a long-term relationship. "Pay-to-post" is influencer advertising, plain and simple.

That said, you should still let an influencer know how you intend to compensate them—the value you will initially provide.

While non-monetary compensation is an option, there are many times—especially with macro-influencers—when an initial payment may be the only way to open the door. You'll have to use your judgment on a case-by-case basis.

THERE'S NO SUCH THING AS A ONE-SIZE-FITS-ALL OPPORTUNITY

Influencers are individuals with their own backgrounds, their own culture, their own goals, and their own perspectives on how they should operate. Go deeper than you think you need to with your research and analysis to ensure you're fully shifting your focus to the needs of the individual or organization you're observing.

After all, slowing down to get things right is not a skill we come by naturally, especially as impatient marketers. That's why the right approach to influencer marketing calls for a shift in how we approach opportunities, evaluate perspectives and plan strategies. It's a shift that requires the discipline to be patient and resist the temptation towards quick 'wins'. Commit to stay in it for the long game—it's worth it!

Recap and Review

KEY POINTS

1. **The first step to establishing a long-term relationship with an influencer is to demonstrate how a partnership could offer them real value.**
   a. If your only offer to an influencer is a transactional payment, you need to shift your perspective and approach to influencer marketing to one of relationship building and mutual value for the parties involved.
   b. Do your homework on the influencer and showcase how you are in a position to create an opportunity where both you *and* the influencer benefit—one which has room to grow and continue into the future.

2. **Creating this sort of irresistible influencer opportunity requires you to be an "opportunity detective".**
   a. Identify your influencer's problems, needs, and challenges and explore all the ways you can offer value to their brand. Then, show them how you can help them grow their influence in ways *beyond* financial compensation.
   b. Think beyond a single transaction. By facilitating growth on both sides, you create a relationship that feeds off its own energy to provide additional opportunities in the future.

3. **The beauty of influencer marketing is that, even if you don't have a big budget (or any budget), there are many**

**ways to craft an opportunity that can appeal to your
selected influencer(s).**

a. Affirmation, exposure to a new audience and/or recognition as an expert advisor helps increase their reach and
relevance in their sphere.

b. Provided there is a plan in place to promote the development of multiple opportunities in the future, an initial paid
business opportunity can be a safe, mutually acceptable
starting point.

c. High-level access to special events or opportunities,
including recognition as a VIP customer or as a true insider.

4. **There's no one-size-fits-all opportunity.**

a. Remember, every influencer is human at the core (even
brand influencers are made up of individuals), and we are
all different. What motivates one, won't motivate another.
Take the necessary time to not just observe your potential
influencer, but to craft a potential opportunity and present
it in a way that will speak to them.

MOVING FORWARD

After investing time and energy researching your potential influencer, identifying their potential goals and objectives, and making the connection between your resources and their needs to
determine the perfect, completely irresistible opportunity. . .it
sure would be terrible to blow it by flubbing the first impression
(or not getting their attention in the first place). Remember: the
whole reason that influencer marketing represents the future of
marketing is because the market is so fragmented and competitive, that it's hard to break through unless you already have the

attention and trust of your desired audience. In essence, you need to influence the influencer to listen to you.

FOOD FOR THOUGHT

How much spam does your email receive in a day? Of the few that make it past your email's filters, how much of it do you read? Most of us don't even read the full subject line before deleting it on reflex. Point is, we know what spam sounds like— which should mean we know how *not* to make our emails set off a person's mental spam filter, yet why is it that so many brands and top marketers are falling trap to this? Let's explore. . .

11

Making the Approach to Your Influencer
How to win—and why so many approaches fail

S
o, you've found "The One." Not just any influencer, but one who aligns with your business *and* your objectives, has real influence over your desired audience, and is perfectly positioned to take advantage of your carefully crafted, mutually beneficial opportunity.

Now it's time to make the pitch—the pivotal point of connection (or not).

Even the most intriguing opportunities won't come to fruition if you don't present it in a way that engages the influencer. The wrong approach will not only fall flat; it runs the risk of turning the influencer off from your brand entirely. Trust me on this; there are several brands with whom I've interacted with or who have reached out to clients of mine, and by coming across as entitled, careless or thoughtless it became an immediate turn-off. While they did achieve their goal of getting the influencer talking about them, it was for all the wrong reasons.

Over the course of several partnerships—and after being on the receiving end of multiple pitches—I've learned how to get influencer alliances started on the right foot. But before I walk you through my process, let's make sure you're in the right headspace to make a connection.

First and foremost: don't skip the warm-up

Just as jumping into a race without a proper warm-up is a recipe for disaster, the same is true for influencer marketing. Get into the athlete mindset, and plan to put in the effort and the time it takes to be successful.

Before you open a window to draft an email outreach, start by putting yourself on the influencer's radar, and showing up in their ecosystem. Lay the groundwork for communication by following them on their social channels, attending their events, or subscribing to their blog.

This is also an important part of your research process, so hopefully you're already there—but if you're not, get started. You can begin engaging with their content by commenting and sharing, but avoid overdoing it—a thoughtful comment or two is better than hammering them with compliments or praise. Make a point of sharing their content from your own accounts or channels, and make sure you mention them when you do it.

The idea is to get their attention and let them know you're genuinely interested in their content. You want them to know that you know what they're about, and to give them a chance to get familiar with you. You might be surprised by how many influencers will reach out of their own accord to ask you about yourself.

One thing I do when I want to connect with an influencer is follow them on Instagram or make relevant comments in their stream. After a period of time, I let them know via direct message that I'm working on a project and would love to send them more details, if they would send me their preferred method of contact. A quick note: even some of the biggest influencers with teams of agents and managers surrounding them are more like to monitor their own Instagram account and get your message directly.

This way, I know they've seen the message, and can gauge whether or not they would be open to further contact. I also learn the best way to make the outreach when they reply, whether that's via phone, email, or an in-person meeting. For academic and corporate influencers, I take this same approach to Linked In. In fact, I ended up acquiring marketing strategist, Shane Barker to co-teach one of my Influencer Marketing classes at UCLA by doing exactly this on LinkedIn.

Always work with the big question in mind: why should they care?

Even if you've crafted the greatest opportunity, it will get lost if you don't know how to articulate the message. This is especially important to convey if the person doing the outreach is different from the person who designed the project or opportunity, which frequently occurs in agencies or with larger companies.

Making a direct ask comes across as desperate and selfish, and sends the message that you're focused on your own needs: "How can you help me?"

Instead, start with this question: "Why should they care?" Put yourself into the influencer's headspace—what about your outreach is going to get them invested to learn more, or even finish reading?

Influencers get asks of all kinds every day, and if you want your pitch to stand out, you have to know what matters to them, craft the 'opportunity' that will offer them real value and then communicate your message in a distinct way that immediately lets them know you are worth talking to.

Put a face on your outreach

It's important to consider who will be the face and voice of your company in regards to influencers; i.e. the person who actually connects with the influencer and who serves as their point of contact for the brand.

Recalling my ZICO experience, the success and longevity of an influencer-brand relationship often has more to do with the person who establishes the relationship than the product or service—because good business is about good relationships

Since influencer marketing is a relatively new methodology, brands often have different people reaching out to influencers for different reasons. A marketing manager might reach out to connect with a new audience to advance a new product, while business development may look to an influencer for new product feedback. The advertising department may want an influencer to attend an event they're promoting.

Suddenly, you have five points of contact. . .and zero engagement.

If you're going to reach out to influencers, make one person your point person to avoid confusing them about who they should be responding to. It's a small thing, but it matters.

Make it personal: no cattle calls

If you think using an automated form email or generic template will help you court influencers, you've clearly missed the point. Not only will you be lucky to even get any responses, the chances that any of those responses will be positive—and profitable—are virtually nil.

Phoebe Mrojeck is frustrated. . .and she's not alone.

As the host and producer of a leading podcast and radio show, *Unbecoming*, she has an all-too-familiar story.

"I regularly receive cold emails from people or agencies pitching themselves to be a guest on *Unbecoming*. Because we reach hundreds of thousands of listeners each month, the inbound emails we receive exceed what we can handle at the moment. But one example stands out amongst a sea of similar examples—and I'd describe it first and foremost as *generic*.

I can always tell who has done their research by the subject line of the email. In this particular case, the subject line ended with "PLEASE RSVP?" Upon opening the email, it was clear the sender was unconcerned with any sort of customization or positive end user experience.

As my show has grown, it's not uncommon to receive an email with inconsistent formatting—different colors, fonts, and sizes. However, this particular email opened with "Hi *First Name*". . .which leads me to believe many other frustrated podcast hosts are having this same conversation.

Rather than creating an intersection point where a guest would add value to my audience, not a single sentence of this email referred to my show, my past guests, or our topics, community, or audience. In a world where attention spans are declining and email inboxes are sacred, s/he who creates the best experience wins. I want to see that you've done your homework, and that you're creating a win-win situation for *me*.

That rarely happens.

Back to the page-long email; it was peppered with links, high-lighted text, odd bullet points, and mention of an attachment that was not attached. The text was incredibly unprofessional, unresearched, and careless.

As a host, I look for well-prepared and well-thought out pitches that feel like a continuation of the story we are already telling on the podcast. I encourage new perspectives, unique voices, and different angles. . .all within the fabric of the overarching theme.

I believe podcasts and their potential guests are missing the mark with their storytelling and communication styles. Any guest can run in the regular speaker circuits, but I find lazy pitches, canned responses, and marketing stories pollute the water and leave hosts with a bad taste in their mouth.

The best guests and hosts handpick their topics, guests, shows, and opportunities to create enormous value, to bring a fresh per-spective, and to share a unique approach to the topic.

My biggest piece of advice is to think one step further down the line from your intended target. Ask yourself, 'What would make them look good, and to whom?' and craft your pitch or show around that concept."

Generic templates are a quick way to lose you respect with any quality influencers, meaning any time you save by going the one-size-fits-all route is just wasted effort. To approach influencer marketing for success is to recognize that creating genuine connection is not about 'lip service' or looking at it for immediate and direct returns. Rather, the smart marketers are creating connection by re-conceptualizing the dialogue, interaction and value creating processes, which, in turn, will optimize the integrative potential of influencer marketing.

Influencer marketing is much more than a sum of exchanges in one-off transactions and it is much more than a set of techniques. It is a new foundation for thinking that requires strategic vision and a sense of the whole. A quality influencer will only respond to a brand that not only gets their attention, but garners their trust by making it personal *to them*, and offering real value.

For example, it may seem basic to use the influencer's name in your outreach, but you'd be surprised how many marketers are still copy-pasting templates into email windows or sending mass emails to a database. As Phoebe pointed out, it's not just frustrating to see an email open with "Hello, First Name"—it can actually turn you off from the brand completely.

(Pro tip: if you've chosen to hire an agency to help you with your influencer marketing, you'll want to ensure you're copied on all their digital outreach to ensure this isn't happening. . .because it often is, no matter what they tell you).

Take Marion, a lifestyle influencer with 129,000 followers on Instagram who lamented a lack of personalization in a Harvard Business Review article:

"When a brand contacts me, I first look at how the email starts. If it says 'Hello' or 'Dear Blogger,' I don't even read it, and I delete the message. My name is Marion, and if you follow my blog then you must know that, otherwise you are just looking to send the email to a large amount of people. Then, I look at whether the person has collected information about me and my blog."

If you've done your homework (the OBSERVE Step of the code), you will know more than enough about your influencer to reference, cite, and praise them in your outreach. Take the time to show *genuine* knowledge of, and *appreciation* for the influencer and their work— they'll appreciate that you've taken the time to understand what they do, and how they do it.

You can also share content pieces of your own that align with the style, values and interests of the targeted influencer to show you're on the same page, and to let them know what you're about (and establish your credibility. . .but more about that in a moment).

Quote the influencer

One savvy way to get their attention and show personalization, thoughtfulness, and care is to include a quote from them in some of your own work. Open communications by letting them know or show-ing them how/where you've referenced them. This is something you can do regardless of budget, and proves firsthand you've done your homework *and* are already committed to elevating their brand. Often, they will even share the reference with their own audience for free.

Many fashion and beauty magazines nail this. For example, look at this blurb taken from an article on lash extensions from Glamor Magazine. In just one paragraph, the writer quotes two influencers:

"That includes not curling your lashes either. 'If they're curled, there's a crease right by the root, and it's hard for the lash artist to apply the extensions—it won't be a smooth-finish job,' says Jessica Shin, founder of Flair Beauty & Lash Studio in New York City, where I've been going for extensions. Other things to avoid: mascara, waterproof eye makeup, oily skin care, and eye cream. You basically don't want anything that'll interfere with the glue. 'If you need to work out, go to the gym and take a shower in advance," Shin advises. "You can't get them wet for 24 hours post-session because the adhesive has to dry completely.' Tirzah Shirai from L.A.'s Blinkbar even recommends avoiding waterproof eye makeup for up to a week before your appointment. 'It leaves an invisible film that will keep the lashes from adhering fully,' she says."

This acts as more than just a "foot in the door" with your chosen influencer; it effortlessly builds a friendly dialogue, showcases your common interests and demonstrates how working together could easily be a highly valuable opportunity.

Act like a human

This is different from making your outreach personal. This is about sounding like a real human being, reaching out to another real human being.

This is business, certainly, but you don't need to sound sterile, dull, or like a barely-updated automatically generated template. If your content and your messages have the look and feel of a spam email, or a tax attorney, you will be treated like one.

It's no secret that people like doing business with interesting people, yet so much of our professional lives find us using language that sounds robotic and distant. People only trust what they can understand, so talk like the real person you are—not a tax attorney.

Odds are, you'll make your recipient more likely to want to invest time and effort into a mutual partnership.

Be specific in recognizing their value

Anyone can say, "I'm an avid reader of your blog" or "I've been following your social media for a while". . .because lots of people do. It's likely why you're contacting them in the first place. But almost *every* outreach email says this in one form or other, so you shouldn't.

Instead, show them that you've actually invested in what they have to say. Something like: "I really liked your post about the difference between advertising and marketing. Your perspective showed a depth of knowledge and real passion on the subject. I actually shared it with our marketing team."

In just a few lines, you let them know you read their content, you understood their message, and you thought it was worth sharing with others. That's a great start to a content partnership.

It's not about you, it's about *them*.

I've seen it so many times. The first email goes on and on about the company or brand being pitched, their great business, and all the benefits of their products or services—because they want you to know how *lucky* you'd be to work with them.

While you may be right in the value and differentiating you offer, the problem is the right *order.* You have all the information that makes a partnership make sense *to you*, but the order isn't the one that will connect with the influencer.

When you're pitching your brand, it's common to use an order that looks something like this: *I have a great [product, service, idea] > Here's why you should work with me.*

You do that because you know the brand/product/service so well, and are an expert in all the great attributes and benefits. Then, because you "know" it's so great, you go on to explain why it's the right partnership for your influencer.

Except that's not how people's brains work. Of course, you want to introduce yourself and your company—but the reality is that most of your recipients aren't going to get interested in you until they know that you can help or serve them.

And they *don't* know why they should care about you.

What *do* they know? **They know what matters to them.** So start here, instead: *Since XYZ is important to you > I have a great opportunity to help you achieve that.*

One of the quotes I try to live by, especially when trying to make new friends at cocktail parties, is this: "If you want to be interesting, be interested."

The same logic applies to your outreach efforts: no one wants a primer on the history and future of your brand before you've told them why they should care. Keep your "about us" to just a few lines to give your influencer some context, and then focus on *them*.

Here's an example of what I mean:

"My name is Caleb from Essentially Healthy, an online store that sells and delivers super nutrient powder mixes. We noticed that you create awesome superfood smoothies that are convenient for the time-starved person—(I personally love how you use pumpkin puree creatively for flavor)—helping healthy people keep balance in their lives, even when they're busy.

Can we share a basket of assorted super nutrient mixes from our online store for you to enjoy with your family?"

The "about" was barely more than a line, but it was enough to let the influencer know they had some brand alignment. Then the focus shifted to the influencer, what the brand had observed about them, and what the brand wanted to offer them.

Many marketers would follow this email up with a request for a review or an image post with a link, but nothing turns an influencer off more than a demand before they've even shown interest in a brand or a product.

You can briefly share the goals of what you're doing on a broader campaign level, but heading in with no strings attached is a good way to put your recipient at ease.

Establish your credibility

This isn't the same thing as going on and on about how fantastic your company is. Rather, this is about establishing authority in your shared space in a tangible way. In other words, you're telling them why they should trust you—but not in so many words.

This is where social proof comes in: sending the message that other influential people find your content or product worthy of a mention. Marketing strategist Shane Barker, advises that if you've already written a guest post for a leading blog in your niche, mention that somewhere in your outreach.

Take a look at how a prominent blogger for Groove subtly mentions how he's done posts for influential websites.

Hey man! Hope all's well.

Been working on a blog post that I think will do really well, and could potentially be a great fit for your blog. Would love to publish there (and help promote to our 7K+ subscribers). Recently did posts on the KISS and Shopify blogs—let me know if you want first crack at this one :)

It's about some interesting results we found from testing stories on our blog. Basically, we took a post, tested a variant where everything was exactly the same, except w e put a story-driven intro at the beginning to pull readers in. I expected it to do better, but I was surprised by how much better (300%) it did.

The post tells that story, and gives tips/strategies for easily weaving narrative into the reader's own blog content.

Mind if I send the post your way for review?

Thx,

David

Don't be entitled

This is the big one—easily the most common and off-putting mistakes marketers make in their outreach: they put in a request for what they'd like the influencer to do. It may be to review their product, or include them in a post, but it's an ask without an offer. After all, what would make someone want to start freely endorsing another brand without any foreseen value?

The influencer doesn't know who you are, hasn't engaged with your content yet, and doesn't owe you anything, including their interest, time, effort, or participation. You have to *earn* their attention and interest, not *expect* it.

Another way many people attempt to make a connection is to ask an influencer for a chance to "pick their brain". I don't know a single influencer or busy person who responds well to this prompt; what does it mean? What will this actually involve? Why me? And why would I?

In fact, in interviewing over 150 social influencers, that statement came up as both "the most irritating" and "most entitled" phrases in brand outreach—asking to use someone's time and expertise without even acknowledging what a big request that is—will get you on the automatic 'no' list.

The bottom line: your primary goal should be to create interest in your potential partner, to let them know that you've taken the time to get to know them and their content, and to briefly establish your credibility so they're ready to continue the conversation.

Now let's get down to the nuts and bolts of your actual message.

THE ANATOMY OF AN EFFECTIVE OUTREACH EMAIL
The subject line

The subject line determines whether or not your email gets opened in the first place. You're competing with a never-ending flood of emails—marketing consultancy Convince and Convert estimates that at least 35 percent of email recipients make a judgement call about what they're going to open based on the subject line alone, so you better make it good.

It's a classic mistake to spend time and effort crafting a great note. . .and then give the subject line absolutely no thought. A Rolex in a paper bag!

The goal is to get your recipient's attention right away, and drag their eyeballs away from all the other messages around yours in an overcrowded inbox. Think of yourself as an email marketer aiming for killer conversion rates on your newsletter—except you care about *just the one open.*

Some parameters to get you started:

- **Stick to 10 words or less:** Your recipient shouldn't need to glance twice at your subject line. Also, use sentence case vs. Title Case (caps at the beginning of each word)—it makes the email feel more personal and natural, and less like a sales attempt.

- **Don't treat it like an internal company email:** You have to do better than "<Brand/Company> Opportunity" or "Need influencer for <opportunity>." This person doesn't work with you, so they're not obligated to open a dull email about company business. The same guidelines about talking like a real person versus a faceless corporation apply here.

- **Use a question:** Specifically, ask a question they're going to want to answer, or else want the answer to. Something like:
  - ▶ "Why is everyone so tired?
  - ▶ "Why are interior designers going wild for this new paint?"
  - ▶ Do you want good coffee?
  - ▶ "What is the most essential tool on your workbench?"

- **Don't use FW: or RE: to trick your recipient into an open:** Yes, I *did* tell you to think like an email marketer. . .just not a scammy, spammy one.

- **Don't craft misleading subject lines:** It might be tempting to create a highly enticing subject line no one can refuse to open. . .but that isn't paid off in your message. If the subject line isn't aligned with your message, you may get that initial open, but you'll immediately lose credibility and trust.

Keep the body of your email short and concise

Don't go on for more than 4–5 paragraphs—ideally *less*—and keep your language direct, simple, and as jargon-free as possible. People tend to scan emails as opposed to reading them in detail, so help them get more of the details you want them to know by breaking up your message with bullets, sub-titles, and bolding any points worth highlighting.

Answer who, what, when, where, why. . .and how

When your influencer gets to the end of your email, they should know exactly **who** you are, **what** you want, **why** you're contacting *them* (and **why** they should care), **when** you'd like to engage, and **how** your partnership would work—along with **how** it will benefit them.

If you leave any of those questions unanswered, you put yourself in jeopardy of losing the attention of your recipient. If they have to follow up with you just to get the basics. . .they won't.

Include a specific—suggested—next step

Often times, we spend so much time crafting the message, we forget to actually put the desired action or behavior we want from our recipient! It's one little detail, but without it, nothing happens.

Be honest and straightforward, without being pushy or entitled:
- "I'd love to set up a call to discuss the opportunity in greater detail in the next two weeks. How does Tues or Thursday anytime between 12 pm and 6 pm work for you?"

- "Can I send you a follow-up email with more details about the project?"
- "I would like to set up a quick meeting while we're both in town for the conference to tell you more. Are you free on Wednesday afternoon, after the keynote?"

This part of your message isn't about making the actual ask for your opportunity, or demanding they give you a response. This is about getting them to take the next step with you, if they're interested.

Don't send without a read-over

Re-read your whole email to make sure you don't have any typos or grammatical slip-ups, because both can lead your recipient to question your attention to detail, or the effort you're putting into your outreach.

Make a polite follow-up

In 5–7 days, follow up on your note with a polite hello, reiterating why you'd like to get in touch, and offering your action step (or the action step of their choice, be it email, phone call, etc.). Sometimes people mean to follow up and then get distracted by life, or they just need to know there's a real human trying to get in touch for a purpose.

And remember: don't be pushy, be *interested*.

The bottom line: You're dropping your fishing line alongside a whole lot of other hooks and bait.

Anyone with any level of 'influence' in a particular category has an inbox full of pitch messages, and that's on top of the insane amount of email we all get on a daily basis. Make yourself hard-to-miss, hard-to-forget, easy-to-read, and easy-to-follow-up with.

EXAMPLES OF INFLUENCER OUTREACH
And where they can be improved

Now let's put it all together with some real-world examples: emails I've sent, and emails I've received—for better or for worse.

The following message is an example of an email sent to an influencer I wanted to work with.

(Note: these were all done after a thorough warm-up by following their work, commenting on their articles, supporting their posts, and, essentially, becoming an Observation detective.)

Subject line: I have 80,000 friends I'd love you to meet.
My goal was to be fun, fresh, and intriguing—who the heck are these 80,000 friends?

Hi XXX

I was recently introduced to your platform via some of my subscribers from my website, Fit, Strong, and Sexy, and had to reach out personally when I saw that you too were a competitive distance runner in a former life (and an "All-American" at that).

Now she knows a) that I've got subscribers, upping my credibility factor and b) we've got something in common with one another—we runners are our own breed!

Your content is rock-solid, clearly, but it's your charisma and how your personality comes out so authentically that grabbed me immediately—I especially love how you open every video with "SMILE! It will make your day better instantly!"

So true!

In just a few lines, I let her know I've seen her videos, and that I appreciate the unique voice and personality she brings to her content.

Opportunity:
I know how many opportunities fly into your inbox every day, but please know I am NOT an agency or marketing company. I'm a fellow creator/influencer who recognizes an incredible way to help us both grow exponentially. . .for half the work and resources!

I want her to know this isn't the typical outreach, and what I want to do for her, on a general level.

Me:
I am an award-winning Partner Creator for YouTube, and the creator of a large online fitness/lifestyle community of women, Fit, Strong, and Sexy (recognized as one of the top female fitness communities for Women by LiveStrong.com), with a dedicated membership of over 80,000 women.

Now she knows we're both in the same industry, and that I've got enough social proof in the industry to make me worth listening to.

I am reaching out to you personally because I think you'd be an incredible partner to be a featured leader on our new fitness show. You can check out more info here (link)

Here's the thing about influencers: they all have a reputation (and ego) to hold up. By presenting an opportunity to feature her as an expert, it immediately speaks to her. Who doesn't want to be a featured leader in their category, and on a platform that is both credible (which I established above) and puts her in front of a new, desirable audience?

It's a brief, straightforward pitch, and I've given her a way to find out more information on her own, if she wants to investigate before she responds.

Why?

- You are already creating exactly the content that aligns with our mission.
- We can share it and feature you to get more eyeballs.
- We can cut out your production costs by covering your expenses.
- You will be free to keep doing what you're doing on your own channel, yet will have triple the exposure, and no cost of production.
- You will have full access to our marketing and social media team to consult with, and our resources to support and amplify any of your initiatives to help you scale.
- We can provide you with equipment, and percentage of any sales you make (though no pressure to sell).

Obviously, you're an inspiration and an influencer, and I know our audience will love you.

I've covered why she is a fantastic fit for our audience, and all of the benefits we can provide her through our relationship. This is the definition of win-win!

So, I guess the bigger question is *WHY NOT?*

This is exactly how I talk—ha! This adds a little bit of my personality, which she'll experience again when we chat.

I'd love to set up a call to discuss the true potential, and see if we may be a fit. Let me know if you are available for a 15-minute call this coming Thursday or Friday afternoon.

And there's the next step.
Sincerely
Amanda
P.S. I truly think this is a life-changing opportunity and a catalyst for positive change for so many women. . .amazing, right? I'm speaking from the heart and would LOVE to do this with you.

I love a good, heartfelt P.S. to refocus the whole conversation!

So, let's recap. You can see that I. . .

- start with a unique, curiosity-building subject line
- affirm the influencer, and let her know I had enjoyed her content
- keep the email scannable by using short paragraphs, bullets, and underlining
- establish who I was and gave her a way to learn more
- establish the opportunity, why it's a perfect fit for her, and how to learn more
- set some solid next steps for follow-up

. . .and wrote it all in my own, very human, friendly voice.

Now, let's check a great outreach I actually *received*—and a few ways they could improve their messaging. . .and in turn, the responses they receive.

OUTREACH EMAIL

Subject line: Not another crappy guest post pitch!

I admit it, I laughed.
Body:

> Hey there,
> How many times have you gotten an email that was like: *"Look I know you get a lot of these, but. . ."* or *"I hope you are doing well!"* or *"Hey There <Name>"* or *"I was cruising the internet and stumbled upon Fit Strong and Sexy. . ."*
> Nobody stumbles around the internet, finds a blog they like, and then pitches free content. All these people are either fake personas or marketers building links for clients.
> I know this because *I'm one of them.*

Now, you might think this is a mistake—who admits this in a pitch!?—but the honesty was a great fit for the tone of the message.

> But I'll spare you all the crap and just say that I have the capability to produce very solid content (that may or may not have a few of my clients' links in it) for your site. The difference is that I'm looking to

start a relationship, so I'm being real with you from the start. I can cover topics you want me to cover. I can pitch stuff. Whatever works for both of us.

They're letting me know I can shape the nature of our relationship, but also suggesting some tangible ways it could work.

Think we can work something out?
Just drop me a yes or no. If it's no, you'll never hear from me again. If it's yes, that's awesome because this job is so full of non-responses and denials that it makes me crazy sometimes. Just send over any specific details and we can get started on this beautiful new relationship together.
Talk to you soon!
Jane Doe
Outreach Coordinator

An awesome closeout. There is zero entitlement and they put the ball in my court. They also addressed the fear of being pestered, which in itself makes me want to respond.

AND THE FOLLOW UP:

Hi again,
I just wanted to see if you got a chance to look over my last email.
I won't bother you with some elaborate follow-up message. If you're interested let me know.
Cheers,
Jane Doe

So, did it work for me?

Pros: This email was *so* not the typical boring outreach. It was humorous, witty, and touched on the exact points that cause us to either dismiss an outreach—or just get annoyed.

Ultimately, it's just great content in general, from the subject line to the email itself. . .it sucked me right in! It has personality and feels personal because the voice sounds candid and human, even though I know as a marketer that it's mostly a template. The thought behind it—and the person doing that thinking—makes me want to get to know them.

Also, and this is key: she doesn't ask me for something up front. Rather, she makes the pitch to start a relationship—which means she *gets* it. Instead of demanding I do something, she states that she wants to provide value for me, and make it a win-win for both of us.

Another big pro was the follow-up, which is *critical* to keeping a connection alive. I thought it was interesting from the get-go, but I was still skeptical. The follow-up gave me the little boost I needed to respond.

Cons: There was no real idea or concept fleshed out, or any evidence they really knew anything about my content or my brand. They also didn't share anything about who they were, or what they do—no website, no sample content, no bio. . .no nothing.

Points for style. . .but it lost the attention it got up front in with a less-than-compelling execution.

TWEAKING YOUR INFLUENCER APPROACH

Finally, let's check out an example of feedback I gave a member of my team about one of their outreach approaches. I always find this style of "workshopping" a good way to get to a better result.

The following back-and-forth from my team started with a comment one of our influencer marketing account managers left on an influencer's Instagram post. Through research and social listening, she found that this particular influencer was most active and responsive to all his viewers on Instagram, so the first post is a comment on his most recent post that tags him and alerts him we've sent him a direct message (DM).

This is important, because if they aren't following, they may not see the direct messages; in other words, it'll get lost in the flood of other messages.

Example: Our comment on the Influencers most recent post: "@ mrfitguy sent you a DM"

Then the direct message: *"Hey XXX, Congrats on the new fitness series! We have an exciting project we think may be an incredible fit, best way to connect?"*

Lucky for us, he responded right away to this Instagram comment with his email. Perfect!

Our same point person followed up on her comment with an email. She's really good at her job, but you will see even subtle changes can have *big* dividends! Below I've outlined the real-time feedback I provided her to edit and improve this email—read and learn!

The original email (with names removed)

Hi John,

My name is Jane Doe. I'm the social media/community manager for Valeo Fit, a fitness/lifestyle platform that Amanda has officially part-nered with to reach an even bigger audience outside of her *Fit, Strong, and Sexy* community.

I currently oversee all social strategies for the brand as well as potential collaborations between Valeo and Amanda.

Valeo Fit started as a name exclusively for fitness equipment, but it is quickly turning into so much more than that, as we are currently re-branding Valeo into a community where people can find recipes, workout videos, advice, health tips, and more. . .all in one place. We are currently building up a team of Influencers to work with for our massive January campaign.

If you are interested, we could further discuss collaboration ideas. I see that you are based in LA, as are we. This would be a perfect opportunity to shoot content together for the coming months.

We look forward to hearing from you.

My feedback for her

"Good initial stab at this! However, I think we need to better position the opportunity so that it appeals to the influencer right away, and does justice to our omnichannel lifestyle platform—a platform that's drawing lots of excitement.

Essentially, it just needs to be reframed to be more alluring as an opportunity to be part of a bigger growth and collaboration. The influencer doesn't care what we are doing or selling—he just wants to know what we can do for him, or how working with us will benefit him.

As soon as we talk about selling product, we will lose him. We need to craft the email by presenting the idea of working with us as an opportunity to build his brand.

Try something like this:

"We are currently curating a (very) short list of esteemed fitness experts to be featured as our favorites on our platform, and you are at the top of that list. Our goal is to support you to grow your own influence and audience through our new omnichannel platform.

We have the resources, mission, values, and team to support your growth—and have fun in the process. . ."

So essentially: we bring you value, we help you grow. . .and we give you a bigger platform and all the resources you need to do just that!"

Now here's a piece of homework for you. Take my feedback to the original email and see what you come up with!

IF AT FIRST YOU DON'T SUCCEED:
TRY, TEST, AND TRY AGAIN

You've learned the best practices of creating an influencer outreach campaign by now, but here's the hard truth: you will still inevitably encounter influencers who decline your offer, or fail to reply at all. Just as you wouldn't expect to win your first race, I'd go so far as to say you shouldn't expect a response on your first try. Persistence is crucial, but it needs to be persistence *without* entitlement or desperation.

Be prepared to send follow-ups; I recommend marking your calendar and following up once per week, for at least 4–5 weeks. Make sure you phrase each follow-up in a friendly, pressure-free way. If you sound impatient, you're going to put them on the defensive. If you assume they must have seen your first email and actively opted not to reply, you ignore how crazy inboxes are these days.

Instead, play it cool, and let them know you're still keeping up with their content. For example: in your follow-up, open with a reference or comment to a recent post they've done, or offer to help them on something they are working on.

If you're not seeing any results, keep reaching out to other (qualified) prospects and testing different subject lines, offers, and content, following the tactics throughout this book. Whatever you do, never assume that the influencer will take up the offer, or that they owe you a response—there are no guarantees. You have to offer value. . .and even then, the fish won't always bite at the line.

Remind yourself that influencer marketing is much more than a sum of transactional exchanges, or a set of techniques. It's a long game—requiring strategic thinking, taking the time to build a relationship, offering real value, and becoming a *real* part of the influencer's community and ecosystem.

Recap and Review

KEY POINTS

1. **No matter how attractive the opportunity, nothing will come of it if you don't present it in a way that engages the influencer.**
   a. You only get one first impression, so it's important to make sure you get it right. Best case scenario, you start your new relationship off on the wrong foot; worst case, you turn the influencer off your brand completely.

2. **Start with a proper warm-up!**
   a. Get on your influencer's radar by meeting them on social media and hanging out in their ecosystem. Ideally, they should recognize who you are when they receive your initial message.

3. **Your message to your influencer should be as well-crafted and customized as the opportunity itself.**
   a. Even if you've created the best opportunity—one they are sure to love—it *will* go unnoticed if the initial message doesn't engage them.
   b. Put yourself in their headspace and ask, "What in this message would make them care? What would immediately speak to them?"
   c. Keep your company sales pitch/history out of it, including no more than a couple lines about your brand/product/

service. Instead, you should seek to establish your credibility, to let them know they can trust you.

d. Instead, put a personal face on your outreach. Skip the automation (or form letters of any kind) and focus on building a relationship.

e. Likewise, make the message personal to the influencer, specifically outlining why you've chosen them in particular. Focus on how you can meet *their* needs, and not vice versa.

f. Above all, don't be entitled. The influencer doesn't owe you anything.

4. **While you do want to make sure your emails comes off as personal and human, they still need to be professional and polite.**

a. The anatomy of an effective outreach email is one with an engaging subject line, sticks to a concise length, answers the who, what, when, where, why, and how, and suggests a next step (without being pushy).

MOVING FORWARD

Once you've successfully reached out to your influencer and they've responded positively, the next step to strengthening your new connection is ensuring that both parties are on the same page. While we want to avoid a relationship where the influencer feels like a freelancer or contract worker, having a mutually approved agreement down in writing helps so much in keeping your fledgling relationship stable and productive.

FOOD FOR THOUGHT

Imagine you've just moved in with a new roommate. You met them a few times in college and they seemed like a perfectly nice person, so when they offered to split the rent, you saw no reason to say no. Now that you're both moved in, you feel like it might be a good idea to lay down some ground rules right at the start, but they assure you that the two of you can just work everything out as you go.

Three months down the line, they haven't done the dishes once, they eat your food right out of the fridge and blast the television at 3AM. Now you're in the awkward position of having to confront them with their behavior, without their having violated even a verbal agreement. Having ground rules, along with an agreed-upon code of conduct, not only helps avoid this type of behavior in the first place—it helps both parties come to an understanding later on down the road if complications arise. In other words, before you try to build a working relationship, you need to construct the foundation.

12

Defining the Relationship
Developing an influencer agreement

magine you own a beautiful boutique hotel, tucked away on a charming little street just minutes from the heart of town. When people find it, they fall in love—but you are struggling in the off season, and would like to be busier all year round.

After plenty of thought and consideration, you decide an influencer marketing campaign will help you reach more people in your target audience to increase awareness and bookings.

Your marketing team researches and identifies a group of relevant travel influencers to build out your campaign. They choose a mix of bloggers and Instagrammers, as they've identified these are the platforms where your desired audience is looking. Each one has an impressive portfolio of high-quality content aligned with your brand, and an online audience that turns to them for travel inspiration, tips, and guidance.

After your initial discussions, everything seems perfectly aligned. The influencers seem to understand your campaign objectives, and are excited about your hotel and what you have to offer guests. You've already agreed upon the terms of compensation, so you greenlight the influencers to execute the campaign.

However, once the content goes live, it turns out it wasn't at *all* what you expected them to publish. One particular influencer completely fails to position your brand in a way that resonates with their audience. Another takes the post down after just 24 hours to shift her audience focus to another brand., and one post is so 'off' that you fear it will negatively affect your brand.

Now you're frustrated. What a waste of time and money! You can't even use the content on your own channels, and yet you're still obligated to pay the influencers, even though what they produced didn't meet your expectations or achieve your desired business objectives.

What's your recourse in this situation?

You could refuse to pay, but word travels pretty fast when an influencer is publicly annoyed at a brand. As far as they are concerned, they did what was expected of them, and produced the content you were looking for.

This disconnect is exactly why an **influencer marketing agreement** is *critical.*

Influencer marketing agreements minimize or negate these uncomfortable and often painful situations, when things *do* go awry you all have a document to refer back to—making it more straightforward to solve the conflict with facts in hand. Otherwise, it's a "you said, they said" situation that turns any relationship sour.

A signed agreement also provides both you and your influencer with protections from a legal perspective. You've agreed to hold up your end of the bargain, and if either side reneges, the other has the backup they need to hold them accountable.

While agreements are becoming more expected and standard, it's still something many shy away from. Why?

- "I don't want to formalize it too much—they might get overwhelmed by all these expectations."
- "I just want to see how it goes for a bit before I commit."
- "I want the freedom to get out of the arrangement without a lot of hassle if it's not working for us."

- "They are seriously excited and motivated. . .I trust them."
- "We've developed a good, genuine relationship; I don't want to hurt it by shoving a contract at them."

No matter how good the intentions may be on both sides, it is a business relationship—and business relationships thrive on structure and clear expectations.

There's an art to this, however. The first thing to know is that not all influencers are created equal, and therefore not all agreements will be the same. Macro influencers have made a career out of their influence, and therefore tend to be more compliant with a brand's needs and requests by virtue of their professionalism. Micro influencers, by contrast, may only be doing this as a side job and don't necessarily *need* their sponsorships because they aren't depending on it for income.

There's also the question of differing perspectives and priorities. The influencer will almost always be focused on engagement; i.e., what image or video is going to get the most 'likes' or views. And don't get me wrong, this is obviously important; but as we've seen time and again by this point, what good are likes or comments if they have nothing to do with your product? This is why, while a brand may acknowledge that the influencer knows their audience better than anyone, *you* know the whole game.

Here's an example. If you give an influencer total control of the content without any guidelines, they are naturally going to make it fit with the rest of their page. This way, the content doesn't come off looking like an ad. However, this could mean putting the product in the background or in the corner—in other words, failing to make it the focus of the image. The final product might get 1,000 comments, but if all those comments are focused on how great the influencer looks, instead of the product you've collaborated with her on, they're not helping drive consumer action to purchase.

The key to success is to strike a balance between allowing your influencer to build content that's creative and authentic but also designed to achieve your brand's goals.

START WITH A CONVERSATION

There are some basic details to consider when detailing the kind of arrangement you want to have with your influencer(s). Some necessary things to consider (which are easy to overlook) include:

- The desired behavior/outcome (both short- and long-term)
- Whether the campaign has a specific end (short-term), or is it intended to be an ongoing long-term relationship?
- Will the campaign have a specific branded topic? Or will the content fall into topics the influencer is already covering?
- Will you engage in a "get to know you" smaller initial project, followed by a more lasting arrangement?
- Do you want the influencer to provide an exclusive mention of your product, or a mention alongside other brands (cheaper, but less focused)?
- Will the content and distribution be on a specific platform, or across multiple platforms?
- Are you working with a single influencer—or several?
- Discuss both the level and type of resources you want and are able to invest.
- Think through all the various ways you see working with them beyond building awareness, such as product development, image management, content production, or in person events. (See Chapter 10 for more ideas!)

Addressing these things up front will give you a better sense of the possibilities open to you, versus trying to force a standardized arrangement with your influencer for the sake of getting something in writing.

This is also the time to confirm that everyone has reasonable expectations for what's possible—in terms of things like depth of content, pace of content posting, timeline of deliverables, anticipated response, and so on—especially if you're working with an influencer who is just starting out.

Canadian Football League television host, digital maven, and speaker Brodie Lawson explains it from the influencer's perspective:

> "The biggest hiccups happen when expectations are not made clear from the beginning—from both sides. Brands often want exclusivity, or for you to be a 'partner', and they come in with huge asks right off the bat.
>
> From an influencer's perspective, you have to be very clear about what you are capable of delivering, so you don't over promise and end up disappointing your brand partner.
>
> Because the space is relatively new, sometimes it feels like you're making it up as you go, and at the end of the day you hope both sides are acting in good faith."

Even if you've developed a strong relationship with an experienced influencer and everyone seems to have the best intentions, remember that you (and they) are only human: the more you can do to anticipate potential pitfalls and risks, the better.

If you've got a solid map to work from together, the more likely it is that you'll avoid miscommunication or questions down the line.

DEVELOPING YOUR INFLUENCER AGREEMENT
Hammer out the basic details

Getting the basics set might seem like a painfully obvious step, but from a legal perspective, it's essential—and many brands and influencers don't take time to nail these basics before they start working together.

The only way you'll have any standing in a court if something goes off course is if you have accurate identifiers for each of the parties and entities involved.

These details include:

- The **legal name** of your business, as well as the name under which you do business (if different)
- Your **legal name** as a party to the agreement
- The **legal name** of the influencer
- The **legal name** of their business, if applicable
- The **legal addresses** for everyone involved, to establish jurisdiction
- The **date** on which you're signing the agreement

Here's an example of what this looks like at the beginning of an agreement:

This Agreement, executed on _____, 20__, is entered into by and between SAMPLE AGENCY, LLC, a Texas corporation with an address of 147 W Main ST, Happyville, DTX 12345 (hereinafter referred to as the "Company") and _____ influencer with an address of _____ (hereinafter, the "Influencer"). Company and Influencer may be referred to collectively as the "Parties."

For good and valuable consideration, receipt of which is hereby acknowledged, the Parties agree as follows. . .

If you regularly work with a lawyer on business contracts, have them draw up a template agreement for you to use going forward. If you don't regularly consult with a lawyer, it's still worth reaching out to legal counsel when you're starting to work with influencers; a couple of hours of their time and knowledge could save you from a crisis in your new partnership.

Outline your campaign parameters

Your next step is to put together a 50,000-foot overview that all of your other agreement details sit under. In business, we call this the executive summary.

Here's an example:

The Sunny Sun Company is partnering with Influencer Irene to create an Instagram-based campaign called "Cool for the Summer" for the month of July 2020. The influencer will post a product-included image and a short (50 words or less) description once a week on Friday afternoons about how they use the Company's products to stay cool in warm weather.

You'll certainly build out more details than this in your agreement (including time zone, time period, platforms of choice, and so on. . .) but this executive summary is a good start to get everyone on the same page.

Map out the duration of the partnership/campaign

This part of your influencer agreement states how long you will be working with the influencer to market your product or service.

It should include any time needed for planning purposes ("two 2-hour meetings via phone to discuss the campaign and content") and the length of time you intend to have them create content for you ("The first post will go up on July 1st, and the final post will be published on July 31st.")

Also, ensure you specify how long the influencer must keep any content live on their end. Many brands have learned this the hard way when an influencer takes down a post after a month, or even just a few days. If post duration isn't specified in the agreement, they can still argue they followed every instruction you gave them.

Establish the level of brand control versus creative autonomy

A major challenge for brands is figuring out how to give the influencer creative freedom in the creation of content. If you provide too much structure for your influencer's content, you'll end up with posts that read as inauthentic or too promotional to their audiences. As ESPN host, and master fitness influencer, Caroline Pearce explains:

> "Some brands make the mistake of trying to micromanage and dictate how an influencer portrays their product or company. I understand there are key words you want included, and a story you want to get across. . .but if you've chosen an influencer you truly believe is right for your goals, then let them tell their own story.
> Their authenticity will be more powerful than your exact wording which the viewers and their following will see straight through."

On the other hand, if you don't provide *enough* structure, you could end up wasting your investment on low-impact content that doesn't achieve your goals—or your influencer's goals. The secret is to achieve a balance of creative freedom and clear expectations with your influencer, and that's where defining the content comes in.

Define the specific type(s) of content you're looking for:

- **What are the crucial points to be included in the content**? This could include specific messaging points, product features or functions, benefits of your product or service, or the name or tag of a specific campaign.
- **What format do you want the content to be in**? A video? An image? A blog post? A tweet? An infographic? Some combination of various types? Be specific.
- **How long or short should the content be?** Give them guidelines to shape their creativity.
- **When should they post the content?** This could be as specific as a time of day on a particular day, or simply posting within a span of time.
- **Sharing Brand Content?** If the influencer is creating content for your brand specifically, do you want him/her to share any content they create for you across their own channels?
- **How long do you want them to leave the content up?** Some influencers will take sponsored content down after a certain amount of time to prevent their platform from being saturated with marketing efforts, or simply do so once a campaign is over. Make it clear how long you want them to leave up the posts they do for you.
- **Will you be able to repurpose the content?** Content can you be used in many ways beyond what it's initially created for. Do you intend to use it across other channels or in different ways in the future?
- **Provide examples.** You can spell out your expectations in detail, but when it comes to inspiring creativity, people learn best from examples, so don't be afraid to showcase several in your agreement. Your examples should include content that has

worked well for you in the past, but you can also show content from other brands or influencers to use as inspiration. The key is to point out what you like and what you *don't* like—and why.

Remember, both sides (the brand and the influencer) need each other, and the key to success is in striking a balance between what each side asks for and what each offers.

None of the fundamental parameters mentioned here should stand in the way of your influencer making their content true to their own brand—rather, it's a way of ensuring they have your expectations as a foundation for whatever they create. Essentially, you give them the frame for the house, and they decorate! To sum it up neatly, marketing expert and author, Joel Backaler terms it "freedom within a framework."

Identify your distribution channels

Be clear about where you want your influencer to post the content they create, including the *specifically named accounts you want them to use*. Many influencers have multiple accounts for different interests or areas of focus, and you don't want to end up on an account where your ideal reader or watcher won't see you.

Here's a close-to-home example: I have five—yes, *five*—Facebook pages:

- One is personal
- One is for my Fit Strong and Sexy brand
- One is for my marketing and consulting agency

- One is for my Valeo Fit company brand
- One is for The Influencer Code

If a brand requests that I post a short video on the benefits of a new supplement for focus and energy, and they don't specify which account, I might post it on my business marketing Facebook page, thinking the mental clarity benefits might resonate with my high-pressure, high-stress executive audience.

However, this page doesn't have *nearly* the audience reach or impact of some of my other pages. Not to mention, the company might have been hoping to target my fitness audience with a beneficial supplement for elite athletes.

Maybe they didn't even realize I *had* a marketing page—and that's why your research matters so much. Gone are the days in which people just wear one hat or title. . .and the bigger the influencer, the more hats they wear.

(Note that I only mentioned the number of channels I have on *Facebook*. We haven't even covered any other social platforms or other online or offline platforms!)

This is also the time to define if you want something unique for different channels, (ex. Instagram versus Twitter versus a video), or if you want the same thing posted everywhere. If you've done your research, you know where your influencer's impact is most powerful, and the audience you want them to speak to—so make sure that's where any content your influencer creates is going to end up.

A NOTE ON OFFLINE INFLUENCE

While the majority of this chapter pertains to the agreements surrounding content creation specifically, the best influencer partnerships are long-term and often require a mix of in-person events, guest appearances, using/showcasing the product in public or during certain times, or public mentions, so be sure to include anything you want done in addition to content creation.

Decide on a dedicated or non-dedicated campaign

Here's a wrinkle that often surprises brands who collaborate on influencer content: when the influencer inserts your content alongside other brand(s) in the same post, ostensibly lessening the impact of their own content. Not every brand will want or need a sole mention, but for many, a dedicated campaign makes sense.

If you're an optical brand working with a fashion influencer, for example, you may initially think an image featuring just your brand (i.e., a close-up of the influencer's face wearing your glasses) is best. But because you've monitored their brand and what works, you know that their followers come specifically for their "outfit of the day (OOTD)" and are looking for a full style breakdown. Their followers want to know how the influencer styles and pairs things *together*. Therefore, you actually stand to benefit more by being mentioned alongside other brands in an 'OOTD" post.

In this case, a dedicated campaign isn't necessary. However, if you're marketing a new model of cell phone, you don't really want another brand's tablet sticking out of a tech influencer's backpack. It's up to you to make it clear what you want, and for the influencer to be true to the content their followers are seeking.

Specify the terms of compensation

This is an area where you'll want to be both detailed *and* specific about how your influencer is going to be compensated for creating and/or sharing content on your behalf.

There are many ways an influencer can be compensated, from a flat-rate cash payment, to free product, to access to services, to performance-based payments. As you agree on your compensation structure, ask yourself the following questions:

- Is this a one-time payment, or an ongoing arrangement? For how long?
- What is the timing of payments during the arrangement?
- Will they be part of an affiliate program? What are the terms?

Whatever the terms, be clear about *what* the compensation will be, *when* it will occur, and *how* it will occur (check, direct transfer of funds, and so on).

Be sure to be explicit about your payment structure to avoid misunderstandings, too. For instance, you could pay 50 percent of the total amount at the signing of the agreement, followed by 25 percent once the content is live, and the final 25 percent at the close of the campaign.

Define the specific tracking methods to be used

Defining what you will measure from the beginning can help you paint a picture of how your campaign is (or isn't) is moving the needle. Here are the most widely used tools, platforms, and strategies (to date at the time of writing this book):

Promotion Codes. This is a personal favorite of mine, which takes the form of a unique text code the influencer can give out to incentivize his/her audience to buy, such as a discount or free shipping. I find this one to be most 'trackable', as people will usually go back to reference the code if it involves anything free or discounted.

 Fit Strong and Sexy ⊘
September 11, 2016 · ⊘

I told you guys before how much I LOVE YUNI Beauty products, which is why I'm THRILLED to be able to offer you guys a 20% discount when you use the code AMANDARUSSELLFSS at http://www.yunibeauty.com/

#SkincareSunday

YUNIBEAUTY.COM
Natural Body Care | Natural Organic Skin Care | Natural Hair Care Products - Yuni

A Facebook post offering my followers a 20% discount with a promo code on a beauty company's website.

Affiliate links and codes. A unique trackable link or text code to use to provide clear data on things like click-through rates, sales, etc., but that doesn't necessarily involve discounts or perks. Any commission or percentage of sales generated by the link or code to the influencer should be specified and agreed upon.

Amanda Russell, @fitstrongsexy · Jun 28, 2015

Teamed up w/ **@LARABAR** to test their preworkout bar-heres how it stacked up #LARABARliving http://goo.gl/fB54uL #ad

This Twitter post from my account contains a LÄRABAR affiliate link.

Tracking Links. At tracking link is simply a dedicated URL created to track actions such as clicks. It can be difficult to tell whether you are about to click an affiliate link or a tracking link—the difference is, affiliate links result in payment for the influencer for every sale made through that link, versus a link that simply tracks the engagement (usually clicks and purchases made) through that link.

Customized Landing Pages. A dedicated landing page created specifically for someone to land on after clicking on an online marketing call-to-action.

About The Focus Project

Whether you're a programmer, mother, executive, teacher, or an entrepreneur.

Best-selling author Erik Qualman has created a landing page
on his website dedicated to his book.

Hashtags. No doubt you know this one: a word or phrase preceded by a hash sign (#), used on social media websites and applications, especially Twitter and Instagram, to identify messages on a specific topic. These hashtags help to collect and quantify engagement, i.e. the number of users searching, clicking, and commenting on posts.

Research suggests that campaign hashtags are the most popular method in current use, with 61% of marketers telling Econsultancy they use them to track the impact of influencer investment.

Coca Cola's #ShareACoke campaign provides an example of using a hashtag to track their campaign efforts: the hashtag was used by all levels of influencers and enhanced by macro and celebrity influencers, such as Selena Gomez.

Whatever tracking method you decide to put in place, it's important to thoroughly define it and to provide your influencer with any tools and guidelines you want them to use to map their efforts, including how and when you want them to be used (or not used!)

Make sure to request access to any valuable measures on the influencer's end.

Some examples include:

- Website analytics, including time on site, pages visited, and exit pages for any visitor connected with your campaign content.
- Post engagement analytics, to give you a sense of how your campaign content fared on social media
- Email list size and open rate, so you can gauge how your campaign content fares in comparison with their usual email engagement numbers
- Results from a previous campaign—to provide a baseline for the performance of your campaign

You need to specify exactly what you expect your influencer to provide from their own analytics programs (such as Google analytics, which every website and blog can access for free), or from the results of other campaigns or partnerships, and how often you want them to provide you with those metrics.

If they're *not* currently tracking anything about their posts or presence—more likely to be the case with micro-influencers—you can help them get set up with a tool or platform to get a look under the hood.

Establish your review and feedback process for all content

It's a good idea to make sure you see the influencer's content before it goes up, and that you have the ability to request changes or revisions of the content *before* they publish it. This should cover errors in details or any sort of misunderstanding around your messaging or product descriptions, as well as anything you might find inappropriate.

Your agreement should cover all of the following:
- When you want to see the post draft
- How long the review period will be on your end
- How long the influencer will have to make any changes or edits
- When final approval will occur
- Terms around vetoing a post, if it fails to meet your standard

Again, if you've done your due diligence around your influencer's content, there shouldn't be any surprises or a huge need for edits—but you should always reserve the right to tweak a bit to make the right impression. This is your brand, after all.

Detail the level of exclusivity and confidentiality—from both sides

When an influencer is witnessed promoting two or more competing brands, it brings their authenticity into question: "Is Product A really the best if they're calling Product B the best a week later?" Not only do they risk hurting their own reputation and the trust of their audience, it can negatively affect the results of your campaign.

"Exclusivity" usually describes an arrangement where the brand doesn't want the influencer working with its competitors, and can include several variations, such as:

- Working only with your brand for the duration of your campaign or partnership
- Not mentioning you alongside other brands in a specific post
- Not working with other brands for a specific time period around the posts they create for you
- Not working with competitors or other brands within specific categories (online or offline)

Be clear and detailed about any restrictions you want your influencer to follow. For example, if your influencer is doing your Ford Fiesta campaign, then it would be typical to include a phrase in your agreement saying they can't work with any other automotive brands for 3 months. Make sure to actually name the brands *specifically* so there's no room for interpretation.

Your influencer may also have some thoughts around exclusivity and who else *you* might be working with on campaigns, in case it creates concerns, competition, or brand issues for them. They may ask you to pause those collaborations while you work with them, or to collaborate on different products or services to make their offer more special or unique.

Regardless of which direction the exclusivity goes, make the boundaries clear for everyone, and get them in writing.

"Confidentiality", on the other hand, refers to private and sensitive information you might exchange with an influencer in the midst of your partnership.

This could include:

- **Actual details of compensation.** Yes, they should disclose they are being compensated, but you don't want them saying for how much—especially if you're working with other influencers (or they work with other brands!). Any disparity, and things could get awkward.

- **Any legal and binding contracts.** Your legal agreements themselves should be considered confidential.

- **Proprietary or intellectual property information.** If you disclose sensitive company information to an influencer, define if you want it kept secret.

The website www.NonDisclosureAgreement.com offers state-by-state templates for confidentiality agreements, so you'll be able to find the appropriate language there for your needs:

This Nondisclosure Agreement (the "Agreement") is entered into by and between _____ with its principal offices at _____, ("Disclosing Party") and _____, located at _____ ("Receiving Party") for the purpose of preventing the unauthorized disclosure of Confidential Information as defined below. The parties agree to enter into a confidential relationship concerning the disclosure of certain proprietary and confidential information ("Confidential Information").

1. Definition of Confidential Information. For purposes of this Agreement, "Confidential Information" shall include all information or material that has or could have commercial

value or other utility in the business in which Disclosing Party is engaged. If Confidential Information is in written form, the Disclosing Party shall label or stamp the materials with the word "Confidential" or some similar warning. If Confidential Information is transmitted orally, the Disclosing Party shall promptly provide writing indicating that such oral communication constituted Confidential Information.

2. Exclusions from Confidential Information. Receiving Party's obligations under this Agreement do not extend to information that is: (a) publicly known at the time of disclosure or subsequently becomes publicly known through no fault of the Receiving Party; (b) discovered or created by the Receiving Party before disclosure by Disclosing Party; (c) learned by the Receiving Party through legitimate means other than from the Disclosing Party or Disclosing Party's representatives; or (d) is disclosed by Receiving Party with Disclosing Party's prior written approval.

3. Obligations of Receiving Party. Receiving Party shall hold and maintain the Confidential Information in strictest confidence for the sole and exclusive benefit of the Disclosing Party. Receiving Party shall carefully restrict access to Confidential Information to employees, contractors and third parties as is reasonably required and shall require those persons to sign nondisclosure restrictions at least as protective as those in this Agreement. Receiving Party shall not, without the prior written approval of Disclosing Party, use for Receiving Party's benefit, publish, copy, or otherwise disclose to others, or permit the use by others for their benefit or to the detriment

of Disclosing Party, any Confidential Information. Receiving Party shall return to Disclosing Party any and all records, notes, and other written, printed, or tangible materials in its possession pertaining to Confidential Information immediately if Disclosing Party requests it in writing.

4. Time Periods. The nondisclosure provisions of this Agreement shall survive the termination of this Agreement and Receiving Party's duty to hold Confidential Information in confidence shall remain in effect until the Confidential Information no longer qualifies as a trade secret or until Disclosing Party sends Receiving Party written notice releasing Receiving Party from this Agreement, whichever occurs first.

Make it clear who owns the content, once it's out in the world

Will the copyright be theirs, or yours? Will you have broad usage of the content after they post it, or will it work according to a particular set of boundaries? Hammer out the details before they write a single hashtag so there are no surprises down the line.

You should also stipulate upfront how, where, and when you expect to be re-sharing or re-posting their content on your own accounts, so the influencer knows where else their content is going to be consumed.

The following is a standard content ownership blurb in a contract, covering what the brand maintains rights over:

Ownership of Materials, Trademarks, Copyrights

1. You acknowledge that you have no right, title or interest, and agree that you will not claim any, in or to any materials produced under this Agreement or in connection with the Program, or in or to any of our trademarks, service marks, trade names, or copyrights.
2. We hereby grant you a limited, non-exclusive, non-transferable, non-assignable, royalty-free license to use the [CLIENT] name, the Program name, the Program logo, and the Program badge in connection with your participation in the Program.

This example, from Fresh Press Media, takes a more detailed approach to laying out the use of the influencer's content:

(b) Grant of Rights. Upon Advertiser's acceptance of Influencer's proof of completion of a Gig, Influencer shall grant to Advertiser the unrestricted, worldwide, perpetual, irrevocable, fully paid-up, royalty-free, fully sub-licensable and transferable right and license to use, reproduce, modify, adapt, publish, translate, create derivative works from, distribute, transmit, display, and perform the results and proceeds of all content created pursuant to a Gig (collectively, "Work"), in whole or in part, in any media, format or technology, whether now known or hereafter discovered, and in any manner including, but not limited to, all promotional advertising, marketing, publicity, and commercial uses and ancillary uses, without any further notice or payment to, or permission needed from Influencer (except if prohibited by law). Influencer agrees and grants to Advertiser the use of Influencer's name/likeness/social media handle or channel/ blog name and any other Influencer attributes in any manner that Advertiser determines supports the Campaign or the Work, including use in any media that accepts advertising or promotional content or communications (such as, but not limited to, digital, print, television or radio).

There are unlimited ways brands can leverage influencer created content—and that shouldn't be a surprise to anyone. We all want to get the maximum return on our investment, but influencers are brands now too and it can come back at you if you aren't crystal clear about it all from the very beginning.

I learned this firsthand during a campaign in the beginning of my career for a brand that was supposed to be distributed online-only. The campaign did very well—so well, in fact, that I was suddenly being sent pictures from people around the world who recognized me from the campaign. Great, right? Except the people recognizing me were finding me all over the place *offline*, from the sides of trucks, to billboards, to in-store displays and magazine inserts! You better believe this quickly became a bigger conversation with the brand, since I was never agreed (nor was compensated) for that level of use.

Lesson learned (from both sides!)

Agree to regulatory compliance

While not new news, it's incredibly important that any influencer campaigns you create is in compliance with the Federal Trade

Commission's (FTC) *Guides Concerning the Use of Endorsements and Testimonials in Advertising.*

The guide gets updated every so often, so to get the most recent version, hop onto Google and search on "FTC endorsement guidelines". Use the Search Tools time filter to ensure you're looking at information from the past month, few months, or within a year.

Be sure to look specifically at the FTC's own pages and published updates--as opposed to summaries from bloggers or other websites--and read them *thoroughly.* You'll gain the understanding you need to move forward with your agreement around the **Four Ps of Disclosure:**

- **Prominence:** Disclosures should be easily visible to consumers and written in a reasonably sized font that stands out from a site's or image's background.
- **Presentation:** Disclosures must be easily understood by consumers—vague or subtle language is unacceptable.
- **Placement:** Disclosures should be posted in places where consumers would typically read or view content. They should not be buried at the bottom of a page or a lengthy post that requires them to click to learn more.
- **Proximity:** Disclosures should be listed alongside the products or services being promoted.

Actress Margot Robbie works with shoe company, Hunter, as a celebrity influencer. On one occasion, they posted a shot of her at the UK music festival, Glastonbury, in her Hunter boots.

Her post confused her followers, because it said #ad when she first posted it. Then, she changed #ad to #glasto.

Why the switch? Margot is Australian, and their standards around disclosure are far more lax than the UK and the US. However, since she was working in the UK, their rules would apply. Hunter was suddenly found themselves in hot water because Margot didn't want her followers to perceive her content as an ad anymore—but with the right agreement in place, it wouldn't have been an option, and thus an issue.

This brings up two points: first, rules for disclosure are different in different places and our digital world makes us feel borderless—but if your influencer is working with a US company in front of a US audience, those are the rules that actually matter to the FTC. If you're dealing with influencers who both live and operate elsewhere, and who will speak to audiences elsewhere, it's important that you are aware of the rules that apply there, too.

Second, people are savvy, and they are usually fine, even happy, to know that an influencer they adore is being compensated, but the opposite is true if they feel the influencer tries to hide being compensated by a brand. The latter comes across as dishonest and untrustworthy, and they will lose credibility and influence.

Take another example: Lewis Howes, host of the *Inspiring Life with Lewis Howes* podcast, provides a list of his sponsors with practically every podcast he records. In doing so, he provides transparency to his followers while acknowledging the advantages he's received from his relationships with these organizations. What you *won't* see is how, on every single podcast, he offers some sort of discount, free trial, or special offer exclusive to his audience—provided as part of the existing agreements he has with his sponsors.

Make sure you articulate the exact expectations you have around compliance in your agreement, too. This includes:

- Specific hashtags
- Specific advertising disclosure language

- The use of your brand name
- Any platform-specific rules around disclosures

Be sure to call out where you want your disclosure to occur—and know that it shouldn't be hidden in comments or so far "below the fold" on a post that it's easy to miss, as the FTC will crack down on you for buried disclosures.

Keep in mind that different industries and different product types also have different rules they need to follow around particular claims or language, especially food and drugs, wellness supplements or consumables, fitness equipment, financial products or programs, and cosmetics.

Don't assume your influencer knows all the rules for your industry (or theirs!)—it's your job to be informed and to inform them. The more informed, clear, and specific about what needs to happen the better. You don't want a great campaign soured because of a technicality or misstep around compliance.

Add any legal clauses or protections you want in place

This is where a lawyer comes in extra handy in anticipating any issues that might arise from an influencer alliance.

A few different types of clauses that might come into play include:

- **Morals clauses:** Sometimes called a "social responsibility clause", this clause is designed to prohibit certain behavior in a person's private life, such as sexual acts and drug use. They were historically used in contracts between actors and actresses and film studios to uphold a particular public image. Morals clauses are now included in influencer contracts.

- **Disparagement clauses:** This clause restricts what an influencer can or cannot say about the brand (and vice versa) during the campaign, and after their contract has ended. These clauses enable you to sever the relationship, refuse payment, or possibly seek compensation should the influencer spread damaging or negative information about your company, or anyone who works for you.
- **Safety clause:** If you are working with an influencer to promote something like a car or sporting equipment, you'll want to agree upon any safety measures you want them to take as they use it, especially given the fact they'll be using it in a public way. This could include a helmet when your influencer is promoting your bike, or a life vest if they're being towed behind a boat to promote your wakeboard.

A GREAT RELATIONSHIP DEPENDS ON A GREAT PROCESS

Let's do a quick review of the most important elements of your agreement:

- **The basic details:** the who, what, when, and all other the basics that define the collaboration.
- **Campaign parameters:** a general overview or summary of the campaign.
- **Duration:** the timeline for the campaign.
- **Creative framework:** the balance between creative control between the influencer and the brand.

- **Channels of distribution:** the places the content will be posted.
- **Dedication:** the extent to which the influencer campaign is focused on a single brand, or is shared with other brands.
- **Compensation:** The nitty-gritty details around payment, sponsorship, or any exchange of goods and services.
- **Tracking and analytics:** The tools you will be using to track your influencer's impact on your campaign objectives, such as affiliate links, coupon codes, customized landing pages, and so on.
- **Review process:** The process of providing feedback and revising content until it's ready for distribution.
- **Exclusivity and confidentiality:** The rules around who your influencer can work with in proximity to your campaign, and what they can share versus keep private about your partnership and brand.
- **Asset ownership and rights:** The guidelines about who owns the content created influencer and the rights around content re-purposing, and usage.
- **Regulatory compliance:** The FTC-mandated disclosures around any content you sponsor with an influencer or pay for in any way.
- Any special legal clauses or protections you want added, such as moral clauses or safety clauses

The amount of ways brands can work with influencers is limited only by the creativity of both sides. Therefore, each agreement—whether at the campaign level or long-term partnership—deserves critical thinking and attention to ensure everyone is on the same page. Every relationship thrives on clarity and solid communication, and your agreement is imperative in ensuring you have both with your influencer.

Recap and Review

KEY POINTS

1. **An influencer marketing agreement is critical to the success of your relationship.**
    a. It's fine to start things off with a conversation, with each party talking things through until you find a win-win arrangement.
    b. Focus on the big goals and desired outcomes (aka SMART objectives)
    c. Discuss clear expectations for both parties each step of the way to avoid any confusion down the road. A great relationship depends on a great process.

2. **Ensure your agreement covers all the important aspects of your collaboration. This is the best way to rule out surprises and avoid unnecessary risks.**
    a. Hammer out the basic details, including an outline of your campaign parameters and the duration of the partnership/campaign.
    b. Establish the level of brand control versus creative autonomy you expect, along with the intended distribution channels.
    c. Decide whether or not you'll be pursuing a dedicated campaign.
    d. Define your tracking methods, establish your review and feedback process for content and detail the level of exclusivity and confidentiality for both sides.

   e. Make it clear who will own the content and specify the terms of compensation.

   f. Outline regulatory compliance, adding any legal clauses or protections you feel are necessary at this stage. Be sure to review the FTC's Four Ps of Disclosure to ensure your agreement is compliant.

MOVING FORWARD

You've assembled all the relevant information, spelled out the terms of your partnership and signed an agreement with an influencer whom you've vetted and determined to the right fit to help you meet your business goals.

Now, how do we get started? And once we're finished, how do we know if we succeeded?

FOOD FOR THOUGHT

If your goal was to save more money this year, you can evaluate how successful you were by comparing your bank account statements from this and the previous year. If your goal was to get accepted into a prestigious university, you can evaluate how you did by looking up at the framed acceptance letter on the wall.

But what about all the intangible things that cannot be directly tracked? For example, you may have become aware of a new electric toothbrush that whitens your teeth via an article written by a dentist in a magazine or blog, but it's not until your personal dentist mentions it that you decide to purchase that toothbrush. In other words, how do you tell the whole story, when so much of influential factors are not easily identifiable or directly attributable.

13

HIIM: High Impact Influence Measurement

A model to reveal results that matter, and help you see— and tell—the whole story

Have you ever tried to lose 10 pounds? The goal is usually to find the most efficient way to make it happen—because let's be real, it's *not* fun—without spending hours at the gym or starving yourself of anything that looks and tastes like real food.

So, in the name of finding *your* most efficient method, you strap on your brand-new fitness monitor and experiment with all sorts of routines to find the most effective workouts to achieve your goal. With that in mind, you take a high intensity interval training (HIIT) class at the gym. You've heard all the buzz about it: in recent years, HIIT has become one of the hottest trends in fitness training. The idea is to make use of repeated bouts of short duration, high-intensity cardiorespiratory exercise intervals, intermingled with periods of lower intensity intervals of active recovery, to burn more calories in less time.

Less time? Check! You give it a try, and your fitness monitor tells you that you burned about 500 calories during a 50-minute session. The next day, you go for a 70-minute run and your monitor says you've burned 1000 calories. Looking at the total calorie burn tracked by your monitor, you conclude that running is going to be the key to your weight loss—after all, it burned twice as many calories! Thinking about your workout from a direct attribution standpoint, the running workout seems like your best option.

But is it?

Here's the thing: the biggest results from your HIIT workout don't occur solely in that 50-minute workout interval. With HIIT, your metabolism spikes for the next 36–48 hours, resulting in a much greater total calorie burn. Even after a lengthy run, your metabolism still doesn't spike to nearly the same level as after HIIT, so your overall caloric burn is actually *less* over those 36–48 hours. Not only that, but long cardio sessions can make you more tired and hungry—and the resulting nap and giant dinner afterwards only serves to put another obstacle in the way of your overall goal.

What all this means is that your fitness tracker isn't giving you the whole picture, and incorrectly interpreting the data it gives you can easily lead you down the wrong path.

Influencer marketing works the same way.

If you focus on short-term immediate return measures, you'll miss out on a much bigger story about the impact your strategy had in the long run. Only when you create a fully fleshed-out narrative to contextualize what impact your influencer partnership has had does it become crystal clear what you've *truly* achieved.

In this chapter, we'll cover my practical method for measuring impact to help you develop that narrative. I call it High Impact Influence Measurement (HIIM)—and the industry is crying out for it.

WRONG METRICS = WRONG RESULTS

The root cause of failure in many influencer marketing efforts is not a lack of access to data via standard web analytics and measurements.

Rather, it's the lack of critical thinking about the long-term impact of a campaign or partnership, and a failure to provide a structured and comprehensive approach for identifying success or failure, which in turn leads to an inability to adequately communicate results.

The industry is largely judged according to what we refer to as **vanity** or **reach metrics** (i.e. 'Likes', follower counts, number of comments, etc.) When you're trying to secure the biggest budget possible from your clients and your company, who are looking for numbers to justify writing the check, we can't help but give them want they want: *a bunch of numbers*.

Yet influence can't be measured that simply—in fact, you actually impede your chances of capturing the full breadth and depth of your results by limiting yourself to these performance measures. It's just like reporting a 500 calorie burn from your HIIT workout, when really you burned exponentially more in the big scheme! Reporting the initial, surface results—these reach and direct-attribution numbers—only tells part of the story, and often not even the correct one.

Don't get me wrong; having been a competitive distance runner, I'm fanatical about measurement. I won or lost based on the numbers alone—right down to tenths or hundredths of a second. But if measuring influence was as simple as mapping things out a spreadsheet, I wouldn't have written this book.

Let's look at it from another perspective, another birthday has passed, and you are feeling lonely and hopeless in the romance department, so you set a goal: to get married *in six months*. You make a list of the traits and characteristics required for your ideal partner, and begin your pursuit.

You'll need to start with a wealth of candidates if you're going to find the one that fits all your "Mr. or Mrs. Right" criteria. Next, you'll need to line up tons of dates, and spend time courting them all to see who you jive with—and who jives back.

Finally—and this is perhaps the hardest part—you'll have to convince the person you select to marry you right away, because the proof of your success will be the marriage license and a ring on the finger.

What would happen if this was your metric to define the success of your marriage?

Yikes.

Yet that's exactly what we do when we prioritize numbers over the high-impact work of relationship building.

You can piece together things like web analytics, financial data, social listening, social network application programming interfaces (API)—basically the programming that allows different applications to talk to one another—and other directional and quantifiable data, but it's not possible to capture the whole accurate story when you're focused on putting direct measures on human relationships.

In fact, fixating on these hard metrics like "revenue-per-social-post" or "direct conversion numbers" most often comes at the expense of recognizing benefits and wins that may not be as obvious or directly attributable—leaving you with an inaccurate or incomplete picture of what actually happened.

Another problem comes from our tendency to focus on immediacy. How can we know we're getting the most out of a relationship inside of six or nine months? How much progress do we need to make to stick with it? Should we move on to someone new at that point, or keep going?

See what's happening?

In the midst of trying to measure the value of the process, we're actually *robbing the process of value.* We're bypassing critical thought, big picture analysis, and all the nonlinear, indirect, yet *powerful* benefits of influencer marketing waiting to be recognized.

If you're not looking to build a long-term, authentic relationship based on mutual success and supporting one another's goals, you aren't doing influencer marketing—you are simply doing influencer advertising. While influencer advertising serves its own purposes, keep in mind—it's still only a transaction; the influencer isn't invested in the future growth of your brand. To optimize your partnership long-term, you want the influencer to be invested in your success, something that that won't come from a one-off transaction. Rather, it comes from creating a mutual beneficial relationship—and doing so requires spending time getting to know the influencer and what matters to them.

This is where we bring it back to the three key steps of the Code:

1. Revisit your business **GOALS** and your business objectives.
2. **OBSERVE** who or what is influencing your desired audience, and then IDENTIFY what will influence those influencers.
3. **CONNECT** and engage with those forces of influence, agreeing on indicators and desired results that will help them track and validate their progress toward their goals (build the partnership).

Then, go tell the story of how that relationship evolves and produces results through **High Impact Influence Measurement.** Ready to get started? Let's go!

UNLOCKING YOUR HIIM RESULTS
HIIM Step One: Setting your baseline

You wouldn't start a fitness weight loss routine without being aware of your measurements and starting weight, would you?

The same goes for working with influencers. Before you begin any sort of partnership with an influencer, take stock of where your brand currently exists in the market, according to your business goals. This will form your baseline from which you will grow. Remember, there's no perfect formula for developing your baseline. Think of it as a snapshot of where you are right now.

Your qualitative and quantitative baseline factors could include:

- **Your social media accounts:** Follower counts, subscribers (i.e. YouTube), average post impressions, likes, shares and replies, engagement ratios, reactions, comments, and shares— and so on.

- **Your web traffic:** Site visits, most frequently visited pages, time on site, bounce rates, and exit pages; anything that provides insight into how your site is being navigated by visitors now.

- **Your paid search results:** Click-through rates, average cost-per-click on your ads, and any other conversion stats you can get access to.

- **Your email marketing results:** Sign-ups, open rates, click-through rates, any share stats you might have, unsubscribe rates.

- **Your brand sentiment:** Social listening mentions, words used to describe you in social and traditional media, and conversations around your brand or industry that include you.

- **Your in-store activity:** If you have a brick and mortar business, your traffic and sales should always be factored into your snapshot, along with average and median time spent in store browsing/shopping.

- **Your print advertising and out-of-home (OOH) advertising results:** If you advertise in newspapers or magazines, or invest in billboards or public signage, factor in those results, too.

- **SEO:** Where does your brand fall in organic search results when variations of key terms for your industry or product are searched?

- **Your (potential) customer feedback:** This could include the results of initial consultations, feedback on your recommendations, follow-up surveys, customer correspondence, testimonials, word-of-mouth, and social media interactions.

- **Your revenue and profit numbers:** If you have multiple markets or locations, you need to break down your numbers by market, rather than just an overall total. That way, your baseline allows you to compare the impact of different influencers in different places.

- **Your product reviews:** This includes both the number of reviews on various review platforms such as Google and Yelp, as well as the sentiment expressed. What did you get right? What were your reviewers' compliments—and what were their objections or challenges?

Not every brand will have *all* of these points of data to choose from, so select the ones that align most strongly with your goals. For example, if you're looking to drive conversions through your influencer efforts, take a closer look at behavior on your website, and any engagement you can track with your outbound marketing, including email and social media.

If you're looking to increase positive brand sentiment, do some social listening and media mention analysis, as well as a more in-depth look at customer feedback. If your goal is to grow your social media presence, get a solid baseline for where you're at today.

Once you've put it all together, it should look something like the following (hypothetical) example.

The Service Brand: H & H Landscaping and Lawn

Where H & H is now: H & H Landscaping and Lawn is a lawn care and landscape design brand based in the Massachusetts suburb of Sharon. They have a roster of clients who rely on them for everything from average yard maintenance to landscape design. Most of their clients are single-family homeowners who want to keep up their curb appeal.

They have set a goal of expanding into the suburbs closer to Boston and Boston itself, and extending their client base to include more small-scale landscaping for urban clients. They predict that, by breaking in with a few small gardens on a brownstone-lined street in Boston, they can get work landscaping the *entire* street, including back gardens and front stoops. Because all of the homes are close together, neighbors quickly take notice when someone does a fantastic job with their landscaping.

For now, most of their portfolio is large in scale, so they're considering collaborating with local real estate agents to landscape the condos and multi-family dwellings being staged for sale. They also want to reach out to urban gardening influencers to offer makeovers and recommendations.

All of their team members are well-spoken and highly informed in their areas of expertise, so they would function well as spokespeople for their services.

Baseline snapshot:
- **Sales activity:** H & H averages 3–4 telephone or email queries per week (12–16 monthly), with a 25 percent conversion on direct inquiries, and strong repeat business. Their customers often recommend them to neighbors, which accounts for about half of

their inquiries. Other sources of inquiries include people who see their signs on clients' lawns, people who call the number on their truck after seeing it in their neighborhood, and Google searches, though they don't do any paid search marketing.

- **Seasonal email newsletter:** 500 subscribers, with a 25 percent open rate, and 1 percent direct queries on average, post mailout. Newsletters are sent quarterly, and usually to announce a discount or seasonal promotion: "Get 1 month free lawn mowing with your summer planting."
- **Social media:**
  - ▶ Facebook page: 1,500 followers with only 0-2 average number of comments, 0–1 shares.
  - ▶ Twitter Account: 2100 followers with an average of 5 likes and 3 re-tweets for each of their tweets on the popular hashtags #gardeningchat and #landscapechat.
  - ▶ Instagram (their most popular platform) has 2,500 followers, and an average of 250 likes and 4 comments on their posts.
  - ▶ Frequency and types of content on each platform:
    - ◆ Facebook: 1–2 posts per week created by the brand and mostly all showing work they have done for current and past clients.
    - ◆ Twitter: 8–10 tweets a week, unless they are in a hashtag chat; then they participate and reply in real time, as needed These tweet numbers include sharing their Instagram posts, and giving out tips to their followers
    - ◆ Instagram: 1–2 posts per week created by the brand and mostly all showing work they have done for current and past clients. The content here is the same as what they post on their Facebook page.

- **Type of comments:** The comments are usually fairly concise and simple: "beautiful yard". They don't see a lot of interaction or conversation, but they do say "Thank you!" to anyone who takes the time to comment.
- **Customer feedback/brand sentiment:** Customers praise them for their attention to detail, elegant and creative design, and flexibility with scheduling. They are also available on-call for emergencies without a change in rate for established customers—a huge benefit in customers' eyes.
- **Service Reviews:** They have a 5-star rating (out of 5 stars) on Google Reviews, with only three reviews. They have a 4.5-star rating (also out of 5 stars) on Yelp with nine reviews. They have not been mentioned on the local neighborhood review board hosted by the Nextdoor platform.
- **Reputation/Press:** They have had two positive mentions in local print publications. They don't yet have any positive mentions or placing on any other website or social media page.
- **SEO:** They are on the first page of results for "landscaper in Sharon" and "lawn care in Sharon", but they don't come up until the third page of google search for "Boston Landscapers" and the fifth page when searching on "best Boston landscapers".

Now that H & H has taken stock of where they're at now, they're better able to measure the impact of their outreach, brand-building, and influencer alliance efforts.

You can also do the same snapshot method for business owners and influencers, because they are brands, too.

HIIM Step Two: **Tracking your progress**

Now you can select the appropriate tracking methods to flesh out your narrative. (Keep in mind, of course, that most tracking measures result in strictly quantitative metrics.)

In influencer marketing, we treat them like puzzle pieces: they give us *part* of the story, but not the *whole* story.

I talked about tracking tools in Chapter 12, but here's a refresher:

- **Tracking pixels:** Tracking pixels are tiny images that will allow you to keep track of how many users are visiting your website from another site. They are a great way to track traffic coming in from blogs and Facebook, specifically, but they're useful across most content.
- **Coupon codes:** It's an old school option, but still one of the best: a coupon code is a nearly foolproof ways to measure the effectiveness of an influencer campaign. Give each influencer a specific coupon code, and tally how many of each are submitted.
- **Tags/hashtags:** Tags and hashtags are a simple way to track mentions and references to your brand on social media platforms. You can also make special campaign hashtags, or a hashtag for a specific influencer.
- **Social Listening and Alerts:** To track brand mentions/media hits, set up Google alerts to know when your brand is mentioned online. Your social listening tasks should include routine searches of your brand name in search engines and across social media platforms to give you a head's up your brand is being mentioned.

- **Affiliate links:** Much like coupon codes, affiliate links are a simple way to tie a site visitor to a particular influencer. Unlike coupon codes, they can also provide you with data about all the actions a visitor takes on your website, including pages they visit, time on site, and where they depart from (if they don't make a purchase).

- **Links within YouTube videos:** YouTube influencers are some of the most effective at driving viewer actions, but it can be difficult to measure the ROI of this medium. Your best option is to include links within the video (or description) that are specific to that influencer—a mechanism similar to coupon codes.

- **Performance-based tracking technology:** By connecting influencers to affiliate networks or SaaS platforms, you can track the entire customer journey from awareness to conversion. This allows you to collect data such as clicks, orders, and sales to help determine attribution of payments for conversions to specific influencers.

- **Curated landing pages:** This is a more labor-intensive way to work with an influencer, but brands are seeing success with dedicated product landing designed around a particular influencer. These pages feature the products they endorse, their favorite product picks, or a special edition of a signature product. If you have a selection of products or offerings that an influencer could curate, or you can create a custom product for an influencer, this is a great strategy for you.

- **Instagram in-app purchasing:** Instagram now allows users to make purchases from influencers or brands directly within their app. This is a crystal-clear way to tie purchases to a particular influencer, and to drill down on the imagery and messaging that drive sales for that influencer.

- **Google Analytics:** Every website operator should be dialed in to their site analytics on a regular basis, but when you do an influencer campaign, you should be paying special attention to any sort of changes or improvements in your overall traffic during an influencer campaign.

Keep this in mind as you go: there are many tracking methods and tools out there, and they continue to become more technologically advanced by the day. Do your research to figure out what's appropriate for your business and your budget and choose the right mix for you and your brand. . .without letting them overwhelm the story you're trying to tell.

For example, you may decide to keep things simple and track coupon codes for sales, as well as create custom hashtags to track any social mentions, the types of comments received, and overall brand sentiment. Keeping it simple gives you some good indicators without overwhelming and pigeon-holing the larger narrative.

HIIM Step Three: Putting it all together with your HIIM narrative

Now that you've:
- Defined your goals and SMART objectives;
- Identified and selected the influencer(S) you want to work with;
- Created a win-win, irresistible influencer opportunity;
- Crafted the outreach and established the connection;
- Made your influencer alliance official;
- Set expectations around content and collaboration;
- Defined your metrics and assessed your baseline;
- Executed your campaign

. . .it's time to deliver the results—what I call the full influencer narrative. This is the heart of the HIIM approach: telling the complete story of your influencer alliance's impact on your business or brand.

THE HIIM MODEL IN ACTION

Just as a high-intensity workout spikes your metabolism to burn calories well beyond your initial workout, High Impact Influence Measurement helps you define and document the success of your influencer marketing efforts well beyond the typical reach numbers—and then helps you identify areas and opportunities to further build and improve on what you've already started.

To implement this framework, take detailed notes of any shifts (for better or for worse) from the baseline you established. Collect the tracking results from the quantitative methods you chose, and then—with all your information in hand—ask (and answer) these five big questions:

1. **What was the objective?** This is the outcome you were aiming to accomplish.
2. **Who were we trying to reach?** This is your target audience— the one that's already engaged by your influencer, but who you want to be engaged by your brand.
3. **What did we do?** This covers the nature of your campaign or strategy with the influencer(s)? What were the details of your agreement?
4. **What happened?** This is where you make a comprehensive list of everything that happened during your campaign. This step is actually my favorite part, because it covers both tangible and intangible measures—because both matter. Did the audience

ask lots of questions at an event? Was their energy positive and engaged? If you're telling a friend how everything went, these are the types of details you'd include, and they most often don't correlate with a number.

5. **What's the narrative?** Using everything gathered in steps 1–4. . .tell the story!

My sincerest hope is that these questions will fuel answers that give you a more practical and impactful sense of how your brand has moved forward than any single type of measurement alone—which is good news for your clients, good for your leadership, and good for the influencers you work with, too

Remember: "Facts tell, but stories sell." As humans, we are more likely to absorb information through a narrative than through a spreadsheet—which is why, from a young age, we both teach and learn through storytelling.

This doesn't mean you don't include all the available metrics; rather, it means using them to support the story, the 'bigger picture', versus using them as results in and of themselves.

Now you've got a much more complete story that includes all the intangibles you've uncovered, and which is supported by the metrics you've chosen. This story enables you to focus on your long-term goals, and to build understanding with the leaders and clients who are ready to see the whole forest. . .versus a few trees.

Let's revisit our (hypothetical) friends at H & H Landscaping and Lawn to see how this works for their influence collaboration:

What was the big focus goal? To increase profit margins and bring in more total monthly revenue by expanding business into the Boston area.

Who were we trying to reach? Real estate agents and urban gardening influencers were H & H's target collaborators—but, by extension, the urban homeowners who wanted exceptional landscaping design, implementation, and maintenance.

What did we do? H & H partnered with local gardening expert, Will B. Thorns, on a series of videos about the challenges and possibilities of small-scale gardening. He shared these videos in previews on his Instagram stories, and then on his YouTube channel. Will agreed to do one video per week for a period of 8 weeks.

What was the result?

- **Sales activity:** H & H saw an increase of 12 new inquiries monthly—on top of their standard volume (12-16 monthly)—with 9 of the 12 new inbound inquiries attributed to their collaboration with Thorns—the callers mentioned his name! 6 out of the 9 opted to work with H & H after receiving proposals for their projects. All of these projects were in Boston proper—another critical growth goal.
- **Seasonal email newsletter:** H& H saw 55 new email subscribers, but their open rate is too early to report on, as their next email is yet to be sent.
- **Social media growth (the "vanity metrics"):**
  - ▶ **Facebook:** Their page followers increased from 1,500 to 1651, with the average number of comments per post increasing to 3, and an average of 2.5 shares per post.
  - ▶ **Twitter:** H & H only saw an increase from 2100 to 2175 followers, but their like average went from 5 to 7 and re-tweets

went up from 3-5 for each of their tweets on the popular hashtags #gardeningchat and #landscapechat.

- **Instagram** (their most popular platform): H & H saw the biggest increase here, from 2,500 to 2707 followers, with the average number of likes per post staying around 250, but with comments increasing from 4 to 7 per post.
- Frequency and types of content by platform:
  - ◆ **Facebook:** 4 posts per week were created and posted through brand and influencer collaboration, covering a mix of client work and gardening and landscaping tips and how-to's.
  - ◆ **Twitter:** 10-12 tweets were posted per week, featuring influencer-developed how-to's and tips.
  - ◆ **Instagram:** 4 posts per week were created through brand and influencer collaboration, showing a mix of client work and gardening and landscaping tips and how-to's. While these posts feature the same content as the ones posted to their Facebook page, the posts have been captioned differently and formatted for Instagram optimization.
  - ◆ **Type of comments:** The comments now include people asking questions and advice, in addition to giving praise.
- There was a brief flurry of social activity around one of the landscapers' dogs in a video, which led to the creation of a special Instagram account for the dog—and customers and followers alike love it. The dog has become a fun mascot of sorts, and as people enjoy the dog's story, they are exposed to H&H as part of that story.
- **Customer feedback/brand sentiment:** H & H's brand sentiment remains strong. Customers continue to praise them for attention to detail, elegant and creative design, and flexibility

with scheduling. They also heard more feedback about their wealth of knowledge and fair pricing.

- **Service Reviews:** Reviews remained the same, but that's to be expected: not enough time has gone by for the new clients work to be completed. H & H expects the reviews to increase, and they have implemented a gift card incentive as a thank you for anyone who posts honest reviews.
- **Reputation/Press:** The head of garden design at H & H was contacted by a local gardening club to do a presentation with Thorns. This is a big deal, because the landscape designers chosen to speak at this club usually make it into Boston's Magazine's "Best Landscapers" list, as well as the Globe and the Herald, so H & H can expect more growth down the line.
- **SEO:** They moved up to the first page of Google search for "Boston Landscapers" and the second page for "Best Boston Landscapers"
- **Innovation + profit margin increase—and other added benefits**
  - ▶ Will B. Thorns, as a noted gardening expert, offered the H & H team some unique insight about using a more cost-effective, and environmentally friendly soil. Not only will they save money on costs going forward, but their customers and potential customers who care about the environment will be happy. This will also enable them to tap into the niche audience of people who specifically seek out "eco-friendly landscaping".
  - ▶ The owner of a local real estate agency saw the collaboration on Instagram as a follower of Will B. Thorns, and reached out to talk about a potential partnership with his agency—an agency with a with a bustling social media presence--to do a

curb makeover for a house they are putting up for sale. If this makeover gets a positive response, an ongoing series might be up for grabs.

- ▶ Several other local real estate agents contacted H & H about various cross-promotion and referral ideas.
- ▶ Since content rights gave H&H the right to use and repurpose the content collaborate with Thorns in perpetuity, they now have a database of great valuable content—saving them production costs long-term, and providing a steady stream of authentic and personal content.

● The bottom line: with an influx of new clients and agent partnerships, H & H has increased their overall revenue for the month by a full 20 percent and cut costs by 10%. They increased revenue AND decreased costs simultaneously, while also increasing customer satisfaction and inbound leads

● H & H also saw many of Will B. Thorns' followers begin to follow them on Twitter and Instagram—a clear indicator that a) they were clicking over, and b) they saw value in their content.

Through each of these bullets and the resulting narrative, the H & H marketing team can tell the whole (and very exciting!) story of their collaboration—one that clearly shows value well beyond vanity metrics.

While our fictional friends at H & H saw some great shifts in those vanity metrics, the larger narrative establishes just how successful their brand-building and lead generating efforts were, and how their specific actions led—and will continue to lead—to specific and ongoing opportunities.

EMBRACE THE POWER OF STORYTELLING

After years of sitting through boring presentations and fielding questions from leaders who don't get what influencer marketing can accomplish, I can promise you that a spreadsheet and PowerPoint deck full of graphs and tables can only do so much to tell the story of a positive and productive influencer collaboration.

We actually stand in the way of our growth and creativity when we expect everything we trade to be documented in such a linear way.

That's why a significant amount of my personal cases are based on this framework. Everything I've told you about my experiences as both an influencer and a marketing consultant comes in the form of a *story*: It begins with a baseline, moves through the details of the collaboration, both big and small—and, most importantly, highlights the impact on the brands—yes, with vanity metrics are included here and there, but not to tell the whole story, rather they are used to strengthen and support the much bigger picture of the tangible and intangible results of partnership.

If your influencer marketing and measurement model does not cover all three areas of the HIIM framework, then it's not complete. Don't accept a mediocre, incomplete picture of what you've achieved—let your success shine through, in a way that everyone from senior leadership to an objective third party can clearly understand to see what's happened and what resulted!

Recap and Review

KEY POINTS

1. **High Impact Influence Measurement is a unique approach that's reflective of how influence and impact really interact.**

   a. Influencer marketing measurement has fallen short of modern consumer habits (until now) by focusing on short-term measures and looking for direct attribution of results.

   b. Vanity metrics should be used to help *inform* our understanding of the bigger picture—pieces of the puzzle, certainly, but not enough to give us a complete idea.

2. **Smart measurement means thinking beyond the numbers.**

   a. Think of your results as part of a narrative, with the numbers there to back up the details as supporting evidence. We comprehend and remember things better when told through story than as plain facts.

   b. Emotion and humanity deserve a place in our measurement narrative, and are necessary to tell us the whole story. Remember, stories inspire as well as inform—something spreadsheets can't do!

   c. Some of the greatest results won't be tracked or measured with hard numbers—you need to observe the tangible and intangibles.

   d. Marketing is not an exact science—so don't treat it like one! Likewise, you can't force a timeline on great relationships. Some results will only be truly felt months or years down the line, and while it's not wise to assume every tree will bear fruit at some point, initial results shouldn't dictate your long-term plans.

3. **Unlocking your HIIM results is a 3-step process that takes you through all the available information—both numerical and otherwise—and provides you with a quantitative and qualitative look at your brand's performance.**

    a. Create a brand snapshot by assessing the current state of your brand, your campaign, and the level of awareness you hold with your target consumers.

    b. Track your progress. There are a host of different programs, tools and metrics available to help marketers track any statistic or aspect of engagement they care to. Just remember that the numbers don't tell the full story, and don't overlook the value of the old-fashioned manual search.

    c. Using all the available information, process everything and present it—not as a collection of data points in a slideshow presentation, but as a story!

MOVING FORWARD

With your influencer relationship established and your first successful campaign in the books, the future is brimming with possibilities. There are virtually no limits to what an influencer collaboration can accomplish and what forms it can take—it all depends on the creativity of those involved. Awareness, engagement and consumer satisfaction are all being created through the amazing content you and your influencer partners create.

But what makes content amazing?

FOOD FOR THOUGHT

Think about your habits while browsing social media, leafing through a magazine, or surfing the web. What typically catches your eye? What holds your attention? What makes you want to share it? Why is it that some content provokes an emotional response that makes it so you can't help but attention, share and/or act, while others just get lost in the clutter—or worse, annoys you?

14

The Keys to Developing *Killer* Influencer Marketing Content
Making content that works—and keeps working—for you

There's an endless sea of content in the form of words, images, video, and voices out there, and it's growing by the second, making it tough for business to get their message seen or heard, let alone stand out.

While this isn't a book about content. . .you can't talk influencer marketing without talking content because every influencer partnership will, at some point, involve content creation. And it goes without saying you want to create the best, highest quality content you can that best represents both your brand and the influencer's brand.

But what actually makes content great?

This is a difficult question with an elusive answer, one that is debated by marketers and influencers alike. We know we need to provide "value" to our followers and consumers—but what does "value" actually mean. . .and how do you get there?

That's why this subject is a book in and of itself—in fact, it's *several* books. Every aspect of content creation has been covered in depth by countless authors, marketers, and content experts—some with true wisdom and originality.

What I want to focus on, specifically, is creating great content with your influencer.

Content marketing and influencer marketing are just different pieces of the same puzzle—and when they're both in the right place, they work brilliantly together. Just as different types of influencers can have an impact at different points in the sales funnel, different types of content will be more (or less) effective, depending on where your potential customer is in their decision journey.

While Influencers can have a powerful impact, it's very rare for them to push people from mere awareness to purchase—rather, the type of content they put out has to *strategically* help move them forward.

You want to embrace the creative style of the influencer—you know, *the reason you chose them*—while still achieving the goals you've set for your brand.

Striking that perfect balance is possible when you've got a keen awareness of what kinds of content work best depending on the specific objective at hand. To do this, let's look at how to calibrate content to best meet where your potential customer is at and achieve the desired result.

USING INFLUENCER CONTENT TO PROPEL PROSPECTS THROUGH THE DECISION JOURNEY

Let's say your objective is to increase the percentage of website traffic you receive from buyers (in other words, turn more of your visitors into customers, or "sales conversion"). Your influencer partner creates a highly shareable video, and her audience loves it: they comment, they share, they 'engage', and seem to do all the things you think you want them to do in response to her content. But wait, none of this led to any conversions for your brand. Why?

In this case, there was no specific incentive given for her followers to actually click over to your brand, to learn more about your product, or to buy. The content generated awareness. . .but wasn't created to drive people to the desired action.

Depending on the specific stage your target audience is at in their journey, there are specific things to look out for when you're directing, collaborating, and approving content at each step in the buyer journey.

Here are some insights into what works at various stages of the consumer journey:

Start of the journey: Awareness

At the start of your consumer's decision journey, your focus is on building brand awareness and affinity. You want to grab your target audience's attention and hold it—but if you try to sell to them at this point, you risk having them walk away. . .never to return.

This point in the funnel is typically where influencers can be at their most creative with their content, so feel free to dive into creating eye-catching, engaging and entertaining content. . .that puts no pressure on your viewer to buy.

If you provide value with a great blog post, infographic, or social post, capitalize on the audience's desire for more of that same quality information with a free e-book or step-by-step guide to something they're dying to know. Keep the sign-up process simple, and you won't lose anyone along the way.

Metrics for awareness are the easiest to gather—clicks, comments, attendees, subscribers, sign ups, and so on. This is your entry point with the consumer, and since the influencer is the one opening the gate, think about what kind of content will make a memorable first impression, or make their lives better.

A great example of prime top-of-the-funnel content comes from **Contently**, one of the leading content marketing platforms. In 2018, Contently launched a video series entitled "Content Marketing Minute", in which their director of strategy, Joe Lazauskas, actually serves as their influencer.

Joe Lazauskas, asking a very good question in a
Content Marketing Minute video.

Each video explores a single topic that comes up with Joe's clients (who happen to be some of the biggest brands out there). Joe has great on-camera charisma, he's a nice-looking guy (a bonus for video content!), and he puts a personal face and voice on an otherwise faceless B2B product.

These videos absolutely nail it, and here's why:

- Joe is an expert, but he's also an employee, so he can deliver influential content with messaging truly aligned with the brand.
- The content is digestible enough to foster awareness, but the right depth for viewers to feel like they've really taken the ideas in.

- They know the content comes from real professionals and insiders at Contently. . .who seem to be worth listening to!

All in all, a prime example of awareness-building content.

Mid-point of the journey: Consideration

This is the point in the journey where you cease being just another store in the shopping mall, and become the one your potential customer walks into. This is also the moment where you can blast past the competition by providing more in-depth education on a topic, a solution to a problem, or an answer to a question.

At this stage, having a strong influencer voice is critical to maximizing your impact. You've got the attention you want, and now you have to show them distinct value through content like product stories, unique use cases, and informative webinars.

It's not so much about changing your strategy at the mid-point; rather, it's about aligning so closely with the customer's values, needs and desires that they put you directly into their consideration set.

My brother is extremely picky. I don't think he's ever worn anything I've bought for him, and I'd like to think I've got pretty good taste (if I do say so myself. . .).

I decided to gift him the services of a personal stylist to build him a wardrobe he would love. However, upon my initial search brought up a countless number of local stylists, and I was immediately overwhelmed. Who should I choose? What was I actually looking for? How would I know if they'd click with my brother?

I poured through everything Google could come up with on stylists in my area, looking through endless blog articles, YouTube videos, Pinterest boards, Instagram feeds. . .essentially *any* content I could find to help me narrow down my choices. And in the process, I was slowly developing an idea of what I was looking for, as I considered what they had to offer.

The following image illustrates the first five hits that came up in my initial Google search—the front page results if you simply type in 'best men's fashion stylist + LA".

The 7 Top Stylists Who Are Dressing Up Hollywood's Leading Male ...
https://www.hollywoodreporter.com/.../7-top-stylists-who-are-dressing-up-hollywoods... ▾
Mar 21, 2018 - Image gurus behind the recent red carpet moments of leading **male** actors discuss ...
Boseman and Michael B. Jordan: 7 Top Hollywood **Men's Stylists** ... he took home the **best** original
screenplay statuette on Oscar night. ... suit and gold- tipped shirt for the Black Panther premiere in **L.A.**
Kim's inspiration?

The 25 Most Powerful Stylists in Hollywood 2016 | Hollywood Reporter
https://www.hollywoodreporter.com/lists/25-powerful-stylists-hollywood-2016-875178 ▾
Mar 15, 2016 - "I didn't know that much about the **fashion** world, so it's **good** to have ..... fun when that
happens with a **men's look**," says the **L.A.**-based **stylist**.

The 25 Top Stylists in Hollywood 2018 | Hollywood Reporter
https://www.hollywoodreporter.com/lists/25-top-stylists-hollywood-2018-1093944 ▾
Mar 20, 2018 - TOP LOOKS The Australian actress, 50, was the evening's **best** dressed in ... WHY
SHE MATTERS Urbinati is a **menswear** tastemaker, putting forth .... WHY SHE MATTERS The **L.A.**-
based **stylist** elevated Janney's style over ...

How To Dress Like An A-Lister, According To Their Stylists ...
https://www.fashionbeans.com/article/menswear-stylists-how-to-dress/ ▾
Dec 19, 2018 - Hollywood's **best**-kept secrets just became public property ... the **good** fortune of being
born within spitting-distance of **La-La** land, UK-born ... Timothy Lord is a British **menswear stylist**
whose CV belies his Yorkshire origins.

Our Favorite Men's Stylists in Hollywood - - School of Style
schoolofstyle.com/blog/our-favorite-mens-stylists-in-hollywood/ ▾
Tags: bradley cooper, Ilaria Urbinati, jeanne yang, **menswear styling**, ... She's probably **best** known
for dressing Bradley Cooper, but her list of **male** clients ... owned a popular **menswear** boutique in **Los
Angeles** from 2008-2013 (you can read ...

As you can see, I'm led mostly to blog posts, lists and review sites, all of which help me narrow down my options to a select subset.

Who wins? The stylists who have the most inspiring content that resonates with me.

Ultimately, I narrowed down my selection based on what I found behind each person, such as who had the most 'stylish looking site', who appeared most well-dressed themselves, and the overall level of expertise their content portrayed.

When the time came to actually make a choice, I turned to the reviews. . .which brings us to the actual purchase decision stage.

The conversion: Driving the decision

This is where an influencer, especially a micro- or nano-influencer, can actually be the most powerful choice. You may have your prospect's email, they may have browsed your services, they may have even opted in to follow your content. . .but now you want to actually *close the sale*.

What happened with my stylist decision? I ended up making my final choice by looking at video reviews from various clients who had worked with the stylists. One of the most powerful pieces of influencer content I came across in that end stage was a fashion YouTuber who did a video documenting his process in working with the stylist, along with his before and after looks—in other words, a review!

I was immediately sold! Not only did I like his style, the differentiator, was that with him, you could clearly see the sentiment of how this stylist made his clients feel. The video reverberated with love for this stylist, and made me want to meet him, too. It was the glowing review I needed to seal the deal.

When talking about championing your best consumers and their real-world reviews, this is the stage at which their content—including sharing information via word of mouth, on social media, on review sites, and so on—is most important. In short: reviewers convert!

Consumer marketing expert Jackie Huba often talks about appealing to your "one percenters." She shares that most of your business comes from the small group of your customers who are your most powerful advocates—your tribe, who don't just buy and love you. . .they can't stop talking about you!

In an interview with Jackie, she cleverly illustrates how Lady Gaga personifies a brand who has focused on her one percenters:

> "Gaga spends most of her effort on just one percent of her audience, the highly engaged superfans who drive word of mouth. Despite her tens of millions of followers in social media, she focuses on the die-hard fans that make up a small but valuable part of the fan base. It's these fans who will evangelize for her and bring new fans into the fold."

Or look at how **Codeacademy**, a company that offers online tutorials for aspiring web coders, applies this concept by helping beginners learn to code, and guides them from the point of knowing nearly nothing to being employable by major companies. Their site offers all the normal details about how the product works and how much it costs, but it also offers a wealth of short testimonials from successful coders.

"I know from first-hand experience that you can go in knowing zero, nothing, and just get a grasp on everything as you go and start building right away."

—Madelyn, a successful Codeacademy graduate employed by top social media platform, Pinterest

"For the longest time I didn't consider myself a programmer and I always put coding on a pedestal. I was like, you need to be like super smart to know programming…"

—Patrick Stapleton, co-founder of Y Combinator-backed Tipe.io

Why are these testimonials so effective?

- They're from real people who used Codeacademy, and were successful in the end.
- They're people who are so happy with Codeacademy that they'll stand behind it publicly.
- They're people who achieved successes in their lives as a result of using Codeacademy.
- They address the fears that a potential user might experience: not knowing enough to get started, and not feeling capable enough to achieve their goal.

So, if you've reached the Codeacademy website and are on the cusp of making a decision, these are exactly the types of voices to help you make a (positive) purchasing decision.

Now let's look at what actually goes into making sure the content we create at every stage of the funnel has the impact and engagement we want it to.

A CHECKLIST FOR DEVELOPING UNFORGETTABLE CONTENT

When you understand what great content is, and the attributes that make it great, you can use those attributes as a measuring stick to:

- evaluate potential content partners
- assess the content you might propose collaborating on,
- better edit and optimize every piece of content in the approval phase

Great content provides answers

And not just any answers—**answers to the questions people are actually searching for.**

Search engines are one of the most powerful tools on the internet. People head to search engines for answers to questions, solutions to problems, or to satisfy some sort of desire:

"What is a good substitute for baking soda?"

"How do I get rid of this spot on my forehead?"

"Where can I find good Mexican food in my area?"

"What music should I listen to if I want to fall asleep?"

"What's wrong with me if I cough like a baby seal?"

"Is there a dating website just for librarians?"

No matter how obscure your request might be, if you type it into that little bar, you'll be presented with an avalanche of links, pictures, and videos. That's why Google is a multi-billion dollar company today: they provide information people are seeking.

You need to think about your content the same way.

You might be tempted to use your content solely to detail the features and benefits of your product.—which means your focus is on you, not your audience. In the process, you fail to deliver anything they actually came to find.

Let's say you sell a piece of exercise equipment called an "ab slider". The device is used to strengthen your core and define your abdominal muscles—two goals *plenty* of people have.

But how many people go online to search for "ab sliders" directly? How many people even know the term "ab slider". . .and if they do, would it ever be top of mind?

Instead, they're searching for "how to lose weight", '"how to lose belly fat", "get a six pack", "tone my stomach". . .you get the idea.

That's why influencers are so powerful as partners: they're already creating the kind of content that answers questions, meets needs, and solves problems. They've figured out what their audiences are looking for and how to keep those audiences coming back for more. And they can help you do the same—building interest, engagement, and loyalty along the way.

Jen Jones, of the popular home organizing blog, I Heart Organizing, uses each of her posts to guide her readers through a particular aspect of getting their homes into tip-top shape, including pantry organizing, drawer organizing, de-cluttering, and more.

She provides detailed checklists—"printables"—that her readers can print out for every step of her plans; she points them to products that support their housekeeping goals; and she guides them through creating kits that make it easy to stay organized.

When Jen works with a sponsor or recommends a product or service, it's always a completely natural extension of the value she's already providing to her readers—because the product she's recommending meets the same needs and solves the same problems *she* does.

If you partner with Jen to showcase your product or service, your brand immediately benefits from the confidence Jen's readers have in *her* brand—that "brand halo effect." Since Jen always provides value, her readers trust the products and services she uses and promotes, and they even look to her for advice and recommendations on all things household organizing.

Great content sparks emotion

If we want people to *do* something, we have to make them *feel* something.

What this means for marketers is we need to *evoke emotion* as much as we need to inform. But for many, the word "emotion" calls to mind the outward signs of emotional response: people bursting into tears, laughing hysterically, etc. But there are many other emotional states besides extreme sadness or complete and utter joy. Great content is content that engages a wide range of emotions, and which is aligned with the creator's goals.

If you don't *feel* anything when you consume content, you won't feel moved to *do* anything with what you've consumed. To quote best-selling author and influence expert Jonah Berger again: "When we care, we share."

Huffington post studied 10,000 of the most shared articles on the internet and correlated each one to different emotions evoked, such as sadness, joy, and anger.

The most popular three emotions invoked were:
- Awe (25 percent)
- Laughter (17 percent)
- Amusement (15 percent)

In other words, when in doubt, invoke awe, laughter, or amusement. Laughter and amusement might seem closely aligned, but the former is much more of an instantaneous response—ha!—while the latter is more nuanced and thoughtful.

Let's say you stumble across a truly awe-inspiring video. If you share that video with a friend, he's likely to feel similarly inspired—and the fact that you both feel the same way, in response to the same content, helps deepen your connection.

You may remember Susan Boyle on *Britain's Got Talent*, singing "I Dreamed a Dream" from *Les Misérables*? When she first appeared on our screens, everyone was a skeptic, because she didn't fit the profile of a typical contestant—and then moments later, her voice blew us all away.

People everywhere felt compelled to share her audition because it was so awe-inspiring. . .and it made us believe *anything* was possible for *anyone*—even the most unsuspecting, shy woman in her 50s who had never left her small town.

That's a message that gives us all hope and joy, and makes us want to share with others.

Many of the most shareable emotions can also be correlated to a *second* dimension of impact: activation, or physiological arousal. Arousal is a state of readiness for action; the heart beats faster and blood pressure rises. Some emotions, like anger and anxiety, are high-arousal.

Funny content stimulates laughter, which is a high-arousal emotional response. Test it for yourself: Go ahead and head to Google and type in "cat cucumber video" and start to watch a couple (there are tons). Not to spoil it for you, but in every video, someone places a cucumber next to a cat—and the cat immediately jumps away like it's been electrocuted (it *is* pretty funny).

When you're laughing, you'll find you want to show someone, or at least *tell* someone about it. Nothing adds to an experience more than being able to share an emotion with someone else.

The *Always* "Like a Girl" video campaign is inspiring on so many levels. First, the simple fact that a female hygiene product brand was able to create such a powerful video says a lot. Not many people would know where to begin if tasked with creating a re-brand campaign for. . .well, pads! The foundational video for the campaign is an example of how to use content to tap into many high-arousal emotions, including awe, amusement, and surprise. . .and the result is the tens of millions of views it's received since they launched the campaign in 2018.

The first part of the video resonates in an often upsetting and personal way. We're shown that the phrase "like a girl"—which we have all heard, and likely even used without giving it much thought—can actually be insulting or belittling to women. This realization leads the viewer to a sense of shame, or even anger—but as the video goes on the focus of the video shifts to how young girls are responding to the phrase without the emotional baggage we attach to it as adults.

The reactions of the young girls are powerful and uplifting, taking us immediately from a negative reaction to a positive reaction—resulting in a powerful state of arousal or activation. Suddenly, we can't help but want to share. . .I know I did!

But not all emotions are created equal. Some emotions increase the probability of sharing, while others actually *decrease* it, so we need to pick the right emotions to evoke.

For example, in that same Huffpost study, sadness was found to be the least shareable emotion (7 percent). Emotions like general sadness, contentment, and calm—such as the feeling after getting a massage—draw low-arousal responses and work against the goal of encouraging us to share. We're neither fired up, nor inspired.

So how do we facilitate high-arousal reactions to our content? As humans, we tend to have the greatest emotional responses to personal stories and anecdotes, including explorations of challenges and obstacles (and victories!); conversations about things that surprise, amaze, or inspire us; debates that expand or change our minds; and real-life examples or testimonials that help us make decisions or choices.

A few years ago, the New York Times interviewed 2,500 people to determine the primary reasons they shared a story online. These were the main drivers:
- To bring valuable and entertaining content to one another
- To define themselves to others (establish or improve their image/reputation)
- To grow and nourish relationships (stay connected with others)
- For self-fulfillment (to feel more involved in the world)
- To get the word out on causes they care about.

Awe-inspiring and amusing content definitely link to the first three motives: sharing entertaining content brings value to our friends, shows others we have great taste, and spurs conversation and reactions—keeping us connected to one another.

Now see how a family-focused healthy living blog post demonstrates how drawing on emotion in content can work from another angle.

It was rainy, blistering hot, and we'd been stranded four, no five, days due to snow. Not all at the same time, of course, but the days in which I've heard "Mom, I'm bored" kind of blur together, you know?

The post starts with a sort of, "Haven't we all been here before?" moment that immediately grabs your attention, which is then followed up by 50 activities and distractions perfect for kids with cabin fever.

When you imagine the mental place many harried parents are in when they land on a post like this, you can also imagine how *understood* they feel when they read that line.

Did the post *need* that opening line to detail all 50-plus activities? No. Did the post need that line to keep a stressed parent coming back for more? *Yes.* It was a simple addition, but one that made all the difference in striking an emotional chord with the reader.

Later in the list of activities, the author begins to recommend some partner products who have sponsored the content. Because the reader believes the author understands exactly how they feel and what they need, they'll be all the more ready to trust those picks—which is good news for the marketer behind those products.

Great content is accurate

This is important, not only from an integrity perspective, but from a legal perspective. If you're espousing particular ideas, making particular recommendations, or making the case in favor of something, sticking with the facts will keep you out of hot water. If you make a claim, it needs to be backed up with data, or strong experiential proof.

An important note: it can be tempting to exaggerate or embellish some facts here and there to make something more entertaining or engaging—especially if you're in the early stages of a collaboration, where both brand and influencer are looking to impress one other.

It's exciting to see a piece of content that inspires you beyond your wildest dreams about your brand. . .but it might be beyond your wildest dreams precisely because it's *too good to be true.* You must vet the accuracy of any huge claims, amazing data, or big promises or exaggerations in influencer content, just in case.

It's like lying about your age, profession or status on a dating app; when you lure someone in on false or inaccurate pretenses, you may get the *first* date (or even a handful) but it will inevitably do more damage in the long run. As a business person, you can't afford to collaborate on content that makes misleading claims about your product or industry—and you don't want to work with someone who does that anywhere else in their content, either.

Great content is optimized for consumption

If you're a veteran of blogging or writing on the web, you know many ways of optimizing your written content to make it easy to read or scan, including:

- Using **bullets and lists** to break up information, and guide the reader's eye from point to point.
- Using **heads and sub-heads** to let the reader know what's coming next.
- Using bolding, italicization, and underlining to make certain words stand out.
- Clearly identifying where links will go by **hyperlinking sentences or phrases**—not just "click here."
- Keeping **sentences to two lines or fewer in a paragraph**, and keeping **paragraphs to 5 lines or fewer.**

This all makes sense, but there's more to optimizing content specifically for public consumption. It also means things like. . .

- **Clearly naming and tagging videos** so viewers know what they're getting in advance—especially via a search engine.
- **Providing clear and brief captions for images**, so viewers know what they're looking at (and where to find it, if it's a product).
- **Linking to any product or service recommendations**, so viewers don't have to do the legwork.
- **Keeping videos or podcasts to a digestible length**—no one has an hour for a YouTube video about how to replace a broken tile in your shower.
- **Keeping short-form content like Instagram and Facebook posts brief—** just enough not to be completely cut off in someone's feed, and to entice a viewer to see more.

Great content is high-quality

As content creators—both you and your partner influencer—want your content to be professional enough to be taken seriously, and high quality enough to establish your credibility.

This doesn't mean you need a master's degree in writing, a whole studio for your YouTube videos, or a $5,000 camera for your images. It means caring about things like clear visuals, clear sound, and well-edited and typo-free content.

If someone is taking time out of their day to watch one of my videos, I want to be certain the product I'm giving them is not only high-quality in terms of what I'm coaching them to do, but also in terms of how I shoot it, so it's easy and enjoyable to watch. If you have to strain to hear the sound, or shift your head in the midst of an awkward angle or fuzzy fidelity, I'm not doing my job.

A good rule of thumb is to take a look at a wide range of content in the competitive space you're in, and then aim to be comparable with the best 25 percent of the producers out there. You may not have everyone's resources. . .but you can try for their excellence.

Great content includes a Call-to-Action

As a marketer, entrepreneur or influencer, we can't overlook the key ingredient in all marketing content: the desired action!

This is what we mean when we refer to the CTA (call to action). We know to start each campaign or advertisement with a specific goal in mind; it follows, then, that our objective must be directly incorporated into whatever content we create to further our goals. The medium doesn't matter; whether it's an email newsletter, a live appearance, a blog post, a YouTube video, or Instagram story, we must start with the end in mind.

In other words, what is the desired action we want to occur when someone consumes our content?

This doesn't mean you always need a "CLICK HERE!" or "BUY NOW!"; it simply means giving viewers a next step to take. You're not degrading them by bluntly telling them what to do; rather, you're showing them how to put any tips, tricks, or ideas they've been given to work in their lives.

Every piece of content should have a purpose beyond just having a viewer see it, too—you want to suggest an action to take that responds to the content, or shares the content, or whatever your goal for that content happens to be. Humans are funny. . .we need to be told what to do! That's where a call to action (CTA) comes in.

You might recall me mentioning how I learned this firsthand when I started my YouTube channel. For every video in which I asked my viewers to SUBSCRIBE, my subscriptions went through the roof. If I changed the call to action to ask viewers to COMMENT, the comments exploded.

Conversely, if I *didn't* give a CTA, I wouldn't get many, if any, comments or subscriptions.

I quickly learned to say it *and* put it on screen.

Bottom line: when reviewing any of the content your influencers create, think about what you want to achieve and edit or insert the appropriate CTA to best optimize it to achieve the intended response.

THREE QUESTIONS ELEVATE AND INSPIRE YOUR INFLUENCER'S CONTENT CREATION

By now, you will have certainly discussed these questions with your influencer(s) during your initial agreement back-and-forth, but there is a certain magic in bringing them up at this stage with fresh context.

They are:

1. "What are you working on—and excited about—right now?"
2. "How can we help you achieve your career goals?"
3. "What can we provide to help you tell our story?"

Not only do these help you build a stronger connection with your influencer—which is something you should always be working on—they reinforce that you expect genuinely valuable, thoughtful content from them. Let them know they're on notice to bring their A-game. . . without sounding demanding or like a micro-manager.

Let's look at each of these questions in a bit more detail. Remember, these are intended not only to start a conversation that will inspire *both* of you to come up with some genuinely creative ideas together, but also create a deeper level of investment in your collaborative relationship.

"What are you working on—and excited about—right now?" Your influencer is not just a source of great content, they're a source of great insight into the market you want to speak to, and what matters to that market. You might also learn about new trends, or how the focus of your market might be shifting. Most of all, you'll tap into what your influencer is most passionate about.

"How can we help you achieve your career goals?" The answer might be anything from access to certain resources for content creation, to a higher profile on your social properties, or the endorsement to speak at an industry event. You've created an opportunity and forged an alliance, but to really build and strengthen the relationship, you must nurture it by continuing to revisit how you can help your influencer meet their goals.

"What can we provide to help you tell our story?" Do they want more background on your company's history or future? Would they like to get to know some of your internal subject matter experts? Do they need info on your mission, vision, or company values?

Different influencers will want to know different things to inform their content, so make sure you're there to provide what they need (and want) to do the best job possible.

COLLABORATE, DON'T CONTROL

If you're a marketer working with an influencer, you are there to provide direction, framework and messaging, while giving creative autonomy to the influencer. If you want to dictate exactly what's being produced, hire a traditional advertising or creative agency.

Influencer marketing is different, you've chosen someone who knows what they're doing. Their content, in whatever form (writing, acting, voice, and so on) is how they've built their community and commanded the influence you're after. They've got a finger on the pulse of their audience, and it's that knowledge that makes them so valuable to you.

Instead, focus on *supporting* your influencer in creating irresistible content—without exerting too much control, or robbing them of the authenticity their audience craves.

CHOOSING THE RIGHT CONTENT FORMAT

You want your content to provide your target audience with information in a manner they find approachable and appropriate—that's just common sense.

"But I've already narrowed down my influencer based on the right target audience and platform, so why are we back to talking about format?"

Every communication channel we have has evolved, and now offers various ways of presenting information—in other words, no longer is Instagram just photos, blogs are not just a feed of articles, and email is no longer just a medium for the exchange of messages.

Almost every influencer can produce a variety of content styles, even if they only use one platform. For example, an Instagram influencer may use a combination of video (live and recorded), photography, sketches, quotes, and infographics—all on a single account. So get creative!

Here is a list of different types of content to consider, regardless of platform:

- Lists
- Infographics
- How-to articles
- What posts (articles with title that starts with "what")
- Why posts (articles that attempt to answer a "why" question)
- Videos
- Live feed takeovers
- Webinars
- Images
- Quote cards
- Collages
- Podcasts
- Audio recordings

But don't be limited to this list, or any list; your content possibilities are only limited to your imagination, and will continue to grow as technology will continue to evolve.

The better you understand your audience's existing content habits, and the better you understand your influencer's existing audience and impact, the easier it will be to choose the right content format for your alliance. There's no substitute for research.

Make things easier on *everyone* with an editorial calendar

When it's time to actually create content, an editorial calendar can be a significant asset in setting expectations, and keeping everything on track. An editorial calendar maps out:

- The platforms selected (social networks, websites, traditional media, events, etc.. . .)
- The content types/formats
- The content creators
- Resources required
- Any information providers (to be included in the content)
- The editors and approvers
- Who is responsible for posting the content (if someone other than the creators)
- Deadlines for different phases of idea development, content creation, content review and approval, and content posting

With all those details in place, creating great content becomes a more linear, positive process for everyone involved—and everyone stays on the same page.

To make it even *easier* on you, we've made a few different templates for editorial calendars available for download on TheInfluencerCode.com/EditorialCalendar.

O NE OF THE BEST parts about writing *The Influencer Code* was having the chance to share amazing conversations with subject matter experts, to add their thoughts and insights to a subject I'm clearly passionate about.

And who better to get advice on creating killer content than the Queen of Content herself?

Ann Handley is "waging a war on content mediocrity"—and as Chief Content Officer at MarketingProfs, a training and education company with the largest community of marketers in its category, it's clear this is a battle she's equipped to win.

If you read Ann's work (and if you haven't, you should!) you will see so much of what I appreciate in great content in general: she's direct, she's witty, she's informative, and she knows how to help people write and create to the best of their abilities.

She is also a monthly columnist for Entrepreneur magazine, a member of the LinkedIn Influencer program, and co-author of the best-selling book on content marketing, *Content Rules: How to Create Killer Blogs, Podcasts, Videos, Ebooks, Webinars (and More) That Engage Customers and Ignite Your Business* (Wiley, originally published 2011. Paperback 2012.) Her most recent book, *Everybody Writes: Your Go-To Guide to Creating Ridiculously Good Content* (Wiley, 2014) is a Wall Street Journal bestseller.

In her capacity at MarketingProfs, Ann is both a digital marketing influencer herself, and someone who works extensively with influencers.

Let's dig in!

As an influencer, what kind of approach inspires you to work with a brand? What doesn't?

I always say no to "one-off" requests from brands I don't know, and generally "one-off" requests in general. It's not because I want someone to hire me for a year and pay me lots of money, but because I want to have a *relationship* with, or a connection to a brand before I work with them. That's what makes the influence relevant, and something I'll actually enjoy working on.

Have I met them? Do I like their products? Do I know the people behind the brand—as in, maybe the owner of a smaller brand, or the marketing team of a larger one?

I get approached a lot, and the ones I immediately say no to arrive out of nowhere with, "Hi, I'm from _____, and we want you to be an influencer for us." You're reaching out to me because you want to benefit from my influence—but I don't know you, and I certainly don't know if you're a good fit for me. How would I create content for you?

As much as you're worried about building *your* brand, I'm also concerned about *my* brand.

What do you want to know about a brand, or have the brand supply to you at the outset of a relationship?

This is why familiarity or some sort of existing interaction and relationship is important to me—because then I'll know what I need to know organically, and I won't need a ton of background.

When I work with agencies, they only bring people to me that I have some knowledge of or affinity with. Then, I can evaluate according to a symbiotic relationship: how will we both benefit?

Do you ever find brands pushing for creative control over what you're saying, or insisting on a particular topic?

I'm certainly open to *suggestions*, but I don't want to be *told* what to write about. As long as you're giving the influencer the ability to say no, I think a suggestion or some inspiration is fine—when the trust and the relationship are there, it doesn't feel unreasonable.

But if I don't know you *and* you want to tell me what I should say? *Nope.*

What do brands and companies who approach you, or who you have a relationship with, actually want you to collaborate on?

The approach or opportunity is really important, because it sets the tone. Here's an example of the kind of approach that really works for me: Oracle has worked with MarketingProfs over the years quite a few times, so I know them well. They asked me to create a video for Women's History Month.

Now, here's the typical play you'd expect in that moment: "Ann, talk about all the great women working at Oracle, and how Oracle hires and promotes them."

Instead, they said, "Tell us a story about a woman who has inspired you." It wasn't about Oracle, and it wasn't even really about me, but about me using my voice to acknowledge somebody who has been important in my life. It was a series as a partnership with a nonprofit called Girl Geeks who work to elevate the role of women in tech.

They sent me a t-shirt to wear in the video that had Girl Geeks and Oracle's names on it, so Oracle *was adjacent* to it, but it wasn't about selling Oracle—so I didn't feel weird wearing it in that context.

The result was such a great, meaningful piece of content that I went above and beyond without them asking me to—I shared it on more platforms, and more often than they'd even suggested. It was something I genuinely enjoyed doing, and the result reflected that.

To me, that's a prime example of doing influencer marketing well: building on a relationship, targeting content toward something that's bigger and beyond both of us. . .but yet aligns me with Oracle in a really unique way.

And I think it really paid off for them—it sent the message they wanted to send about how important the voices of women are, and how important they are to Oracle.

Is there any kind of influencer content you think *doesn't* work?

It's really situational—the content should fit the audience. The only thing I would call a "don't" is a one-off sponsored post; it feels interruptive and inauthentic. You get a feeling from it right away, and not a feeling that inspires you to want to learn more about the product or the company.

I would tell brands and influencers to think about authenticity first, before you come up with an idea or an approach: what's going to be real, and feel real to the people seeing that content? That will change from audience to audience, so give it thought.

Any other advice you'd give to brands working with influencers?

I talk to a lot of brands who ask how they can find or evaluate influencers to work with them.

Here's my advice: go to the next tier from the top. Everyone wants to work with the A-Listers and "rockstars" in their space, but I tell them to go for the "almost rockstars". That's what I've always done on with MarketingProfs and at our conferences—I want to *help* people become rockstars.

Typically, the people I reach out to are adding value to me already—retweeting me, or participating in conversations I'm a part of, or showing up to our seminars or B2B Forums. They're not the ones shouting the loudest, or the ones only showing up when they want to pitch me—they're already a part of my community.

I think those people are more motivated to help you do something great, and you can level up *together* through your collaboration. That's what I've always done as an editor, too, but it applies equally to working with influencers: your ability to help one another is what makes for the most successful relationship.

Thanks, Ann!

PUTTING IT ALL TOGETHER
Sperry: A content case study

Sperry, a classic American shoe retailer, is no stranger to influencer marketing; in fact, the brand is noted by marketing experts for their work with micro-influencers in particular. One of their first successful campaigns was #OdysseysAwait, where they featured content created for them on Instagram by micro-influencers—for free.

The campaign concept was simple: influencers and social media users were encouraged to share photos of the adventures and journeys they took in their Sperrys, using the #OdysseysAwait hashtag Sperry created.

The super-short "creative brief" couldn't have been more simple or easy to understand, but it also provided users and influencers with tons of freedom to interpret what "adventures" and "journeys" they could capture. Everyone could be part of the fun, regardless of how cool or famous or gorgeous or internationally traveled they actually were—a key aspect of making the campaign approachable and accessible.

If Sperry liked the content, they would share it with their (significantly large) audience—not just in the United States, but on all of Sperry's country-specific accounts (in multiple languages), too.

Sperry worked directly with influencers across different categories to signal-boost the campaign, and featured content on Twitter, Facebook, YouTube, and blogs—and Instagram, which proved to be the favorite platform for Sperry fans.

Given the ongoing success of #OdysseysAwait, Sperry has continued to encourage content creation amongst their followers, and to work directly with influencers. Other hashtags include #Sperryence, #SperryMyWay, #RockYourBoat, and #SperryStyle. Today, much of their Instagram imagery features non-Sperry photo credits from Instagram users who are now Sperry fans.

The #SperryForGood campaign was created to promote their new BIONIC line, made with recycled plastic recovered from marine environments. A partnership with Waterkeeper Alliance and BIONIC was a perfect fit for another digital marketing blitz. On site, Sperry shoppers were invited to share pledges to make more environmentally friendly choices:

As with #OdysseysAwait, Sperry fans were invited to share images of their BIONIC shoes in the wild on the #SperryForGood hashtag, with the hope of seeing their image shared on Sperry's main social accounts.

Sperry also worked with musical artist and influencer Josie Dunne and internet retailer Zappos to create a cross-channel, cross-brand

The Keys to Developing Killer Influencer Marketing Content

social good campaign, with Josie designing her own line of BIONIC shoes to be sold on Sperry.com and Zappos' own social-good focused website.

Why is Sperry's influencer marketing content so great?

Earlier in this chapter, we talked about creating content for the different stages in the sales journey, as well as the attributes of great content—and Sperry is winning on both fronts.

- **It creates content at every stage:** Everyone from macro influencers to happy customers could participate and in doing so they created a mix of content that bred everything from awareness (simple product placement), to social proof and conversion—real life reviews from other people.

- **It provides Sperry with a UGC goldmine. . .for free.** All Sperry needs to do is track, curate, and give credit for content they know their followers will enjoy.

- **It tells authentic stories about real people—which resonate with other real people.** Sperry's potential customers can "recognize" their lifestyle or values in their content. "Hey, those people look like my friends when we go camping!" or "Hey, I've been to that ballpark!"

- **It tells stories that inspire, amuse, excite—and other high-arousal emotions.** Whether the content is about an incredible travel experience, a dream-worthy day away from the stresses of life, or Josie Dunne's #SperryForGood collaboration, it inspires viewers to seek out an adventure of their own.

- **It broadens Sperry's brand perception.** As a brand best known for their preppy boat shoes, Sperry only stands to benefit from elevating fans of different ages, different backgrounds, different interests, different cultures, and different lifestyles. Again, real people seeing *real people*.

- **It encourages participants to bring their "A-game".** Great content spurs on great content, and makes everyone want to capture their Sperry moment in a memorable, high-quality way.
- **It introduces Sperry to new influencers—and valuable collaborators.** Several of Sperry's Instagram followers and hashtag users went on to do paid campaign work with the brand.
- **It encourages involvement from non-digital influencers, too.** *Anyone* can use the hashtag to celebrate their Sperry-wearing adventures—not just influencers. Many Sperry lovers and Sperry newbies alike took part.
- **It provides Sperry with rich market research data.** Which shoes get the most shots? Which influencers start rich conversations versus simply gathering likes? What brand sentiments— for better or for worse—can they extract from the content their fans create? What can they learn—lifestyle, interests, other hashtag usage, other brand affinities and purchasing behaviors— about their audience?
- **It provides both targeted *and* evergreen content.** Sperry can put the focus on a particular style or line of shoe, or simply keep their audience sharing the adventures they have in their Sperrys, all year round.
- **It continues to churn out content, years later.** Every marketer dreams of a campaign that lives on, remaining relevant and active without additional input from the brand itself. To this day, Sperry continues to see fresh activity on their hashtags daily, without needing to push too hard for engagement.

Recap and Review

KEY POINTS

1. **Influencer content should be tailored to propel prospective customers through the consumer decision journey.**

    a. Different types of influencers will work best at different stages:

        i. Awareness: Content is focused on providing the viewer value and engaging them. Content shouldn't try to push the product or service yet; there is a need to build trust first and *that* starts with value.

        ii. Consideration: Content needs to propel the viewer past awareness of your brand into actual interest and desire. Case studies, valuable information and expertise, unique product/service use cases, and inspiring stories work well in this stage.

        iii. Action: This is where micro, nano, and personal influencers are most powerful, writing reviews or telling others about their experience with your brand. People trust people, and you can move someone from consideration to a definite 'yes' when they see the social proof of others loving the brand.

2. **Great content works overtime for you.**

    a. It provides the answers to questions and solutions to problems—it does not try to convince you of its value, it simply satisfies a need.

    b. It sparks emotion—and emotion leads to action. Emotion also leads to sharing; whether your content elicits joy,

amusement or interest, people want to share their reactions with others, which increases your reach.

   c. It establishes credibility and value, which is critical to building trust. Think of great content as a freely available portfolio demonstrating your willingness and ability to provide value to others.

   d. It's easy-to-digest and enjoyable. While not all content need necessarily be completely absorbable in a glance, your content should be consumer-focused—meaning people should *want* to consume it.

   e. It has a purpose. Just because you're creating content in Step Three of the Influencer Code does not mean you shouldn't be keeping your goals in mind! All content you create should work towards driving the desired behaviors in the end consumer.

3. You can continue to foster and strengthen the relationship with your influencer during the content creation phase by asking these three questions:

   a. What are you working on—and excited about—right now?

   b. How can we help you achieve your career goals?

   c. What can we provide to help you tell our story?

4. Streamline the process with an editorial calendar.

   a. The structure that comes with having target dates and deadlines for key deliverables ensures that all the different pieces of any campaign continue running smoother. The more detail about process and production you can include, the better—setting clear expectations will save you from unpleasant surprises.

APPLYING THE PRINCIPLES OF INFLUENCER MARKETING

15

The Code in Action
The Power of Social Good and Charitable Partnerships

From the daily news bombarding us with bad tidings to the continuing rise of social media, it can sometimes seem like we're in the midst of an epidemic of negativity and narcissism. Yet most people, at their core, want to do good, help others and improve society—and they are increasingly expecting the same from both private and public companies.

In response, brands are forming what are sometimes called "brand synergy partnerships": collaborative agreements between a business and a civic organization or charity. These partnerships are designed to be mutually beneficial, with both sides sharing resources and audiences. A charity might receive funding, sponsorship and awareness-raising, while a business benefits by everything from positive media coverage to a more engaged workforce and customer or client base.

You don't have to be a massive global company to form a charity partnership. Small, local partnerships can be just as advantageous for your business.

Corporations need more than just revenue

With 55% of consumers willing to pay more for products from socially responsible companies and 93 percent of the world's companies now publishing annual Corporate Responsibility reports (CSR), it's clear that for-profit organizations should be looking to social good causes to form potential influencer alliances—alliances that will set them apart from their competitors.

Although the direct goal of the program should not be tied to revenue, a strong corporate responsibility program is one of the best moves a brand can make toward their future growth and positive business outcomes. More and more companies are using CSR and brand synergy partnerships as a way to push innovation, cost savings, brand differentiation, customer engagement, and employee engagement.

If you've ever attended a charity event, you've likely seen signs that advertise a set of sponsors or corporate partners that have helped make the event possible in some way; they might give money to secure a venue, contribute to the costs, or provided needed goods and services to ensure the event goes off without a hitch.

This is how brands have been involved in charitable work for decades: offering their resources to help nonprofits with events or operations, plain and simple. Many major brands will partner with several organizations at the same time, depending on their resources, their philanthropic goals, their alignment with the organization's mission—and, often most pointedly, public relations.

If a business is having reputation issues, they can strategically choose a charity partner to help re-shape and/or counter-balance any negative perceptions that exist about them, and move their brand perception in a more positive direction.

This is how you end up with marathons sponsored by Coca-Cola, or auto manufacturers aligning with environmental groups, or banks contributing to anti-poverty charities.

But where once it was enough to join the logo farm on a gala sign, their customers and employees—even their stockholders—expect less logo and more *action*.

Lip service won't cut it, because consumers are increasingly making it their business to know *exactly* where their money is going and to demand authenticity and integrity from the brands they choose to invest in.

According to a 2018 study from Accenture Strategy, 63 percent of consumers are actively buying products from companies that reflect their personal values and beliefs, and 62 percent want companies to take a stand on the social, cultural, environmental and political issues that are close to their hearts. 47 percent of those surveyed have stopped doing business with a company that *doesn't* reflect their values.

A 2018 Sheldon Group study found that a mighty 86 percent of consumers believe that companies should take a stand on social issues—64 percent of those who said it's "extremely important" for a company to take a stand on a social issue said they were "very likely" to purchase a product based on that commitment.

This means that companies need to consider a greater purpose beyond making money. In a time when businesses are mostly commodities, a clear, active commitment to social good can become a major differentiator.

Sir Richard Branson, the billionaire mogul and Virgin Group founder, released a book entitled, *Screw Business As Usual*, where he trumpets the impact of social good involvement on our planet's wellbeing. . .and on a company's bottom line.

According to Branson, businesses who get involved in social causes have more satisfied and motivated employees, see higher profits through increased customer engagement, save resources, and see a greater impact than any nonprofit could, operating on its own.

In an interview with *Fast Company*, Branson offered his Virgin Air subsidiary as an example of how their social commitment is making a very straightforward impact on how they do business: Branson is aiming to have 100% clean-burning fuels by 2020. "The airline industry could become one of the cleanest industries, rather than one of the dirtiest industries in the world."

If you're a consumer who cares deeply about the environment, and Virgin is flying where you want to go, odds are that you'll opt to buy your ticket with them versus an airline that doesn't have an environmental stance—even if it costs a little more. Virgin employees are also incredibly proud of their commitment to reducing fossil fuel use, which makes them more likely to stick around, versus heading to a less socially responsible company.

The depth of the impact goes beyond the obvious

Aside from the very real feeling of making a positive difference in the world, the right charity or social good cause campaign or partnership can also act as an influencer by bringing you:

- **More engaged customers and increased sales:** This is the big aim for many businesses, and the core idea in cause market- ing (more on that a bit later.) Accenture's study and the Sheldon Group findings indicate that a majority of consumers not only pay attention to company values—they choose to stay or go *depending* on a company's values. When you boldly state those values through your actions as a company, you inspire custom- ers who share those values to align their own brand with yours. This is going to be an area of impact for years to come, too: two- thirds of millennials and Gen Z express a preference for brands that have a clearly expressed set of values or point of view.

- **More engaged—and profitable—employees:** As Branson told *Fast Company*, "They realize that we are more than just a money-making machine. And, I think, because they're proud of working for the company. Because they're proud of going out in the evenings and having a drink and saying that they work for Virgin. I think they'll make that little bit of an extra effort, which is good for the bottom line."

- **Brand halo—and exposure to new audiences:** Companies who partner with charitable organizations can definitely see a "brand halo" impact from their involvement—and the donors and supporters of the charity are much more likely to look into, and buy from businesses who support what they support.

- **Public relations storytelling:** Publicists love charitable involvement because it's an easy public relations win, and a shortcut to creating content that will enlighten and inspire, rather than just promote.

- **Crisis rehab:** Companies who have gone through a crisis can see a rebound in their reputation through their charitable involvement, especially if there's a direct line from the crisis to the cause's vision and mission. This is a tricky one, however—charities and consumers alike can see a PR whitewash from a mile away, as opposed to a serious commitment to improve. The actions you take, and the time and resources you give to them, will be critical in overcoming skepticism.

- **Increased sales:** If you opt to donate a percentage of the profits from the sales of a particular product to a charity, the community support you experience through your charitable partnership could have a serious impact on your bottom line. Suddenly you have a whole army of new brand advocates—so even after donating generously to a cause, you'll end up with a healthier bottom line. Everyone wins!

Putting your money where your values are and how brands can get involved

Now let's look at some of the ways brands can get involved with influential social good causes. Depending on the size of your business, and the resources you have to devote to your social good efforts, some options may be more appropriate or accessible than others.

Partnering with a nonprofit or charity: This is the most straightforward way most brands get involved in social good. . .but nowadays, their employees and customers expect a little more than a check sent to earn a tax deduction. If you want to team up with a charity, consider the following steps to create a seamless partnership:

- **Consider what makes sense with your industry and your brand:** As with the example of Coca-Cola sponsoring marathons, sometimes organizations choose a charity to "make up" for a negative impact they may have. While this can sometimes be a good strategy, it can also encourage skeptics to question your altruism. Make sure whatever organization you choose can live with who you are as a business *and* you can live up to their values as a charity.
- **Get your employees involved in the choice:** You could do a survey of different causes or organizations, or invite your employees to submit organizations they're already involved with for your consideration.

- **Be clear on your commitment:** Are you going to give a certain percentage of your profits from a particular product or campaign? Are you going to donate a lump sum toward a particular initiative? Are you going to encourage your employees to give or volunteer, too? Make sure you map out what's going to happen—and then live up to your end of the bargain.
- **Be careful about tooting your horn too loudly:** The best possible public relations for your brand will come from the charity or cause itself, when they tell the story of the impact of your contribution to their supporters. You can share what you've done through your own communications, but through the lens of sharing the *charity's* good work—not yours.

Establish your desired mission impact, and back it up with action: Whole Foods Market gives 5 percent of their proceeds to causes they're passionate about each year—but the actual causes they support change each year, according to the impact they want to make that year.

They might opt to provide small business loans to indigenous women to increase their autonomy, or provide resources to an environmental group dedicated to preserving wetlands, or fund a free school breakfast program in a low-income area—all past initiatives they've supported—depending on their bigger philanthropic goal.

Make a change from within: Virgin's renewable fuel goal is a perfect example of a company's commitment to a bigger benefit than their bottom line. Patagonia, the clothing and outdoor equipment retailer, made headlines in 2019 with their declaration that they prioritize the sale of their personalized or branded clothing options to organizations with a positive social impact. . .upsetting the scores of finance and investment brands who can't get enough of their signature Patagonia vests.

Some consumers thought they were "cutting off their nose to spite their fleece", but the positive response to their choice from B Corporations and different social good organizations confirmed they'd made the right choice.

Pay your employees to use their time to do good: Many businesses are offering their employees paid days to volunteer with either a particular charitable partner, or the cause of their own choice. According to a 2018 Fortune Magazine study, firms like Salesforce.com, Intuit and Deloitte allow their employees to volunteer for organizations as part of their paid work week. Many also contribute or match donations to their employees' favorite charities, which brings us to the next option. . .

Create a donation matching program: About 65% of the Fortune 500 offer employee donation matching programs to their employees, per DoubleTheDonation.com, but businesses of all sizes can get involved. If you want to offer a donation doubling program, consider:

- **Your matching ratio:** Do you want to stick with a 1:1 match, or go bigger?
- **Your maximum match:** If your employees have a significant ability to give because of higher salary rates, you might want to consider a "match up to ____" limit to keep yourself from putting your bottom line in bad shape from over-commitment.
- **Your standards for matching:** A good rule of thumb is that the charity needs to be a registered 501 (c)(3) and in good standing with the IRS to earn a match. This information should be readily

available from the charitable organization in question—and if it's not, it should probably be a no-go.

Create a foundation: Starting a nonprofit arm of a company for charitable giving is popular option on a major corporate level, but might be a little too intensive in terms of preparation and time and financial resources for a smaller company. If you do opt to start a nonprofit, your tax obligations will change—as will the requirements around transparency for your business operations. Your best bet is to hire a foundation consultant to help you navigate the ins and outs.

Become a B Corporation: Benefit corporations, widely known as "B corporations" are companies that make a set of commitments to corporate responsibility and transparency as a foundational element of how they do business. These corporations are re-certified regularly according to their adherence to B corporation standards, and undergo an intensive impact assessment process to even be considered for certification.

Companies of all sizes and in a wide variety of industries have opted to become B corporations, and many consumers who put a premium on social responsibility go out of their way to work with brands who have made this commitment, including major players like Athleta, Patagonia, Ben & Jerry's, Method, and Seventh Generation.

CAUSE MARKETING: GOOD FOR THE WORLD, GREAT FOR YOUR BOTTOM LINE

Sir Richard Branson is clear about how his commitment to social responsibility has made a positive impact on his bottom line—and that's also why brands from every corner of industry are actively pursuing what is often called "cause marketing."

Cause marketing, simply defined, is when a business develops a charitable program, initiative, or campaign that not only raises their profile, but makes an impact on their profitability through increased consumer or industry engagement. The best cause marketing creates a win-win relationship between a change-making organization of movement and the brand that champions it: the cause is amplified, and the brand sees an uptick in positive sentiment, customer loyalty, *and* sales.

While cause marketing has been around for years now in some form, consumers are increasingly eager for social good alignment with brands by the year According to Edelman's 2019 Trust Barometer, "73% of people agree that a company can take specific actions that both increase profits *and* improve the economic and social conditions in the communities where it operates—a nine-point increase from 2018."

Let's take a look at a recent cause marketing effort by MGM Resorts where the depth and authenticity of the alignment between the cause and the brand made for a successful campaign.

"Universal Love": MGM Resorts takes a stand for equality

In 2019, advertising giant McCann New York partnered with MGM Resorts, to release a special album called "Universal Love" on all of the major music streaming services, as well as a vinyl release. Each of the songs on the album was a reimagining of classic wedding songs with new pronouns to make them more LGBTQ-friendly.

The artists involved included both heavy hitters like Bob Dylan and Zoey Deschanel's hipster-beloved musical partnership, She & Him.

What were the goals of the campaign?

MGM Resorts' goal was to send a message to the LGBT+ community that they were welcome at MGM Resorts properties, and that they wouldn't have to endure the indignities and insecurities that LGBT+ couples often face in traveling together.

A Virgin Holidays study from 2017 looking at how LGBT+ couples feel while on holiday revealed that, while 84% of straight couples felt comfortable showing affection to a partner while they were abroad, only 1 in 20 LGBT+ travelers felt comfortable showing open affection with a loved one.

LGBT+ couples also expressed concerns about judgment from the hotel staff—for example, many had been offered rooms with two single beds versus a couples' arrangement. They also feared abuse from their fellow vacationers, and a lack of response from security, should any abuse occur. MGM Resorts is committed to doing better by their LGBT+ customers.

On top of that, according to a recent Google study, 84% of self-identified LGBT consumers in the U.S. are readily engaged by LGBT+ friendly advertising and almost 60% of millennial women on YouTube say they are more likely to remember a brand that's LGBT+ friendly.

Why was the campaign a good fit for MGM Resorts?

MGM Resorts not only believes in the cause—they live it as a company. Human Rights Campaign has recognized the company as one of the most LGBT+ friendly employers in the United States—while also maintaining those same standards with their overseas employees, even in areas without standard diversity practices.

They actually received a perfect score of 100 on the 2019 Corporate Equality Index (CEI), a benchmarking survey on corporate policies and practices related to LGBTQ workplace equality administered by the Human Rights Campaign Foundation.

In addition, for more than ten years before same-sex marriages were legalized, they were performed at MGM Resorts.

What were the results?

In the end, "Universal Love" generated 2.5 billion media impressions, with the album ranking 9th place in the pop category on iTunes. It also increased positive perception of MGM Resorts among the LGBT+ community by 40%.

Why was the campaign a success?

- **It targeted both a cause *and* a consumer:** LGBT+ equality is a cause currently very much in the zeitgeist—but behind the attention and debates around LGBT+ freedoms, there are LGBT+ consumers with a considerable disposable income looking for companies who respect their lifestyles and needs.
- **It struck the right tone:** The "Universal Love" album offered like-minded people the opportunity to celebrate the advancement of LBGT+ freedoms in a fun, approachable, and celebratory way—an approach that feels true to a resort company.
- **It skipped the hard sell—but it hit it out of the park in terms of marketing:** There was no direct sales push or purchase associated with the campaign, but the nature of the strategy highlighted many of the positive attributes MGM Resorts would

want to elevate through any of its marketing efforts: accessible, celebratory, inclusive, fun, and romantic.

- **It was true to the company's ethics and beliefs:** Again, as an award-winning model of LGBT+ inclusivity, MGM Resorts was perfectly positioned to deliver the critical message of the campaign.

Now that we've talked about:
- How social good causes and organizations are influencers in and of themselves
- How brands can get involved with social good organizations and causes, and about,
- The power of well-executed cause marketing

Let's look at how a charitable organization has capitalized on influence to advance their goals.

Using influence to boost nonprofit performance: charity: water

Social good campaigns that capitalize on influence can clearly have a positive impact on your business outcomes and the strength of your brand—but when nonprofit organizations put influencer marketing to work to achieve their goals, the results can be just as high-impact.

When Scott Harrison founded **charity: water** 13 years ago, he was two years into a break from his work as a club promoter in New York— two years he'd committed to working with the poor and marginalized in Liberia alongside the charity, Mercy Ships. While his career had delivered all the material goods and outward success he'd thought he wanted, he felt an emptiness, and believed that a step back from the "glamorous life" would do his heart some good.

His desire to bring more meaning to his life wouldn't end with that two-year commitment, however—rather, it would change the entire trajectory of his career. In the midst of his volunteer work, he recognized that many of the issues and obstacles he was seeing in Liberian communities came from a basic lack of access to clean water and sanitation.

He founded *charity: water* in 2006 with the goal of increasing access to fresh water for communities across the world. To date, the organization has funded over 23,000 clean water projects in 24 countries, to the tune of over $252 million in funding.

charity: water has long been recognized for its exceptional branding and marketing savvy—no surprise, given Harrison's own image-focused background. The organization focuses on straightforward, consistently branded, highly visual communications that give donors and potential supporters a compelling look into every aspect of the work they do.

They invite their viewers into the stories of the individuals and communities they serve, and make them feel like they're genuinely a part of their journey toward a better life.

One of the most successful aspects of charity: water's marketing and development efforts has been their work with both macro- *and* micro-influencers to reach out to their communities.

Many of these have begun with charity: water's signature birthday campaigns, where followers are encouraged to donate to specific projects as a way to celebrate a charity: water supporter's special day. Those who pledge to give to their campaign are encouraged to pledge their own birthdays, too.

Celebrity philanthropy website *Look to the Stars* lists more than 43 actors, artists, and musicians who have worked with charity: water to promote their efforts, including Justin Bieber, Julia Roberts, Blake Shelton, Alicia Keys, Tony Hawk, Will Farrell, and Zac Efron. These people were connections (or connections of connections) that Scott Harrison had made through his career prior to charity: water—and likely would have been enough to keep his cause going for the foreseeable future.

But his vision didn't end there.

charity: water reached out to social media celebrities like pioneering YouTuber Felix Kjellberg, known as "PewDiePie", helping him celebrate hitting 10 million subscribers. . .in a campaign that ultimately raised funds for over 20 water projects, and helped foster a sense of greater social responsibility in his followers.

Again, these types of high-profile partnerships keep charity: water in the headlines, but much of the money they raise comes from inspiring their less high-profile supporters who think of themselves as influencers, too.

After seeing both celebrities *and* friends with just a few followers donating to charity: water, Laura "Pistachio" Fitton of Hubspot and author of *Twitter for Dummies* was inspired to create a holiday campaign where she raised money for a water filter project in a Cambodian village, which included the promise of a special handmade pendant—crafted by Laura—for the first 11 people who gave $65 to her project.

Laura ultimately raised a greater number than her goal amount for two reasons: her followers trusted her choice of charity, and they loved the personal touch and commitment she brought to her campaign—and she continues to partner with charity: water at special moments to this day.

On charity: water's website, would-be fundraisers are given the training and tools they need to set up their own campaigns, whether for a special occasion or milestone, or just because.

By encouraging their supporters to make a personalized, targeted pitch to their own communities, charity: water is able to overcome some of the resistance and disconnection that nonprofits often face when reaching out to potential supporters. They capitalize on each individual's sphere of influence—whether 20 people, 200 people, or 200,000 people—to overcome skepticism.

In a 2018 interview with Brene Brown, Scott Harrison summed up how charity: water encourages their supporters to influence *others* to take positive action:

> "Optimism and hope are essential components of the charity: water brand. We use positive imagery and uplifting storytelling, and work hard to never guilt or shame our community into donating. Our goal is to inspire people by showing them what's possible—the transformative outcome of radical and selfless generosity, changing lives of those in desperate need by providing access to clean water.
>
> We let the joy that comes with the act of giving speak for itself and attract the right people and the right type of generosity to our cause."

Three takeaways to inspire you from charity: water

Consider the power of influence at every level. Yes, charity: water works with major mainstream and social media celebrities—but the vast majority of their campaign creators have significantly smaller followings.

They are inspired to become involved because charity: water's pitch validates *everyone's* capacity to make a difference, at every level; and the value of every single dollar that comes their way to have an impact on a project, a village, and a family.

Give influencers the tools to tell their story—and then encourage them to get personal. charity: water offers influencers at every level the means to make their pitch and raise funds in a safe and secure way, but they also encourage them to make their campaign personal by tying it to a birthday celebration, a major milestone in their life or career, or the beginning of a challenge, like a marathon.

By tying each campaign to something unique in the fundraiser's life, they give their supporters another reason to care—and to give.

Keep it simple. The most effective fundraising campaigns keep their pitches simple and straightforward, clearly tying the actions and contributions of their supporters to a measurable impact on the organization's mission, or a tangible result.

When you invite thousands of people to spread your message through their own efforts, a simple ask and a clear impact are essential. charity: water accomplishes this by keeping their messaging short and sweet, and tying each dollar contributed to a specific project in a specific place with a specific goal.

Our global economy demands corporate responsibility, which is why smart brands are establishing partnerships with nonprofits, and actively moving to engage their community in the good work they are doing together.

And as with every mutually beneficial influencer alliance, a charitable partnership will be most successful when both the nonprofit and the corporation are deeply invested in one another's success—and when the impact goes far beyond a token act of volunteerism.

16

The Code of Tomorrow
The Future of Influencer Marketing

Thinking about the future of marketing and figuring out what's next is one of my favorite things. Some people have "futurist" in their job title, but the desire to look ahead—and act in response—is part of any good marketer's DNA. Not only do we need to be creative and analytical in our approach, but we need to be on top of a rapidly changing landscape that has given way to the democratization of everything from creativity and media to education and commerce. Never before has marketing been more challenging. . .*or* more exciting.

We have more ways to connect with one another than ever before, with new platforms, new applications, and new devices showing up by the day . . .giving brands more opportunities to connect with us, too.

While technology is the main driver for this pace of change, we can't overlook some of the principle social shifts that have been evolving for years.

Influencer marketing—done right—can help brands and business owners address many of the technological and social shifts in our society, and address them *more effectively* than many other marketing methodologies.

It has already changed the game for many brands and businesses, helping them to connect with today's consumer, and win not just their attention, but their trust.

I've divided my predictions into three influencer-specific categories:

- How technology is evolving influencer marketing
- How the influencer-brand relationship is evolving
- How influencer marketing is evolving the marketing world

By the time you read this, some of these predictions may be in the works as functional reality, but at the end of this chapter, I'll tell you where you can go to learn how marketing *and* influencer marketing are evolving—from the perspective of your colleagues, peers, and marketing experts.

TECHNOLOGY CONTINUES TO TRANSFORM INFLUENCER MARKETING

Neuromarketing: Your brain is telling on you

As humans, we're not terribly good at predicting our future actions, or explaining why we make a particular choice or decision. As much as we want to think we can, we often don't know what truly influences our decisions. We have so many messages rattling around in our brains at any given time, how could we possibly narrow it down.

Until now, the only way companies have been able to understand what influences our behavior has been by observing or asking them directly. Not anymore.

Say hello to **neuromarketing.**

By definition, neuromarketing (sometimes known as consumer neuroscience) is a new field of marketing that leverages medical technologies like functional Magnetic Resonance Imaging (fMRI) to study the brain's responses to marketing stimuli.

While it could still be considered a "frontier science," neuromarketing has built some buzz over the past five years via several groundbreaking studies.

In an academic trial led by INSEAD's Hilke Plassmann, the brains of test subjects were scanned as they tasted three wines with different price points. Their brains registered each of the wines differently, with their neural signatures indicating a preference for the most expensive wine. In actuality, all three wines were the same.

In another experiment, an MRI revealed that *when* consumers see price may have an impact on their mental calculation of value. When the price of a product was displayed before the consumer was exposed to the product, the neural data differed from when it was displayed *after* exposure, suggesting two very different mental calculations: "Is this product worth the price?" when the price came first, and "Do I like this product?" when the product came first.

One of the biggest struggles in influencer marketing is choosing the right person to deliver the right message to encourage the right action with your desired audience. Even when you do your due diligence, and select an influencer who has the trust of your target customer, you can't predict whether they will be able to transfer their audience trust to your brand. Additionally, even a high-impact influencer may fail to encourage the desired action if they're operating within the wrong context, or with the wrong content. So how do we find out what works?

Neuromarketing can help marketers select an influencer who empirically resonates with their audience, and strategize the type of content that fosters the reaction they want from their consumers. By taking a look at the brain's reaction to specific stimuli, they can minimize error in their collaborations and content, and discover who will influence their target market to action.

Neuromarketing has the credibility to become much more widely adopted by brands and businesses. Companies will now have access to powerful tools to predict what and who will *biologically and psychologically* influence people—making neuromarketing one of the most valuable tools companies will have to strategize their marketing efforts, and to choose what and who to align with.

However, while some innovative companies are already tapping into this technology, it is still much too expensive for most, and the technology could use some refinement—but in the future, it will no doubt become cheaper, easier and more widespread.

Your watch is watching you: Wearable tech and bots as influencers

Plenty of us are already dependent on wearable tech to map our vital statistics, to gauge the success of our workouts, to track our caloric input, to tell us when we need to slow down and take a breath, and to keep track of our screen time.

But all that data we're feeding into our devices will ultimately impact more than our health; marketers are going to take full advantage of what they can learn from our devices. I predict that wearable technology will continue to advance to the point where the data they produce is so accurate, specific, and customized that we'll actually start to become our own influencers, via our devices.

Here's an example: your FitBit or Apple Watch indicates to you that you burn the most over the course of 24 hours on the days you choose to swim versus any other workout.

If weight loss is your goal, this bit of data will make you partial to swimming, versus CrossFit or cycling or circuit training, or whatever trendy fitness thing you could opt to do instead—no matter who is leading it, no matter who is asking you to go, and no matter which influencers are touting it. You've got all the confirmation you need that you're making the right call.

Let's say you're out for a walk, and you happen to pause in front of a car dealership to check out the new Honda CRV. Suddenly your device chimes in to let you know that this vehicle is a smart choice for you, given your current auto costs—and that you could save money if you buy one. Further, it will let you know that an upgrade to the CRV is a smart move given your driving patterns, and will actually save you money in less than 12 months.

Or how about the moment you order a glass of wine at your favorite restaurant? Your device knows you have a sensitivity to sulfates, so it suggests a new organic vintage that filters out the sulfates. . .and lo and behold, it just happens to be on the menu where you are.

While we already have targeted advertising based on our buying and search history. . .but in the future, those recommendations are going to get *much* more personal and specific—based on our real-time biometrics and daily health.

"Amanda, how is that helpful to influencers? Are you telling me that people are listening to their watches. . .not other people?"

This is where our ability to think differently about influencer marketing makes us stand out and succeed because we don't limit our influencer marketing strategies to *people*. Instead, consider how you could insert yourself into that person-device interaction by having your brand or product featured in the recommendations that pop up for device wearers.

What if a fitness tracker recommended your electrolyte drink on a hot day when someone's workout takes a turn for the sluggish? Or if Siri recommends your brand of toilet paper to individuals making grocery lists with the incentive that you offer $1 of every purchase to a charity?

But the possibilities don't end with devices—because we do a lot of interacting with applications ("apps") and automated chatbots these days, too.

Think about how you search for travel plans: the "Hello Chat" bot that pops up becomes the influencer by giving you real time recommendations.

Chat bots have already become acquainted with casual language, emojis, and GIFs, which makes them approachable and engaging to their audiences. it's time to start thinking about the potential for collaboration with the bots who are chatting with, and guiding your customers.

Digital influence is, and will continue to be an entirely valid form of influence—if we're ready to think differently and embrace it. And that brings us to the *next level* of digital influence.

Digital avatars that feel just as real as the people who follow them

Computer Generated Imagery (CGI) influencers aren't technically real *or* human (other than the humans who envision and program them), but they are already starting to revolutionize influencer marketing.

Miquela Sousa, or Lil Miquela, is a 19-year old verified Instagrammer from California with cool clothing, social causes she supports, and a devoted following of people who listen to her on Spotify and follow her every move on social platforms. She was chosen as one of TIME Magazine's 25 most influential people on the internet in 2019. . .and she's not actually a real person.

Lil Miquela even sells custom merchandise with her face and name on the products—including a $30 pair of socks. Her fans are willing to shell out. . .and that's why we need to pay attention to the potential of CGI influencers.

There is already a blurred line between reality and artificiality in the online personas of many influencers, celebrities, and social media stars. That's how we ended up with "Instagram Life": a phrase that refers to how we edit and curate our lives for public consumption.

But there's a whole other level of curation and idealization possible when you take the real humans out of the influencer.

You might want to scoff, but these CGI influencers are only marginally less real than some of our living, breathing influencers. With the right lighting, filters, Photoshop editing, a little help from estheticians and plastic surgeons, and the right camera angle, *anybody* can make themselves look like an entirely different person online.

Yes, they're technically humans, but what they're sharing with the world is a construction. We only see many celebrities and influencers from particular angles, in particular poses, wearing particular clothing, in particular environments—without exception. Kim Kardashian is so deeply in control of how she's seen that she might as well be a cartoon. . .so why couldn't a cartoon possess the influence that Kim does?

As marketers, we need to be developing relationships with the companies and individuals who create these CGI influencers. Just like every brand, each one has a team of real people behind them. By building a relationship with that team, you'll be able to influence the CGI influencer to build a relationship with you.

Artificial reality (AR) and virtual reality (VR)

We're about to enter a world we can barely envision at this point, as the big digital marketing platforms begin to adopt real-time virtual reality technologies.

People won't just want to *consume* content, they'll want to *experience* it first-hand. We will move on from Facebook Live and Instagram

Live, and a new wave of social platforms will emerge that put VR and AR to work—and people will start actually living the experience provided by portable technologies.

Influencers are now using VR to live stream their day-to-day existence. Whether they're putting on makeup or travelling the world, influencers will continue to provide viewers with a deep window into their lives—turning them not just into spectators, but participants.

For brands (especially marketers) this highly sensory and specific experience allows for a much more authentic depiction of products and services than even the most valuable traditional content could ever bring.

This is an answer to the reality that social media is extremely limited in terms of live experience. AR & VR sessions allow followers to communicate personally, directly and instantaneously with the Influencer.

Marketers and brands will include more live experience require-ments for collaborations with influencers through the use of VR head-sets—which also allows more collection on consumer insights and data, a big win for marketers in which insights are often still vague and hard to track.

Real-time content that you can almost reach out and touch is going to be the next step in the influencer marketing revolution, and will change the game as we know it.

The inevitable backlash: keeping the human in influencer marketing

With wearable tech, bots, and digital avatars becoming influencers, there will inevitably be a craving for real human touch—and thus a shift for marketers to emphasize the human aspect of influence.

Brands will work to bring more human elements into influencer activities, including more live events where fans can meet and interact with influencers both in person and virtually.

If humanity is what people are hungry for in an increasingly digital world, go the extra mile to make this a part of your marketing strategy. This will be what makes the compassionate and savvy brands stand out from the crowd.

INFLUENCERS AND BRAND RELATIONSHIPS ARE EVOLVING

I invited my friend, futurist, speaker, author, and marketing expert, Rohit Bhargava, to weigh in on this section, and he offered some great insights into how brands will choose the influencers they work with.

Influencers will seek out "content peers"

From Rohit:

"The brands who will get influencer marketing right will be the most content-driven brands who've put the time and effort into providing value to their audiences.

If they're already creating great content, have a solid perspective, and are regularly putting value out there, they'll be able to interact with influencers from the vantage point of a *peer*.

That's a much more powerful place to collaborate from, and amplifies what both of you are doing."

Sound familiar? This perspective is at the core of the Influencer Code. Forward-thinking, goal-oriented marketing created by marketers working *together* with impactful influencers—not on commission, but through collaboration. Relationships, such as the ones we've stressed throughout this book, are inherently between equals—between *peers*—rather than between client and contractor.

Influencers as long-term partners and ambassadors

As brands and businesses come to understand the power of influence to create connections with their ideal audiences, I predict one-off, short-term contracts will become a thing of the past. Granted, short-term arrangements will remain a great way to test whether an influencer is a good fit—but one-offs as a primary influencer marketing strategy will be perceived as short-changing influencers and brands alike.

With so many social influencers speaking into the void and consumers becoming sensitive to the fact that many of these product placements are simply advertising, brands will recognize that human billboards *aren't* the way to go.

A big part of yielding long term influencer/brand relationships will be an increasing shift to co-branded merchandise, or special collections built in collaboration with smart influencers who already have the audience and trust of the target audiences for brands.

Savvy marketers will instead use single engagements to make initial contact, start a conversation, and gain awareness, leveraging a specific campaign to act as a testing ground for working together and creating a long-term partnership.

We're already beginning to see the earliest forms of this practice take root in corporate practice through brand ambassadorship programs, as well as programs that look to cultivate existing influence from within, rather than conscripting from without. Refer back to Chapter 9 to see a number of examples of just how powerful it can be to provide a platform for those most familiar with your brand to speak on the positive impact you've had on their lives.

As influencer relationships grow, so will the contracts that define them

I talked in Chapter 13 about how influencer marketing agreements need to be intricately detailed, but the expansion of agreements won't just end with minutiae around content and compensation.

Today, brands are liable not just to continue to pay an influencer who loses the respect of the public, but having to clean up the reputation damage caused by association with the influencer who has misbehaved—making the arrangement doubly expensive in the long run.

Movements like #MeToo and 'Time's Up' have forced a number of industries to recognize, and become accountable for influencers' conduct. A new move to include morality clauses will mimic the contracts celebrity ambassadors and spokespeople have had to negotiate for years—both as a way to deter misconduct, and to provide them with a means of protecting their investments.

Brands will get smarter about recognizing "pre-influencers"

From Rohit:

> "People seek out other people who do great stuff. It's a beautiful thing to find someone who is a pre-influencer—someone with all the potential, but who hasn't broken through yet.
>
> In other industries, we expect that there are people out there looking for greatness—in the music industry and in sports, there are

scouts out there looking for great talents, and hoping to discover them before they get snapped up. It's starting to happen on YouTube, too: who's talented? Who should we be paying attention to? Who can we grow with?

Yet when it comes to influencer marketing, we've been looking for the person on the hashtag with a million followers, and throwing money at him or her. It's lazy thinking, and it leads to lazy marketing.

The most successful brands will learn to be influence *scouts* first."

Influencers are ready for the biggest stages in marketing and advertising

It's clear that the stereotypical influencer role—focused solely on social media posts and online content—is giving way to a broader perspective on what influencers can do for brands, and where they belong in the business world

Many influencers are now receiving offers to be:
- Equity partners
- Co-owners or co-brands of new merchandise or product lines
- Featured in major brand commercials
- Featured guests at events
- Subject matter or audience experts for marketing and messaging brainstorms
- Consultants and advisors in product development meetings
- Strategists on all new business ideas, and growth opportunities both internally (B2B) and to end consumers (B2C)

. . .and that's just the beginning. Smart brands recognize that the influencers who are experts at connecting with their audiences also bring an expert perspective to conversations around what the audience wants, needs, and responds to, as well as the types of products, services, distribution, and brand messaging they are drawn to.

Influencer opportunities will expand into a mergers and acquisition model, especially for bigger more established influencers. Influencers are brands now--and brands are influencers.

INFLUENCER MARKETING IS DRIVING CHANGES IN MARKETING
Enough is enough: Changing how we measure influence

Throughout this book, I've talked about how much of the marketing world is still stuck on direct attribution and other measurement models that lead to misleading and partial results. We used to be skeptical about how much data could really tell us about our efforts. . .and now we're *so hung up* on the sea of data we're swimming in that we're not making strategic choices about what we measure.

It is my hope that the marketing world will finally figure out that data alone will not uncover the full picture. Marketers will come to appreciate that understanding the human element of influence *that takes place over time* will become critical to being successful in influencer marketing—not just the rusty old direct attribution model we have a hard time letting go of.

Relying solely on data ultimately distorts *any* marketing strategy. The judgment of true experts—*actual human beings*—who blend their understanding of data with experience and instinct to make smart decisions are going to prevail.

The best marketers will moonlight as social scientists, and will select the *right* data factors to pay attention to, according to their goals. Then they'll marry that data with their very *human* observations and learnings gained over time.

And in cases where data and human reasoning don't align, *the latter will prevail.*

I believe—with all my being—that the measurement model I provided in Chapter 13 will give the power for spectacular success because it's a structured way of thinking that will adapt no matter the technology or platform you are dealing with.

Bad news for fakers: It's only going to get tougher

Fraud is unfortunately still a very real part of the influencer marketing landscape. Anyone with a social media account can purchase followers, and there are companies that generate millions of fraudulent account followers that might actually seem real or organic to the untrained eye. They perform the same actions that real accounts do, like commenting and liking and sharing. . .but there's nothing to them but a name and a profile image.

While brands and marketers are also starting to use a critical eye when they assess influencers—new software tools are making it easier for them to detect the fakers. In addition, more social media platforms are focusing on verifying their real users, and penalizing opportunists who create fake accounts and promote fake engagement.

Platforms will have to be the leaders in eradicating the problem, and returning legitimacy to their brands. Implementing technology measures to safeguard future marketing campaigns proactively and allow brands and businesses better assessment of influencers from the beginning will be pertinent to their success of these social platforms.

A new era of ever-more-dedicated marketing teams

Growing a brand is going to get even more challenging—not that it's easy now—as the market continues to become even more fragmented. If you want to align with quality influencers, you're going to be up against plenty of competition—and it's not going to be cheap, both in terms of time and resources.

Savvy brands will make the shift to investing in influencer creator roles: bringing together the right people, teams, technology and resources to develop their individual brands as influencers, in and of themselves. Some brands will respond by championing their internal team members as true, human influencers—such as their CEO or founder, or beloved employees. We're already starting to see success stories (and cautionary tales) from this approach, and you can bet more and more brands will be taking notice. Our discussion of Elon Musk in Chapter 9 is just the beginning; soon, visible, personable and engaged CEOs will be a virtual must-have.

Others will take a different approach to giving consumers a personal connection to their brand by creating engaging, alluring bots, or CGI influencers. The beauty of new options like CGI influencers is that brands can have complete control over their narrative—and if companies are having to spend major cash and time to build influence, they will begin to see more value in new approaches and technologies.

Final Words

The future is already here. Are *you* ready for it?

The only thing that's certain in the world of marketing is that change is a constant. And while we as marketers have done our best to keep up, in this new era of incredibly rapid advances and shifts in technology, communications, and our society as a whole, our hyper-speed evolution—which shows no signs of slowing down—is starting to leave us behind.

But I don't want you to feel overwhelmed by this, or to close your mind because you think you *can't* keep up. You should feel energized by all the possibilities to come! Now armed with the Code, you possess the knowledge, framework, and mindset to craft and execute influencer marketing at the highest level to affect real, long term growth and success.

These are fundamental marketing principles, and no matter how much the world changes, the Code will remain the same:

1. Define the **RIGHT** goal
2. Observe and identify the **RIGHT** influencers
3. Create the **RIGHT** connection

With a goal-oriented mindset, a keen and observing eye, and an ability to connect with others on a personal, individual level, there is no market evolution or paradigm shift that can leave you behind.

Stay infinitely curious. Keep asking questions. Keep experimenting and being willing to adapt. Don't settle for simple fixes or measures or shallow data points, and be *relentless* about keeping the big picture in mind.

Influencer marketing isn't a standalone tactic, it's a long-term business investment, and takes a lot of time and work, but I assure you that it's worth it.

You now know what's important, where to start, and what to focus on. You know how to strategize, implement and execute. You know how to communicate real results to your boss or client that connect your business objectives to your overall goals.

In short, you know how to think differently about all of this, and approach it from a much more focused lens. That's what's going to make you a success at influencer marketing today, and for the future.

But now I'd like to know what you think about the years to come: tell me what your predictions are for the next few years—or longer!—in this new influencer economy. We all bring different experiences and insights, and your perspective is one our community of experts and marketing pros would like to hear—in the spirit of collaboration, let's collaborate!

Use the hashtag #influencercode to share your predictions with me across social media, and visit our website, TheInfluencerCode.com to see what others have shared. I'll collect them there on their own page at theinfluencercode.com/futureofinfluence.

You didn't think I'd forget the CTA, did you?